Computer Tools, Models and Techniques for Project Management

This book is dedicated to the memory of:
OMOLADE BADIRU

Computer Tools, Models and Techniques for Project Management

Dr. Adedeji B. Badiru
University of Oklahoma

and

Dr. Gary E. Whitehouse
University of Central Florida

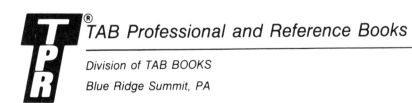

TAB Professional and Reference Books

Division of TAB BOOKS
Blue Ridge Summit, PA

FIRST EDITION
FIRST PRINTING

TPR books are published by TAB Professional and Reference Books, a division of TAB
BOOKS. The TPR logo, consisting of the letters ''TPR'' within a large ''T,'' is a registered
trademark of TAB BOOKS.

Library of Congress Cataloging-in-Publication Data

Badiru, Adedeji Bodunde, 1952 –
    Computer tools, models, and techniques for project management / by
Adedeji B. Badiru and Gary E. Whitehouse.
      p.   cm.
    Includes bibliographical references.
    ISBN 0-8306-3200-X :
    1. Industrial project management—Data processing.
I. Whitehouse, Gary E., 1938 – . II. Title.
T56.8.B3 1990
658.4'04—dc20   89-28580
                        CIP

TAB BOOKS offers software for sale. For information and a catalog, please contact TAB
Software Department, Blue Ridge Summit, PA 17294-0850.

Questions regarding the content of this book should be addressed to:

    Reader Inquiry Branch
    TAB BOOKS
    Blue Ridge Summit, PA 17294-0214

Acquisitions Editor: Larry Hager
Technical Editor: Mark D. LeSuer
Production: Katherine Brown
Series Design: Jaclyn J. Boone

Contents

Acknowledgments

We thank our families for bearing with us and giving us all their support and understanding throughout the preparation of this book.

We express our gratitude to our colleagues in the College of Engineering, University of Oklahoma and the College of Engineering, University of Central Florida for their continuing support and cooperation.

We thank the entire staff of TAB BOOKS for their expeditious handling of the publication of this book. Our special thanks go to Robert Ostrander, Larry Hager, Suzanne Cheatle, Mark LeSuer, Katherine Brown, Linda Cramer, Nadine McFarland, Dick Hawkins, and the entire production staff.

Preface

Both large and small organizations are buying more and more project management software. The market for project management software has grown by more than 30 percent in the last three years alone. This healthy gain in the market has resulted in a broad diversification of project management software capabilities. In addition to performing the traditional functions of project scheduling, many project management packages now offer such tools as time management, resource allocation, resource leveling, budget analysis, presentation graphics, and work breakdown structure.

In addition to packages designated as project management software, other software tools, such as spreadsheets and database managers, are now finding their own niche in the project management environment. Any of the existing computational or decision support software packages can find a useful application somewhere in a project life cycle. Traditionally, the life cycle of a project covers items such as the ones listed below:

- Need Analysis
- Problem Definition
- Specification of Project Requirements
- Request For Project Proposals
- Bid Analysis and Vendor Selection
- Proposal/Cost Justification
- Project Approval
- Contract Development
- Organization of Project Team
- Design Specification and Approval
- Project Initiation

- Project Scheduling, Monitoring, and Control
- Transfer to End User
- Project Phase Out
- Post-project support and maintenance

It is not difficult to imagine how any existing software, even a word proces-sor, can be gainfully utilized in at least one of the areas listed above. But, as it turns out, most of the present computer software and hardware resources are not being used as effectively as they could in enhancing project management functions. For example, the increasing proliferation of local area networks can be exploited to allow users in a project management environment to access, update, and share data, and enable project managers to monitor and control project events more effectively.

Conventional software packages can be interfaced with project manage-ment software to enhance the planning, organizing, scheduling, monitoring, reporting, and controlling of a project. Conversely, project management soft-ware can find potential applications in conventional ''non-project'' functions. For example, city planners can use the cost analysis capability of some project management packages to handle the community budgeting function.

This book presents a guide to the available computer tools, models, and techniques that could be used to enhance project management functions. Topics covered include using spreadsheets for project management analysis, using database management techniques for project management, integrating conven-tional application programs with project management software, using data com-munication protocols for project management functions, using computer simulation as a project planning tool, developing local area networks for project data communication, and organizing a project environment conducive to com-puter application.

The primary audience for the book includes project management practitio-ners, managers, consultants, and supervisors. The book also should appeal to educational and training institutions. Students of project management will find the book to be a valuable reference as they prepare for the real world of project management. The topics in the book are presented in easy-to-follow and step-by-step formats. Graphic representations and drawings are used whenever appropriate to clarify the concepts presented.

Chapter 1 presents a general introduction to computers. The impact of computers in the decision making environment is emphasized. The mainframe computer environment is discussed in contrast to the microcomputer environ-ment. Some of the specific topics covered by this chapter include hardware, software, and operating systems requirements. Subsequent chapters expatiate on these topics in the context of project management needs.

Chapter 2 presents many of the general aspects of computer hardware and software that are relevant for project management functions. Project manage-ment functions are discussed and potential application areas for computer tools are identified. The factors to consider when selecting project management software are also discussed.

Chapter 3 presents examples of how an electronic spreadsheet can be used for enhancing many of the numeric analyses that are often encountered in project management. Such analyses may include budgeting, resource allocation, cost estimating, development of presentation graphics, and many more.

Chapter 4 presents basic database management concepts for project management applications. As with the spreadsheet discussions in Chapter 3, no particular database program is recommended. The presentations are generic enough to illustrate how the reader can utilize his or her present database management program for project management applications.

Chapter 5 presents some special analytical tools for project management analysis. Topics covered include computer simulation as a project planning tool, engineering economic analysis for project cost versus income evaluation, and basic statistical techniques for evaluating decision parameters involved in project management. A BASIC computer program developed by the authors is used to illustrate the effectiveness of computer simulation for project planning. Other BASIC programs developed or codeveloped by the authors are used to illustrate the economic analysis aspect of project management. The commercial STAT-GRAPHICS software is used to illustrate some of the statistical analyses available for use in project management.

Chapter 6 discusses computer networking and communication tools to coordinate and enhance project management functions performed at different locations. Networking and remote communication links make it possible to share information on a timely basis for prompt decision. Some of the newer communication technologies are discussed to enlighten the reader about what tools are available and how the tools can be used in the project management environment.

Chapter 7 discusses the emerging technologies of artificial intelligence and expert systems as potential tools for project management. The basic characteristics of expert systems are discussed. The benefits to be derived from the application of expert systems to project management are presented. Some of the prevailing knowledge representation and reasoning models are discussed with indications of how they may be suitable for project management application. An example of a decision model is presented to illustrate how conventional project management approaches and expert systems might be integrated with state space representation to enhance project monitoring and control.

Chapter 8 presents a brief evaluation of some selected project management systems. The use of computer software in project management and control is also discussed. The significance of computer information flow for project monitoring and control is emphasized. A few selected case studies are presented to illustrate the use of computer software in managing projects.

Adedeji B. Badiru
Gary E. Whitehouse

Introduction

Over the past few years, the interest in *project management* has increased dramatically. Because any function can be defined in terms of project concepts, project management has emerged as one of the core efforts in many organizations. Business, industry, and academic institutions have been committing more and more resources to project management efforts. Many professional organizations now offer regular project management training workshops. Nowadays, a major component of any project management effort is the use of computers. The annual project management software market is quickly approaching a billion dollar industry. The market for reference books to go along with the software tools also is growing rapidly.

The authors have combined their extensive experiences in the project management field to write a book that outlines the capabilities of computers in enhancing project management functions. The book concentrates on the computer tools, models, and techniques for project management analysis. These items include such things as conventional project management software, spreadsheets for project cost analysis, database for project information management, local area networks for project communication, and so on.

The rapid development of technology has continued to fuel the momentum for project management efforts. Unfortunately, the pace of generating text materials for project management has not kept up with the prevailing interest. While many books are available on the subject of management, relatively few focus on project management in particular. Even fewer books focus on computer applications for project management. This book makes a contribution by helping to fill the void that is now existing in project management publications for practicing professionals and managers.

Introduction

The primary audience for the book will be practitioners and managers in business and industry. These include engineering, data processing, research and development, production, maintenance, finance, marketing, administration, and so on. Typical readers will be those who plan, schedule, control, organize, staff, and manage projects of all kinds.

Some of the specific practitioners that should benefit from the contents of this book include Industrial and Systems Engineers, Industrial Engineering Managers, Corporate and Business Planners, R & D Managers, Project Supervisors and Coordinators, Plant Managers, Production Supervisors, Project Managers, Manufacturing Engineers and Managers, Management Consultants, and Computer Consultants. In addition to practitioners, the contents of the book should also appeal to students and teachers of project management as a reference guide. This book covers the basic things you need to know about computers in order to better manage your computer operations and, consequently, be a more effective user of computer tools for project management.

1

The Computer
Revolution

This chapter emphasizes the impact of computers in the decision-making environment. The mainframe computer environment is discussed in contrast to the microcomputer environment. It is expected that most of the future uses of computers for decision making will be carried out in the microcomputer environment. As such, more emphasis is placed on microcomputers in this book. Some of the specific topics covered by this chapter include hardware, software, and operating systems requirements. Subsequent chapters expatiate on these topics in the context of project management needs. Check the glossary for unfamiliar computer terms. Readers who are already familiar with computer operations may wish to skip to chapter 1.

1.1 IMPACT OF COMPUTERS ON TECHNOLOGICAL CHANGE

The driving force behind our society's transition to an information-oriented society is the computer. The computer is having a profound impact on the industry and business communities. Computers are becoming the practical partners of decision makers (Whitehouse 1985). The unprecedented technological advancements in the computer and information fields have caused computers to become a part of our daily lives. The rapid growth in the number and variety of computer applications have permeated all aspects of human endeavors. Computers are now frequent players in our professional and personal activities.

1.2 MAINFRAME COMPUTER ENVIRONMENT

Minicomputers and mainframes are computer systems. Desktop computers are also computer systems. Each kind offers a variety of input and output alternatives, and each is supported by a wide variety of commercial software. There are significant differences in size, speed, and capabilities. Minicomputers and mainframes are larger in scope: program executions are generally faster; on-line disk storage has more capacity; printer speeds are much faster; the number of concurrent users is much larger and costs also are higher. Besides the size and capabilities, the most distinguishing characteristic of minicomputers and mainframes is the manner in which they are used. Mainframe computers, with their expanded processing capabilities, provide a computing resource that can be shared by an entire company, not just a single user. For example, the project management, finance, personnel, manufacturing, and accounting departments can share the same computing resources on a minicomputer or mainframe simultaneously.

Prior to the late 1960s, virtually all commercial computers were mainframe computers. They were expensive and required a large amount of space. Only very large companies could afford them. As the market continued to grow, computer manufacturers saw the need for smaller computers that would be affordable to smaller companies. So, a new line of computers called *minicomputers*, or simply minis, was introduced. Minis are scaled-down versions of mainframes. Even though some of today's minicomputers are more powerful than the largest mainframes of the early 1970s, their nickname of "mini" continues to prevail.

There is no clear-cut or generally accepted definition for a minicomputer. The rapidly changing computing technology has made any clear distinction impossible. In fact, some of the more powerful microcomputers are now making inroads into the territories of minicomputers as far as computing power is concerned. Likewise, the increasing capabilities of minicomputers continue to push them into the traditional mainframe power range. As if involved in a technological race, the traditional mainframes are now pulling away into the so-called supercomputer domain.

In general, minicomputers have most of the operational capabilities of mainframe computers, except that they perform at a slower speed. Minicomputer input, output, and storage devices are similar in appearance and function to those used on the larger mainframe systems. However, for minis, the printers are slower, the storage capacity is smaller, and fewer number of workstations are supported. All computers, whether micro, mini, main, or super, perform their operations in the same fundamental steps of: *input, processing, output,* and *storage*.

The specific mechanisms used in each step are often the distinguishing characteristics of the caliber of the computer system. The major advantage of minis and mainframes is the large number of simultaneous remote workstations they can support. Microcomputers, in general, support only one user at a time. But the emerging technology of micro networking is beginning to make it possible for more than one user to access a single microcomputer system in what is called *simultaneous processing*. As a rule of thumb, any computer that supports over 100 remote workstations has surpassed the minicomputer range. Some systems in the present generation of supercomputers can support as many as 10,000 remote workstations.

Processing

Mainframe computer systems and some minicomputers are normally configured to include one mainframe (host processor) and several other processors. The host processor has direct control over all other processors, storage devices, and input/output devices. The other processors relieve the host of certain routine processing functions. For example, the back-end processor performs the task of retrieving data from storage locations. The front-end processor relieves the host processor of communications-related processing functions such as the transmission of data to and from remote workstations and other computers. In this configuration, the host processor can concentrate on the overall system control and the execution of applications software. This is why it appears that the system is performing several operations at the same time at an incredible speed. Although the host could handle the entire system without the assistance of subordinate processors, the overall system efficiency and productivity would be drastically curtailed. You can imagine why a microcomputer, doing everything all by itself, appears to run so slowly.

Storage

All mainframe computer systems use similar direct and sequential storage media. The larger ones simply have more of the media and work faster. In a typical configuration, there might be 4 magnetic tape drives and 10 magnetic disk drives. The disk drives are usually dual density and can store twice the data in the same amount of physical storage space as the single-density media. The total data storage capacity might be as much as 800 megabytes of sequential storage (tape media) and 16,000 megabytes of direct-access storage (magnetic disk media).

Input

The primary means of entering data into the system is the same, no matter what the size of the computer system. The only differences between a large and a small system are the number and location of the workstations. For example, on a mainframe, as many as 100 workstations might be dedicated to service and administrative functions, 50 workstations to programming, 20 ports to microcomputer linkup (dial-up/log-on), and 10 workstations to project monitoring and control.

Output

The *hardcopy* of the output of a computer process is produced on printers, while the *softcopy* is displayed on the computer monitor screen. For a mainframe, one might have a high-speed line printer with a speed in excess of 2000 lines per minute and a page printer with a speed as high as 40,000 lines per minute. Plotters also can be included in the configuration for producing hardcopies of graphs, charts, and drawings.

A handful of the available commercial project management software packages are designed for use in the mainframe environment. Such packages offer the flexibility of on-line interactions between project work stations. However, their size and cost often restrict use to only very large projects in large organizations. In addition, the independence of the microcomputer environment is often preferred by practitioners for quick project decisions without susceptibility to mainframe down times.

1.3 MICROCOMPUTER SYSTEM

If you are like the typical project management professional, you will be operating your project management software on a *microcomputer*, sometimes called a personal computer or a desktop computer. It is very important that you become conversant with the capabilities of your computer.

A microcomputer system consists of electronic and mechanical devices that can be directed or programmed to react in a desired way. The electronic and mechanical devices are known as *hardware*. The directions or commands that control the hardware are known as *software*. Hardware and software working together make up your total computer system. A microcomputer system contains a device capable of recognizing and following instructions properly presented to it from an external source. A complete set of instructions, organized in a specific manner to solve a given problem, is called a *computer program*. Computer programs that turn your computer into a special-purpose tool, are called *applications software*. Your project management program is an example of an applications software package. The software tells the hardware how to perform particular tasks. The process of carrying out the instructions in a program is called *running the program*. FIGURE 1-1 shows an example of a typical configuration of a microcomputer system in a project management environment.

Most applications software packages consist of an attractive, eye-catching box containing an instruction manual and one or more computer disks where the program is electronically stored. The computer program is the software component of the application package. The instruction manual is the *documentation*.

Microcomputers are small enough to sit on a desktop or fit in a briefcase. The development of silicon chips led to the compact "micro-level" size of small computers. That explains the name microcomputer. The terms *personal computer* and *desktop computer* are derived from the fact that the small computers

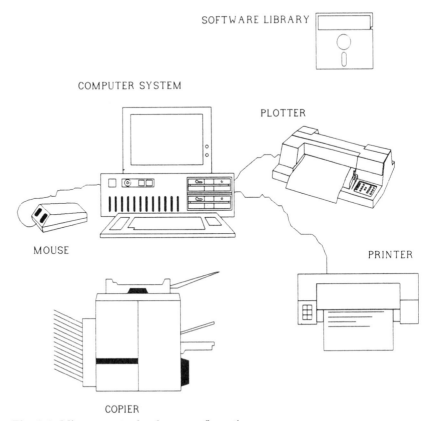

SOFTWARE LIBRARY

COMPUTER SYSTEM

PLOTTER

MOUSE

PRINTER

COPIER

Fig. 1-1. Microcomputer hardware configuration.

are intended for the personal use of one person at a time and to fit on a personal desktop.

Mainframe computers can be used by many different people at the same time. Actually, the many users are accommodated one at a time in a *batch mode*, this means the computer attends to all users so fast that the consecutive operations appear to be simultaneous. A mainframe computer together with its peripheral equipment (printers, terminals, tape storage units, etc.) can occupy a large room. These computer rooms are usually found in large corporate offices. In the hierarchy of computer sizes and power, mainframe computers are considered to be large while microcomputers are considered to be small. A *minicomputer* is a computer of intermediate size and power between a mainframe and a microcomputer. The cost of a computer is almost always directly proportional to its size and power.

The increasing need to run independent operations and the proliferation of powerful desktop computers have created an unprecedented push toward microcomputer usage in areas ranging from corporate offices to the family living room. A typical microcomputer system consists of the following components:

- Keyboard—Resembling a typewriter, the keyboard allows you to send information to the system.
- Monitor—The monitor resembles a television set and is used to display the information that you present to the computer or that the computer presents to you.
- System Unit—The system unit is the central control unit for the system. It contains electronic circuitry for performing data manipulation and memory for holding data that is being manipulated. It is usually referred to as the *Central Processing Unit* (CPU).
- Data Storage Devices—Data storage devices store information on a long-term basis. For example, when the computer is turned off, you can have your information saved for later retrieval. The most common data storage devices are diskettes and hard disks, although other devices are in use as well.
- Printer—The printer is an indispensable optional item in your computer system. This component produces printed copies of the results of a computer operation.

Microcomputer systems are quite flexible and generally allow for extensive user customization. Installing additional circuit cards to the system unit allows you to add new system components, such as a *mouse* or a *light pen* for pointing to the screen, a *plotter* for making high-quality graphics, or a *controller device*, for controlling an instrument such as a thermostat or a burglar alarm.

Within a very short time, microcomputers have changed their status from a new technological invention to a standard problem-solving tool. Their widespread acceptance can be traced to a number of factors, including:

- Problem-solving Capability—Microcomputer software solves problems. Many of the computational problems that used to take hours to solve now can be solved conveniently within minutes or seconds on a microcomputer.
- Low Cost—Microcomputers are relatively inexpensive. The advent of cheap microprocessor chips continues to drive the cost down. Consequently, greater problem-solving capability can be obtained at decreasing prices.
- Compact Size—Microcomputers are small and can be accommodated within most work environments. It is even possible to have a microcomputer system set up in a corner of your bedroom.
- Speed—Microcomputers process data with remarkable speed. They can perform hundreds of thousands of operations in a second. They also can retrieve data from storage memory in less than one-millionth of a second.

- User Friendliness—One of the greatest attributes of microcomputers is that they are very easy and convenient to learn and use. Developers have strived to make microcomputer software easy to use. You do not need to be a computer scientist or a computer programmer in order to use microcomputers.
- Accessibility—With the "personal" nature of microcomputers, an individual can own one for himself. Therefore, access is enhanced.

In the early 1970s, semiconductor technology progressed to the point where the circuitry for the "brains" of the computer (*CPU*) could be manufactured on a single semiconductor chip. These miniaturized computers, called *microprocessors*, are still manufactured by corporations such as Intel, Motorola, Texas Instruments, and Hitachi. Microprocessors made it possible for the first time to build computers that were small enough to fit on a desk top and inexpensive enough for individuals to afford.

Application programs began to appear around 1980. First-generation programs for word processing, data management, spreadsheets, and communications allowed novice users to experience the power of microcomputing. At first, major corporations viewed microcomputers as electronic toys. Compared to the power available on mainframes, the early microcomputers were, indeed, like toys. As it turns out, most corporations underestimated the significance of bringing computing power down to the level of the individual user. IBM, which later captured the microcomputer market, was one of the corporations that initially scorned the microcomputer industry. However, the industry changed forever in 1981 when IBM itself entered the microcomputer market. The company introduced its own microcomputer, nicknamed the IBM PC. (PC is an acronym for *personal computer*.)

The fact that IBM, a company of high corporate prestige, would enter the market convinced businesses that the microcomputer was more than a temporary fad. Within a short time, the microcomputer was recognized as a productivity tool that could be used at all levels to process, store, retrieve, and analyze information. Almost every business could find a legitimate place for a microcomputer. IBM's hold on the market was so great that it immediately set a standard for the industry. There are now scores of microcomputer brands that are *compatible* with IBM computers. These computers are sometimes referred to as IBM *clones*, meaning that the computers can run the same programs written for IBM computers.

Full compatibility is an issue that has generated a lot of controversy. Some manufacturers claim that their machines are 100 percent IBM compatible when, in fact, the machines are only partially compatible. However, many IBM clones have proven to be fully IBM compatible. The advantage of IBM clones is that they are usually cheaper and in some cases more powerful than true IBM machines. If you plan to buy an IBM clone for your project management analysis, make sure that the computer is fully capable of running your software, as well as supporting your peripheral equipment such as printers and modems.

1.4 APPLICATIONS SOFTWARE

Application software is developed by two main sources:

1. Users themselves
2. Professional programmers

Programs written by users are referred to as *user-written programs*. Those written by professional programmers and sold to users are referred to as *pre-written application packages, canned programs,* or *commercial packages*. Commercial packages can be purchased from a vendor or distributor, or directly from the developer. Unless you embark on the ardous task of developing your own project management package, the package you will use most likely will be a commercial product.

The advantages of commercial application packages are:

1. They can be purchased for immediate use.
2. They are relatively inexpensive.
3. They are available for many applications.
4. They have already been tested.
5. They can sometimes be customized to fit user needs.

The major disadvantages of commercial application packages are:

1. They might be too general to fit specific user requirements.
2. They might have been developed for a computer not compatible with yours.
3. Frequent updates can disrupt operations.

The advantages of user-written application packages are:

1. They can be written to fit the exact needs of a user.
2. They can be sold to others if successful.
3. There is a pride in generating the computer code.

The disadvantages of user-written application packages are:

1. A high level of programming expertise is required.
2. They require much development time.
3. They can be frustrating to the user.
4. There is a lack of formal testing.

The most popular application packages fall into five categories:

1. Word processors
2. Data managers
3. Electronic spreadsheets
4. Graphics
5. Communications

Word Processor

A *word processor* is a program for manipulating text. It allows you to type a document into the microcomputer's memory. You can view the document on the screen as you type. You can move directly to any point within the document to add, delete, copy, or move sections of text. You can save the document for later retrieval, or you can print it. WordPerfect, WordStar, and Lotus Manuscript are examples of commercial word processing packages.

Data Manager

In many business situations, you will need to deal with sets of data. For example, you can maintain an inventory of your organization's equipment as a database stored in computer memory, or you can create a database of your clients and invoices. When necessary, you can analyze or update such a collection of data by using a database management program. The program allows you to add to the data or retrieve data using some specific criteria. For example, you can retrieve only those data elements, say invoices, that were generated in a specified year. dBase III, R:Base 5000, and Reflex are some of the most popular database programs.

Spreadsheet

A spreadsheet program turns the microcomputer into an accountant's worksheet. It can be used to plan budgets, perform accounting tasks, and analyze investments. A spreadsheet allows you to define relationships between numbers. For example, you can define one entry as the sum of a column of numbers. As numbers in the column change, the sum is automatically updated. Lotus 1-2-3 is, no doubt, the most popular spreadsheet program available today.

Graphics

Graphics packages display data visually in the form of graphic images. For example, after using a spreadsheet or data manager to manipulate and organize data, the user sometimes can find difficulty in seeing the data relationships or interpreting the information that is generated. Presenting the information visually (graphically, in the form of pie charts, histograms, etc.) is one way to make the information clear. Business managers use graphics packages to present statistics and other data and their relationships. Graphics programs allow you to create images on a screen and print the images on a printer or plotter. Lotus Freelance Plus and Harvard Graphics are two of the most popular graphics packages.

Communications

You can use communications programs to access information in distant computers. This is sometimes referred to as *remote access*. As more individuals and organizations use computers, the need to transfer data from one computer to another has increased. For example, law-enforcement officials can exchange information on criminals; home users can access stock market information; or businesses can exchange sales information via a remote computer linkage.

Electronic mail is another application of computer communications. Commercial services such as MCI Mail and Western Union's EasyLink provide electronic "mailboxes" into which people can deposit mail. Using electronic mail, you can send or receive memos, reports, letters, and other documents to and from anywhere in the world. For example, word processing service centers can deliver their clients' completed manuscripts via electronic mail. Of course this assumes that the client has compatible hardware and software to generate a hardcopy of the manuscript. Some of the popular communications packages are PC-Talk and ProComm.

Although project management programs will be the primary application software for your projects, you might find it helpful to have the other types of software previously discussed. You can use Lotus Freelance Plus for drawing charts and figures for project presentations. The graphics files can be merged with word processing documents to produce complete publishable project reports. Spreadsheets can be used to format numeric tables of project information. Spreadsheets, like graphics, can be merged with reports. Sometimes, project analysts have database files that they would like to include in their word processing documents to create integrated reports. These database files can be retrieved with a database management program, organized into an appropriate format, and then exported to the word processing document.

If you would like to have all your application programs right at your fingertips, so to speak, you might want to procure an *integrated application software* package. This kind of single program might include modules for several applications programs like word processing, communication, database management, spreadsheets, and graphics. An integrated package permits easy manipulation and interchange of data in several different applications. Moreover, an integrated package allows the user to learn one consistent set of commands for accomplishing a variety of tasks, instead of learning the individual sets of commands for independent packages. Lotus Symphony is an example of an integrated package that contains word processing, spreadsheet application, graphics, database management, and communications.

1.5 THINGS YOU SHOULD KNOW

This section presents some of the basic definitions you should know about your computer so you can discuss more intelligently with your clients, suppliers, and other professionals in the industry.

Computer Memory

Primary Storage Unit. The primary storage unit refers to the internal storage unit of the computer, where programs and their data are stored. Primary storage or primary memory provides temporary storage during program execution. Part of primary storage might also contain permanently stored instructions, such as those that tell the computer what to do when it is turned on. Because primary storage is located inside the computer, it is linked directly to the other components of the CPU. Thus, access time to data located in primary storage is very fast.

Most primary storage is comprised of semiconductor technology. Semiconductor memory is made by "etching" electronic circuits onto a silicon chip. Primary storage is typically of two types: random-access memory (RAM) and read-only memory (ROM).

Random-Access Memory. Random-access memory is the part of primary storage where data and program instructions are held temporarily during program execution. This kind of memory allows the user to enter data into memory or retrieve data from memory. The process of entering data into memory is called *writing*, while the process of retrieving data from memory is called *reading*. Information stored in RAM is volatile because it is lost as soon as the computer is turned off or when new information is read into memory.

Read-Only Memory. Information can only be read from read-only memory. You can read from but cannot write into ROM. Read-only memory may contain information on how to start the computer and even instructions to operate the entire operating system. The actual contents of ROM are usually set by the computer manufacturer. They are unchangeable and permanent. Contents of ROM are retained even when the electric current is turned off. Therefore, ROM is nonvolatile.

The amount of primary storage determines the capabilities of your computer system. The more primary storage you have, the more data you can load into memory. Many application programs require a specific amount of memory to run. For example, many of the present generation of word processors require at least 512K of RAM. If you plan to run more than one program at a time, such as your word processor and a graphics program, you might need as much as 640K of RAM for both to run successfully.

Bit. The smallest piece of data that can be recognized and used by the computer is the bit. A bit is a single binary value, either a one or a zero. The computer identifies signals in the form of digital pulses, which represent either a high-voltage state, known as the "on" state, or a low-voltage state, known as the "off" state. The "on" and "off" conditions are conventionally labeled with the numbers 1 or 0, respectively. This number system is called the *binary system*. The 1's and 0's can be arranged in various combinations to represent all the numbers, letters, and symbols that you will ever want to enter into the computer. As far as the computer is concerned, the numbers and letters that you see on your computer screen are actually codes of 1's and 0's. The items you type into your computer are first encoded into 1's and 0's before the computer can understand them.

Byte. A grouping of eight bits is called a byte. The byte is the basic unit for measuring the size of memory. You will frequently hear the terms *kilobyte* (K or KB) and *megabyte* (MB or MEG). A byte is the amount of storage needed to hold one character in computer memory or on a disk. For example, the letters *ABCS* would occupy 4 bytes of memory (one byte per letter). A double-spaced, typewritten page will take approximately 1500 bytes. One kilobyte equals 1024 bytes and one megabyte equals 1024 kilobytes, or 1,048,576 bytes. Thus, 1500 bytes is actually 1.4648K (or simply 1.5K), 1024 bytes is 1K, 1048576 bytes is 1024K which is 1Mb or 1M.

By the same reasoning, a *Gigabyte* is estimated to be 1,000,000,000 (one billion, "giga") bytes. If the technological developments in the electronics industry continue at the current rate, we might soon see memory capacities on the order of a *terabyte*, which is estimated to be one trillion bytes. Depending on the typeface you use, a one-page, double-spaced document will occupy about 2K of storage memory.

Depending on your computer system, which version of DOS you are using, the type of disk drives you have, and whether your drives use one or both sides of the disk, a disk can hold anywhere from 163,840 bytes (160K) on some basic PC's to 368,640 bytes (360K) or to 1,228,800 bytes (1200K or 1.1719M) on the PC AT. Confused? Well, you are not alone. To avoid dealing with the extra digits in all these bits and bytes, they are usually rounded off to the nearest thousand. Thus, 1000 bytes (which is actually 0.9765K) is referred to as 1K and 1200K (which is actually 1.1719M) is referred to as 1.2M.

Word. One word, in computer parlance, represents the number of adjacent bits that can be stored and manipulated as a unit. Some of the newer and more powerful microcomputers have 32-bit word capability. The older computers, by comparison, have word lengths of 8 and 16 bits. Word lengths can range up to 128 bits for supercomputers. Generally, the longer the length of the word that a computer can handle, the faster it can process data. When you evaluate the hardware to be purchased for project management purposes, ask your dealer about the word length of your prospective computer. The need for faster computers in your project functions will become evident when printing long documents or when generating graphics images.

Generating Outputs

You can produce graphics and text material with a wide selection of printers and plotters. A *printer* produces output on paper; a *plotter* produces graphics on paper. Some printers also have the capability to print graphics. The print quality available on your printing equipment can vary considerably. Some of the terms you will hear in connection with print quality are *near-typeset quality, letter quality, near-letter quality, standard quality*, and *draft quality*. You should experiment with your equipment to find out the levels of quality you have available. The quality level at your disposal will definitely depend on the capabilities of your equipment, both hardware and software.

Impact Printers. An impact printer produces characters by using a hammer or a set of pins to strike an ink ribbon, which in turn presses against a sheet of paper to leave an impression of the character on the paper. This is the same way that an ordinary typewriter works. Dot-matrix and daisy-wheel printers are the most common impact printers available on the market now. Both kinds of printers print one character at a time. The dot-matrix printer uses print heads containing from 9 to 24 pins. The pins produce patterns of dots on the paper to form the individual characters. The higher the number of pins, the better the quality of the printout. With the pins structure, most impact printers can print graphics. Some printers print in only one direction (*unidirectional*), while others print in both directions (*bidirectional*). Bidirectional printing is faster than unidirectional printing.

To obtain the letter quality of a conventional typewriter, a daisy-wheel impact printer can be used with your computer system. The print head of a letter-quality printer is a mechanism that looks like a daisy. At the end of each petal of the "daisy," a fully formed character is available. This full-form character produces a solid-line print. A hammer strikes a "petal" containing the desired print against a ribbon, and the character is printed on paper.

If a large volume of printing needs to be done, the one-character-at-a-time printer might be too slow to meet the required productivity level. For large jobs, *line printers* can be more helpful. A line printer prints a whole line at a time. The speed of line printers typically ranges from 1,200 to 6,000 lines per minute. Drum, chain, and band printers are examples of line printers.

Nonimpact Printers. Nonimpact printers do not use a striking mechanism to produce characters on paper. These printers run much quieter than impact printers. Major products in this line of equipment are the *ink-jet, thermal-transfer,* and *laser* printers.

Ink-jet printers form characters on paper by spraying ink from tiny nozzles through an electrical field that arranges the charged ink particles into characters. The speed of ink-jet printers is typically around 250 characters per second.

Thermal-transfer printers use heat to transfer ink to paper. These printers bond the ink onto the paper by heating pins, which press against a special ink ribbon.

Laser printers generate printouts with a quality comparable to typeset material at high speed. Laser printers produce images on paper by directing a laser beam at a mirror, which reflects the beam onto a drum. The laser leaves a negative charge on the drum to which positively charged black toner powder will stick. As the paper rolls by the drum, the toner is transferred to the paper. A hot roller then bonds the toner to the paper. The images of characters are formed by selectively charging portions of the surface of the drum. The formed character images are then transferred to paper. The HP LaserJet laser printers are the most popular of the desktop laser printers currently on the market.

Plotters. A plotter produces high-quality graphics in multiple colors using pens that are attached to movable arms. The pens are directed across the surface of a stationary piece of paper. Some plotters combine a movable pen arm with paper that also can roll back and forth to make the drawing. The dual movement facilitates the generation of highly complex drawings. A plotter can be used to prepare large documents, such as blueprints and posters.

Plotters reduce images to a sequence of lines, rather than individual pixels. For example, diagonal lines produced by a plotter don't have the jagged appearance they often do in non-letter-quality printers. However, letter-quality printers using fixed print heads cannot generate graphics outputs. You pay the price for the high-quality output of plotters in terms of cost and speed. A single plotter drawing may take 10 to 20 minutes to complete. If multiple colors are desired, the print time is expected to be longer. The Hewlett-Packard (HP) plotters are the most popular brands now on the market.

The HP PaintJet printer is an example of an ink-jet printer that some organizations are using as an alternative to the higher-cost plotters. PaintJet offers the advantages of a lower price with a higher print speed, but there is a slight degradation of print quality.

Monitors. The monitor, also called a computer screen or display unit, is used for viewing the output of your computer work—for displaying information. Monitors are combined with keyboards so that the data you input into the computer can be viewed and checked as it is entered. This combination of an input device (keyboard) and an output device (monitor) is known as a *terminal* or *workstation*.

Monitor quality is typically expressed in terms of *resolution*, a measure of the number of picture elements, or *pixels*, that a screen can contain. A pixel is the smallest increment of a display screen that can be controlled individually. The number of pixels a monitor has will determine the clarity and sharpness of the image. A 640-x-460-pixel monitor means that there are 640 horizontal pixels and 460 vertical pixels.

Color monitors are more expensive and are of two types: *composite color*, which is much like a TV monitor; and *RGB* (red, green, and blue), in which the colors are more definite and the resolution is higher. Neither monitor is well suited for word processing, although RGB monitors display text much better than composite monitors do. A color monitor is often preferable for outputs containing graphics. Three colors of phosphor dots form a pixel on RGB color monitors. These colors are blended to make other colors by varying the intensity of the electron beam focused on the phosphor dots. The new generation of color monitors known as video graphics array (*VGA*) and extended graphics adapter (*EGA*) offers good colors and better word processing text resolution than conventional RGB monitors.

Monochrome monitors are single-color monitors that are used when output is mainly text and numbers. Monochrome monitors usually display either green, amber, or white characters on a black background. They display text and graphics very well. For applications requiring color, however, such as presentation charts, you might want to investigate the option of a color monitor. Of course, color monitors are more expensive.

Secondary Storage

Because RAM is volatile and limited in capacity, *secondary storage* is normally used to permanently store information external to the computer. Secondary storage is usually used for storing large amounts of data or long-term retention of programs.

Magnetic Tape. A magnetic tape is typically a $1/2$- or $1/4$-inch ribbon of mylar (a plastic-like material) coated with a thin layer of iron oxide material. In the tape drive, an input/output (I/O) device, the tape passes by a read/write head. The read/write head is an electromagnetic component that is used to read from and write to the tape. Data pieces are stored on the tape in the form of magnetized iron oxide particles. The magnetized spots represent patterns of 1's and 0's that, in turn, represent data. To read the tape, the drive passes the tape by the read head and the patterns of 1's and 0's are interpreted as data. Magnetic tapes can be used with all sizes of computers. They are made in reel-to-reel, cassette, and cartridge forms. Each kind stores data sequentially and magnetically, but their storage capacities and access times are different.

Magnetic Disk. A magnetic disk is a mylar or metallic platter on which electronic data can be stored. Data files on the disk can be read sequentially or directly. Magnetic disks are manufactured in both floppy diskette and hard disk styles. The main advantages of magnetic disks over magnetic tapes include:

1. The ability to access the data stored on it directly
2. The ability to hold more data in a smaller space
3. The ability to attain faster data-transfer speeds

A *floppy diskette*, also called a diskette or disk, is a small, flexible, mylar disk coated with iron oxide on which data is stored. Floppy disks are available in three sizes: 3.5-inch microdisk, 5.25-inch floppy disk, and 8-inch floppy.

The 5.25-inch and 8-inch disks are covered by a stiff, protective jacket with various holes and cutouts that serve special functions. The hub ring is where the disk drive holds the disk to rotate it. The elongated read/write window allows the read/write head of the drive to write data on or read data from the floppy disk. The small hole next to the hub ring is the index hole through which the computer determines the relative position of the disk for locating data. The cutout on the side of the floppy diskette is the write-protect notch. By covering this opening with a piece of tape, data on the disk is protected from being accidentally erased or written over.

The 3.5-inch disks, sometimes called *microdisks*, have a hard plastic covering and a protective metal piece that covers the read/write window when the disk is not in use. This additional protection makes the disk less prone to damage from handling, dust, or other contaminants. The 3.5-inch disks are growing in popularity because of their larger storage capacity and durability.

Each disk must be prepared for use before data or programs can be stored on it. The process of preparing the disk for use is called *formatting*. You should consult your computer's manual for instructions on formatting disks.

Hard Disk. A hard disk is a hard and inflexible device made from materials such as aluminum instead of mylar. The I/O device that transfers data to and from a hard disk is called a hard-disk drive. Hard disks are sometimes called *rigid* or *fixed disks*. The read/write head of a hard-disk drive floats above the surface of the disk at a height of about 50-millionths of an inch (0.00005 inch), a distance less than the diameter of a human hair. Hard disks have tremendous data storage capacity compared to floppy disks.

The high rotation speed of hard disks is about 3,600 revolutions per minute (rpm). If the read/write head runs into any particles of dirt, dust, or even smoke, a head crash might result. When this occurs, a foreign particle is pushed into the disk and the head actually bounces and comes into contact with the disk. This is what happens when people say that their hard disks *crashed*. Severe damage can result to the head or the disk, thereby destroying the data stored there.

A hard disk has several advantages over a floppy disk. The rigid construction of a hard disk allows it to be rotated at 3,600 rpm, compared to 360 rpm for a floppy disk. Thus, data can be transferred much faster to or from a hard disk because it takes less time to find the storage location. More data can be placed in a smaller area of a hard disk because of its hard construction.

Hard disks are available for all sizes of computers. They can be one of the following:

1. Fixed-disk systems that are permanently installed in a drive
2. Removable cartridges
3. Disk packs which can be removed from the drive

Optical Disk. In recent years, microcomputer designers have done a great deal of experimentation with optical disks, also called *CD ROMs* or *laser disks*. These disks use a laser to write data onto a hard magnetic platter, which is the same technology used to record sound on a compact audio disk. Future optical disks will hold vast amounts of long-term storage, typically 1,000 megabytes per disk. At the present time, most optical disks can be written to only once. However, some of the more expensive optical disks can be written to and erased. Optical laser disks are hard metal disks ranging in size from 4.72 to 14 inches in diameter.

Laser beams encode binary data by burning microscopic "pits" to represent patterns of 1's and 0's. This process makes a permanent recording on the disk. Therefore, optical disks are usually used only for applications requiring access to a large prerecorded collection of data, such as an encyclopedia. For example, the *American Academic Encyclopedia*, a 9 million-word (20-volume) encyclopedia, is stored on one compact disk less than 5 inches in diameter. A 14-inch laser disk can store as many as 20 reel-to-reel tapes.

Optical tape is similar in appearance to magnetic tape, but data is stored by optical laser techniques. Optical tapes, which are in cassette form, can store over eight gigabytes of data each.

As the technology continues to improve, there will be new developments and products to enhance your computer system. You should try to find out what is available before you prematurely commit a large investment. What we have presented should give you the basic understanding you need to shop intelligently for computer equipment. If your dealer finds out how much you know, he or she will respect your judgment more and will go all out to help you. Your basic knowledge should help you in negotiating better deals for your project management equipment.

1.6 COMPUTER DISK OPERATING SYSTEM (DOS)

DOS offers a very powerful environment for controlling your computer's operations. With DOS commands, you can direct your computer to perform nifty tricks and functions. Your application package gives you the avenue for performing specific functions. But there are a myriad of other functions, particularly those performed on files, that you can only perform from the DOS level. Some application programs that are specially designed will offer you a way to temporarily escape the program to the DOS level so you can perform DOS-level functions. The following sections present some of the basic things you might need to know about taking full advantage of the power of DOS. For full details on DOS, you will need to consult your official DOS manual.

What Is DOS?

DOS is a program. But it is not like any other program. Most of your other programs most likely will need the help of DOS to run because DOS controls every part of the computer system. DOS gives you complete control over whatever your computer does and how it does it. It is the link between you and your computer. DOS is called the disk operating system because much of its work involves managing disks and disk files. You might call it the "enforcer" of the computing environment.

What DOS Does

By using DOS commands, you can use DOS to manage your files, to control the work flow, and to perform other useful tasks that might otherwise require special utility programs.

The A>, B>, or C> that you see after you boot up your computer is called the *system prompt*. It is a prompt from the computer to tell you that it is ready to accept input from you. The prompt identifies the *current drive*, or *default drive*. The default drive is where DOS will look for a file unless you explicitly specify where the file is located. You can change the default drive by typing the desired drive followed by a colon and then pressing Enter. For example, to change from the A drive to the B drive, you will type B: at the A> prompt and press Enter.

1.7 BASIC DOS COMMANDS

Following are some of the basic DOS commands that you might encounter or need to use in your day-to-day project management operations. The commands are briefly described. You must consult your DOS manual to get the full explanation of each command.

Copy

COPY copies files from one location to another. For example, if your project management package has a temporary DOS exit facility, you can momentarily escape to the DOS level and make a copy of a file. Some examples of the format of the COPY command are:

COPY a:*.* b:

Copies all the files in drive a: to drive b:.

COPY a:*.DOC b:

Copies all the files in drive a: with the extension *.DOC* to drive b:.

COPY a:abcs.* b:

Copies all the files in drive a: with the name *absc* and any extension into drive b:.

COPY a:absc.doc>prn

Copies the file named abcs.doc to the printer. If the file is a standard ASCII text file (i.e. not compiled into computer machine language), this is a quick and dirty way to get a printout of it.

COPY CON: newfile.doc

Creates a text file named newfile.doc. This is a fast way to create small text files, such as config.sys, autoexec.bat, and command document files. After you issue this command and press Enter, you can start entering text lines. Press Enter at the end of each line. When you are done, press Ctrl-Z and then press Enter. The Ctrl-Z command signals the end of the file.

Diskcopy

DISKCOPY copies all the contents from one disk to another. In the process of diskcopying, all the previous contents of the target disk are erased through the process of formatting. You must make sure that no desired files are located on the target disk.

DISKCOPY a: b:

Copies the disk in drive a: to drive b:.

Format

FORMAT is the command for preparing a new disk for use with your computer. If you format a previously used disk, all its contents will be erased.

FORMAT b:

This command formats the disk in drive b:. The computer will prompt you to insert the disk into drive b:. If you issue this command from the A> prompt, you must have your DOS disk in that drive because the FORMAT.COM program is located on the DOS disk.

Type

The Type command prints the contents of a file onto your computer screen. This is a quick and easy way to take a look at the contents of a file before regular processing.

TYPE filename.doc

Prints the contents of the specified file onto the screen.

TYPE filename.doc > prn

Sends the contents of the specified file to the printer.

CLS

The CLS command clears the computer display screen while you are at the DOS level. If the screen is already filled with commands, responses, and other unwanted materials, you might want to use CLS to clear everything before you continue your work.

Shift-PrtSc

The PrtSc command prints what is currently displayed on the screen to your printer. Make sure that your printer is already on. Press the PrtSc key while holding down the Shift key. If your computer does not have the PrtSc key, check your computer manual for the procedure to use for your own particular system.

Ctrl-PrtSc

The Ctrl-PrtSc command simultaneously sends information to both the display screen and the printer. Make sure that your printer is on. Whatever is displayed on the screen is also printed on the printer. This command remains in effect until you cancel it. To cancel it, simply issue the command again.

DIR

The DIR command is used to display the file directory on a disk. Whenever you ask DOS to show you the directory of a disk, it lists your files by filename. It also shows you the size of each file in bytes, and gives you the date and time the file was either created or last updated. If you are interested in the date and time information, you should always give the current date and time when DOS prompts you for date and time after you first turn on the computer. Some examples of the DIR command are:

A>DIR

To display the directory of the disk in the current drive, you simply type dir. Type the command and press Enter. To display the directory of another drive other than the current drive, type the drive designation after the DIR command. For example, DIR B:.

A>DIR/p

This command displays the directory one screen at a time. If your file directory is very long, the /p (pause) option will enable you to momentarily stop the scrolling of the directory listing.

A>DIR/w

This command displays the directory in a wide format across the screen. It permits you to get more information on the screen at one time. However, the file size, date, and time information will not be displayed.

Restarting DOS

There are times when you might want to restart DOS, such as when the computer hangs up and the only way to get out of the dilemma is to restart DOS. You can start all over by turning the computer off and then turning it back on. However, there is a command that restarts DOS without turning the computer off: Press Ctrl-Alt-Del simultaneously. Note that whatever you have currently in the computer memory will be lost when you restart DOS.

Freezing the Display

DOS has a command that lets you temporarily freeze the display screen so that you can read displays that otherwise would scroll by too quickly, such as a long directory listing. Press Ctrl-Num Lock. The display remains frozen, giving you time to read whatever is on the screen. To start the display scrolling again, simply press any key.

Cancelling a Command

The command Ctrl-Break cancels whatever the system is doing. Use it when you really don't want the computer to continue what it's doing. In many cases, the command Ctrl-C will perform the same function of cancelling the ongoing operation.

1.8 TYPES OF FILES

A file contains either a program or data. A program is a set of instructions for the computer. Data are the text and numbers that the program needs to accomplish its goals. Three types of files are important to your work; *text files, command files,* and *application program files*. They are all different, both in content and function.

Text Files

Text files normally contain characters you can read, such as letters, numbers, and symbols. Many word processors save their document files as text files. Software that saves its files in machine-readable code (unintelligible to users) often has a conversion utility that converts machine-readable files to text files.

Command Files

Command files contain the instructions DOS needs to carry out commands. These instructions can be a program, such as the format program (FORMAT-.COM) that is used to format new disks for use with your computer. Not all DOS commands are command files. Some commands, such as the Copy command, are built into the main body of DOS. When you load DOS into memory, you automatically load these commands with it. When you want to use these commands, DOS has them ready for immediate use. It does not need to look up a separate command program to run.

Built-in commands are called *internal* commands. These commands are executed simply by requesting them. In contrast, commands that are kept in command files until they are requested are called *external* commands. When you use an external command, you type the name of the command and DOS loads the program and runs it.

Application Program Files

An application program, such as a word processor, is stored in a command file. The application program stores your work, such as documents, in data files. Each file has an extension that identifies which type of file it is. Your application program will use its own peculiar extension, such as .DOC, .TXT, or .ASC.

Special File Extensions

Some file extensions have special meaning to DOS. These extensions are either created by DOS or cause DOS to assume the file contains a particular type of program or data. You should not give any of your files these extensions unless the function of the files fit the descriptions given in TABLE 1-1.

How Files Are Tracked by DOS

Information is recorded on a disk in narrow concentric circles called *tracks*. There are 40 tracks on a standard disk and 80 tracks on the high-capacity disks used on the IBM/AT and compatibles. A track is divided into smaller areas called *sectors*, each of which can hold 512 bytes (0.5K) of information.

The disk side, track number, and sector number of the beginning of a file are stored as part of the directory entry for the file. You don't see this information when you use the DIR command to check the contents of a disk. DOS uses the side, track, and sector numbers information to locate any file on a disk. The 40 tracks on a standard disk are numbered 0 through 39, and the nine sectors are numbered 1 through 9.

Double-sided disk drives use both sides of a disk for storing information. Single-sided drives, which are now almost extinct, write on only one side of a

Table 1-1. Special File Extensions.

Extension	Meaning	Type of File
COM	Command	Identifies a command file that contains a program DOS runs when you type the file name.
EXE	Executable	Identifies a command file that contains a program that DOS runs when you type the file name. Application files that are compiled into machine-readable code usually have the EXE extension.
SYS	System	Identifies a file for use by DOS only.
BAK	Backup	Contains an earlier version of a text file. Many word processors and other application programs automatically make a backup copy of a file and give it this extension at the start of an editing session.
BAT	Batch	Identifies a text file you can create that contains a set of DOS commands that are run one after the other (in a batch mode) when you type the name of the file.

disk. A double-sided disk can store 360K, while a single-sided disk can store only 180K. The high-capacity disks used on IBM AT have 80 tracks numbered 0 through 79, each of which is divided into 15 sectors numbered 1 through 15. Because a sector stores 512 bytes, a high-capacity disk can store 1.2 megabytes.

The items covered in this chapter have touched briefly on some of the many aspects of computer systems. There will, undoubtedly, be some specific components of your own computer system that were not discussed in this chapter. The procedure for the implementation of project management functions on your own computer will depend on the configuration of your computer hardware and software. We have, however, presented the general topics that should be very valuable in your evaluation of computers for use in project management. Subsequent chapters go into more details of what computer tools, models, and techniques are available for use in project management functions.

2

Computers and
Project Decision Making

Project management is both a science and an art. It is a science because it uses
scientific techniques that have been proven to enhance management processes
(Whitehouse 1973). It is an art because it relies on the good judgment, expertise, and personal intuition of the project manager. A good project manager uses
his or her personal expertise and experience and the tools available to manage
projects effectively. Computer hardware and software together constitute one
group of tools that is available to the project manager. This chapter presents
many of the general aspects of computer hardware and software that are relevant for project management functions. Check the glossary for unfamiliar project management terms that you might find in this chapter.

2.1 PROJECT MANAGEMENT FUNCTIONS

To appreciate the capabilities of the computer tools, models, and techniques discussed in this book, you must understand the basic functions of project management. This understanding will facilitate the selection of the proper
tools for specific project management functions. Presently, the most frequent
uses of computers for project management involve activity scheduling and
resource allocation. However, many other aspects of project management are
amenable to computer implementations: communication, project planning and
organization, project coordination, personnel motivation, budget analysis, project control, and performance evaluation. There are numerous computer software packages and tools other than the conventional project management
software packages that can be used effectively in all aspects of project management.

Elements of Project Management

Project management is the process of managing, allocating, and timing resources in order to achieve a given objective in an expedient manner. The objective might be in terms of time, monetary, or technical results. Alternately, project management could be defined as the process of achieving objectives by using the combined capabilities of project resources or assets. It also might be viewed as the systematic execution of tasks needed to achieve project objectives.

A project can range from the simple, such as painting a room, to the very complex, such as the construction of mass transit routes. The technical differences among project types are of great importance when applying project management techniques. For example, an application of project management principles, if carried to the extreme, will probably slow down the room-painting project. Even if the painting process is not slowed, it is doubtful that the improvement in the result will be significant enough to justify the effort. On the other hand, the success of the mass transit system can be seriously hampered by a lack of proper project management techniques.

As a historical perspective, the project management concept was initially concentrated on defense-related and construction projects. Many of the notable developments in project management occurred during and immediately after World War II. Since those early years, the concept has spread to virtually all industries. Project management techniques are now widely used in many human endeavors, including construction, banking, manufacturing, marketing, healthcare, sales, transportation, and research and development, as well as academic, legal, political, and government establishments. The construction industry has been the most noticeable in the project management movement. In many applications, the completion of a project on time is the overriding factor. Punctuality in delivering the completed project is a crucial aspect of many undertakings. Delayed or unsuccessful projects not only translate to monetary costs, but also impede subsequent undertakings. The notion of ''a minute waited is a minute wasted'' should be an overriding concept in project resource management. Resources should never be allowed to wait for something to do.

Within the several industries that embrace project management concepts are unique practices and requirements that relate only to particular industries and situations. However, there are certain unifying characteristics of the various applications. Standard project management elements and definitions include (Badiru 1988):

- *Program*—The term commonly used to denote very large and prolonged undertakings. The term is typical in many government endeavors that span several years. The U.S. space program is a good example. Programs are associated with particular systems; for example, a nuclear armament program within a national defense system.

- *Project*—The term generally applied to time-phased efforts of much smaller scope and duration than programs. Programs are sometimes viewed as consisting of a set of projects. However, it is not uncommon for practitioners to use both terms interchangeably. The government sector generally tends to refer to its efforts as programs.
- *Task*—The elemental content of a project. A project is normally composed of contiguous arrays of tasks that all contribute to the overall project goal.
- *Activity*—The atom of a project. Activities are generally smaller than tasks. In a detailed analysis of a project, an activity can be viewed as the smallest practically indivisible work element of the project. Such minute details of a project can become very crucial in identifying project bottlenecks.

To clarify the relative descriptions of the terms presented so far, we can consider a manufacturing plant as a system. A plantwide endeavor to improve productivity can be viewed as a program. The installation of Flexible Manufacturing Systems (FMS) is a project within the productivity improvement program. The process of identifying and contacting various equipment suppliers is a task. The actual process of placing an order with a selected supplier is an activity.

- *Resource*—The manpower, tools, equipment, and physical items that are available for the pursuit of the project goal. Not all resources are necessarily tangible. For example, conceptual knowledge and skill can be broadly classified as resources. The lack of or untimely availability of resources can be a major impediment to project management efforts.
- *Top Management*—The class of company personnel responsible for company policies and final decisions. Top management generally has the final say in the initiation and implementation phases of most projects, especially when budgetary commitments are required for the project.
- *Project Manager*—The individual who oversees the execution of the project plans. He is the most likely person to need computer tools for performing his project management functions.

Functions within Project Management

Modern project management encompasses several functions, including those found in traditional project management and general management. Some of these functions are outlined in this chapter. For further details on project management functions, consult any of several available texts on the subject (Badiru 1988, Whitehouse 1973, Meredith and Mantel 1985, and Kerzner 1986).

Project Birth and Death Process. The birth and death process of any project covers the following steps. Note that the computer can play a significant role in each step:

- *Project Conceptualization*—The stage at which a need for the project is identified, defined, and justified.
- *Project Definition*—The phase at which the specifications of the design elements are developed. The specifications converge on the overall project goal.
- *Project Development*—The operational aspects of getting the project on track in accordance with specified goals. Project development covers items such as activity definitions, resource procurement and allocation, personnel organization, and scheduling.
- *Project Monitoring*—The diagnostic process of checking whether or not project results conform to plans and specifications.
- *Project Controlling*—The corrective actions implemented to steer the project in the proper direction based on established objectives.
- *Project Termination*—The phase-out stage of the project. A crucial component of terminating a project is the need to communicate with those who will be affected by the termination.

Resource Management. Project objectives are accomplished by applying resources to functional requirements. Resources, in the context of project management, are generally made up of people and equipment. These two items are typically in short supply. The people needed for a particular task might be tied up with other ongoing commitments, and required equipment might be under the control of a rival department. The project manager must organize both the physical and human resources to ensure they are available when needed. Resources need to be carefully budgeted during the definition phase of a project and are usually considered in the light of the scheduling function, which relates to the commitment of resources against time for the project activities.

Project Planning. *Planning,* in a project management context, refers to the process of establishing courses of action within the prevailing environment to achieve predetermined goals. Planning is needed to:

- Minimize uncertainties
- Clarify project objectives
- Provide basis for evaluating project progress
- Establish performance standard for operations
- Notify personnel of responsibilities

The project planning process varies, depending on the organization involved, the particular project under consideration, and the prevailing environment. The established policies and procedures of the organization do, however, play a key role in the planning process. The standard elements of project planning should include the following:

- *Project Overview*—An enumeration of the objectives of the project. The scope of the overall project and its relevance to the company goal should be specified. The major milestones, with a description of the significance of each, should be documented. In addition, the managerial structure to be used for the project should be established.
- *Project Goal*—A detailed description of the overall project goal. A goal can be regarded as the result of a series of objectives. Each objective should be detailed with respect to its implication in the project goal. The major actions that will be taken to ensure the achievement of the objectives also should be identified.
- *Project Policy*—The general guideline for personnel actions and managerial decision making. The project policy, in effect, dictates how the project plan will be executed. The chain of command and the network of information flow are governed by the established policy for the project. A lack of policy creates a fertile ground for incoherence in the project resulting from individual conflicting interpretations of the project plan by the personnel.
- *Project Procedures*—The detailed methods of abiding by the project policy. An example is the requirement for written documentations for all approvals. For example, a policy might stipulate that the approval of the project manager be sought for all purchases. A procedure then might specify how the approval should be obtained (e.g., oral or written).
- *Project Resources*—The manpower and equipment required for the project. Currently available resources should be identified, along with "procurement" resources. The time-based availability of each resource should be specified. Very careful attention should be given to the resource requirements because resources determine the structure of the project schedule, which in turn determines the project performance. Issues such as personnel recruiting and training should be addressed in the analysis of resources.
- *Project Budget*—Usually represented in dollar amounts. The budget also might be listed under *Resources,* instead of being listed as a separate entity. One-time and recurring costs should be identified separately. If possible, budgetary requirements by tasks should be specified.
- *Project Performance Standards*—The yardsticks against which project outputs can be compared. In addition, the methods by which the performance will be analyzed also should be defined to avoid ambiguities in monitoring, recording, and evaluating the project status.
- *Project Organization*—The correlation of duties, responsibilities, and interactions of the project personnel. The project organization serves as the coordination model for the overall project. Decision and communica-

tion relationships should be carefully developed and enforced in the project organization.

- *Work Breakdown Structure (WBS)*—The partitioning a project into convenient small work packages. This method facilitates a more efficient and logical analysis of the required events and activities involved in the project.
- *Potential Bottlenecks*—The areas or phases of the project that could cause the project to be slowed down or stopped. As a part of the planning process, potential bottlenecks should be identified. This identification will alert all personnel and the project analyst to possible problems during the life cycle of the project.

Project Scheduling. Project scheduling is a major function in the project management process. It is usually a source of problems and controversies for organizations. The project schedule shows the timing of the efforts of the project personnel. It outlines when individual activities are to begin and end. Reliable estimates of durations of the project activities should be developed. A master schedule should be developed and properly distributed to both the managerial staff and the functional employees.

Project Control. Project control is the process of reducing the deviations between project realities and the project plan. The control function is the culmination of the planning, monitoring, and controlling cycle. Project performance should be regularly monitored and compared to established standards. Corrective actions become necessary whenever observed deviations from plans are significantly higher than permissible limits. A computer tool offers the means by which performance can be quickly evaluated so corrective actions can be identified. Some possible corrective actions include:

- Alteration of activities
- Elimination of activities
- Addition of resources
- Expediting of activities
- Termination of activities
- Improvement of operation procedures
- Resolution of personnel conflicts
- Elimination of waste
- Reduction of cost
- Consolidation of functions

The controlling process is usually carried out in the following three steps:

1. *Measurement*—The process of measuring the relationship between planned performance and actual performance with respect to project objectives. The variable to be measured, the measurement scale, and

the measuring device should be predetermined in the planning stage. The fundamental variables for control are the project cost and schedule. The cost can be measured, for example, in dollars. The dollar amount then can be expressed in terms of overall budget depletion relative to project status. The status of the schedule might be expressed in terms of relationship to important milestones.

2. *Evaluation*—The testing of the measured magnitude of the performance variable against performance standards. The analysis of the appropriate actions to take is included in the evaluation. Different levels of deviations for the same variable sometimes can warrant different corrective actions.

3. *Action*—The implemention of the corrective actions identified in the evaluation process. The implementation of corrective actions often leads to at least a partial replanning of the remaining portion of a project. A corrective action in itself might be a potential source of the need for some auxiliary corrective actions.

The Triple C Principle. The Triple C Principle (Badiru 1987) states that project management can be enhanced by implementing it as three distinct managerial functions of:

1. Communication
2. Cooperation
3. Coordination

The principle facilitates a systematic approach to the planning, organizing, scheduling, and controlling of a project. Each of the three steps advocated by the Triple C Principle can be implemented with the aid of computer tools.

Communication. Proper and timely communication is needed to keep project personnel apprised of what is going on in the project environment. Components of project communication include the following:

- What is being planned
- When the plan will be executed
- How the project will be organized
- Who is in charge
- Why the project is needed
- What the potential direct and indirect benefits are
- What alternatives are available
- What is the expected cost
- What personnel contribution is needed
- What the possible negative impacts of the project are
- What penalties are associated with the project
- What precedents are available for the project

- Who else already knows about the project
- Who will be affected by the failure of the project
- What the scope of the project is

In addition to in-house communication, external sources also should be included in the communication loop as appropriate. The communication effort could be simplified if the project analyst would do the following:

- Demonstrate personal commitment to the project
- Create multichannel communication networks
- Identify communication hierarchy
- Develop a communication responsibility matrix
- Identify internal and external communication needs
- Endorse both formal and informal communication links

Cooperation. Not only must people be informed, but their cooperation must be explicitly elicited. Merely signing off on a project might not result in their full cooperation. A structured approach to seeking cooperation should help identify and explain the following items to the project personnel:

- The cooperative efforts needed
- The time-frame involved
- The criticality of cooperation to the project
- The rewards of cooperation
- The organizational impact of cooperation
- The precedents for future projects
- The implication of lack of cooperation

Coordination. After the communication and cooperation functions have been successfully initiated, the efforts of the project team must be coordinated. Coordination facilitates harmonious organization of project efforts. The development of a responsibility chart can be very helpful at this stage. A *responsibility chart* is essentially a matrix consisting of columns of individual or functional departments and rows of required actions. Cells within the matrix are filled with relationship codes that indicate who is responsible for each task. The responsibility matrix can easily be implemented on a computer by using an electronic spreadsheet or a database file. The responsibility chart helps to avoid overlooking essential communication requirements as well as obligations. It can help resolve questions such as:

- Who is to do what?
- Who is responsible for which results?

- What personnel interfaces are involved?
- Who is to inform whom of what?
- Whose approval is needed for what?
- What support is needed from whom for what functions?

FIGURE 2-1 shows an example of a responsibility matrix for a software development project.

		Individuals Responsible						
Code:		Domain Expert	Knowledge Engineer	Programmer	Project Manager	Documentation Specialist	Plant Manager	Clerical Staff
R = Responsible								
A = Approve								
C = Consult								
I = Inform								
S = Support								
Actions								
1. Problem Definition							R	
2. Personnel Assignment		C			C		R	
3. Project Initiation					R		A	
4. System Prototype		C	R	R	I		S	
5. Full System		C	R	R	I		S	
6. System Verification		R	R	R	C	I	C	
7. System Validation		R	R	R	R	I	C	
8. System Integration		R	R	R	R	I	A	
9. System Maintenance		R	R	R	C	I	A	
10. Documentation		C	C	C	C	R	A	I

Fig. 2-1. Example of a responsibility chart.

2.2 SOFTWARE AND PROJECT MANAGEMENT

A large number of procedures and methods have been developed to enhance the application of project management to a vast range of industrial and administrative functions. This rapid spreading of project management is largely a result of the availability of computer software packages that make it possible to implement project management techniques quickly. Using a computer should not replace the conventional planning, scheduling, and controlling functions of management, however; nor should it be expected to replace traditional management decision-making processes. The computer should be used only as a tool to facilitate the implementation of proven techniques. The primary value of the computer is the speed at which it will perform the quantitative analysis needed to develop schedules and generate a variety of outputs and reports.

Computer programs for project planning and control have been available for a long time, but the cryptic designs have made general use difficult. The first generation of project management programs was complex, expensive, restrictive, and difficult to use. However, new hardware and software technologies have opened new possibilities. The increasing popularity, acceptance, and use of project management software are evidenced by the number of commercial programs that have been introduced in the past few years. Many computer trade publications such as *PC Week* and *PC World* now regularly carry advertisements and software reviews on project management packages.

Project management software is designed for use not only by the project manager, but by any person involved in managing a group of resources in order to carry out a set of tasks. In larger projects, the overall project leader cannot be aware of all activities going on in the project. A decentralized organization of the project management environment is often more helpful in coordinating the various activities in a large project. The project leader sets the objectives and time frames for accomplishing the objectives and then delegates the actual functions to different groups.

A software package must be able to meet the needs of a decentralized project organization. It must be an aid to both the middle- and lower-level management personnel. Today, it is not necessary to use a mainframe computer to meet these needs. These needs can be met by using flexible microcomputer software tools with facilities that make it possible to send and collect relevant information in a local area network. The personal computer can help you enjoy your work more and facilitate greater project profit. With just a few keystrokes, you can screen tasks and identify possible bottlenecks.

Instead of spending a lot of time performing conventional tracking, you can get the facts about project progress much easier from a computer, rather than having to make a series of phone calls. Without leaving the office, you can get detailed project reports within minutes. With a PC and a modem, you can have instant access to information located at remote project sites. Regular software tools can be combined with dedicated project management software to create a powerful information control environment. During the past few years, project management software packages have become available for desktop computers.

2.3 SOFTWARE EVOLUTION

The present stage of project management computer software has been achieved through an evolutionary process that spans several developments. Five distinct generations of software evolution (Badiru, 1988) have been identified:

1. First Generation (Pre-World War II)—The era of unstructured project analysis when managers executed their project plans (if there was one) by raw gumption and the so-called "seat-of-the-pants" rules.
2. Second Generation (From mid-1950s)—The era marked by the emergence of PERT/CPM techniques. Project analysis in this generation was performed manually.
3. Third Generation (From early 1970s)—The era mainframe computer implementations of PERT/CPM became prevalent. However, access to the programs was limited to only those with the necessary hardware.
4. Fourth Generation (From early 1980s)—The period marked by the development of more accessible project management programs on mini micro computers. The increased access gave managers the tool for timely project monitoring and control.
5. Fifth Generation (From mid-1980s)—The era marked by the introduction of integrated project management packages. These advanced programs combined the traditional PERT/CPM network analysis with project graphics, report generation, spreadsheets, and cost analysis.

The sixth generation is still on the horizon. This generation promises to incorporate real-time communication and networking capabilities into project analysis. Some of the elements of this sixth generation are already available in some project management packages.

2.4 SOFTWARE SELECTION

The proliferation of project management software has created an atmosphere whereby every project analyst wants to have and use a software package for every project situation. However, not every project situation deserves the use of project management software. You should first determine whether or not the use of a software package is justified. If this evaluation is affirmative, then you must determine which specific package of the many available should be procured. If you can answer at least five of the following questions in the affirmative, then you can conclude that you do need project management software.

1. Do you manage more than one project at a time?
2. Do your projects typically contain more than 20 tasks?
3. Is your project scheduling environment very complex?
4. Are more than five resource types involved in each project?
5. Do you perform other numerical analysis in your project management functions?
6. Is the generation of graphics outputs such as Gantt and PERT charts important in your project management functions?
7. Do you need to perform cost analysis on a frequent basis?
8. Is it necessary to generate forecasts from historical project data?
9. Is automated reporting important in your organization?
10. Is computerization one of the goals of your organization?

A close examination of any modern project environment will reveal that it fits the criteria for using project management software. Nowadays, only the unreasonably narrow projects will not need the help of software for effective management. The issue is usually not that of whether or not software is needed, but which software should be used and how.

When evaluating project management software, you need to evaluate several factors and questions. Notable among them are:

1. Cost
   • Can the software be procured for a reasonable amount relative to the organization's budget and intended use?
2. Need
   • Is a computer program really needed for the project involved?
   • Is there or will there be a knowledgeable person who can run the software?
3. Project Plan
   • Ease of entering and storing the plan
   • Full precedence capability
   • Limitations on number of activities (network size)
   • Work breakdown structure capability
   • Work splitting
4. Resource Management
   • Capability of assigning partial resources
   • Resource leveling
   • Assignment of costs
   • What resource allocation heuristics are available?
5. Progress Tracking
   • Display of time-based project schedule
   • Project replanning (network editing)

6. Report Generation
   - Network diagram (limitation on size, ease of understanding)
   - Gantt Chart
   - Milestone schedule
   - Resource reports
   - Cost reports
   - Performance variance analysis
7. Ease of Use
   - On-line training and help
   - Input format
   - Output format and contents
   - Quality of documentation
8. General Characteristics
   - Software version. Later versions of a program, for example, version 3.2, tend to have fewer bugs and more enhanced features. However, excessively high version numbers, for example, version 8.1, could mean that the developer has been slow in responding to customer complaints and implementing all needed upgrades.
   - Compactness (e.g., three disks versus ten disks)
   - File import/export capability
   - Availability of trial package
   - Copy protection and backup procedures. Does the program permit limited or unlimited hard disk installations?
   - Speed of execution
   - Compatibility with the computer hardware and other software used in the project environment
9. Software Capabilities
   - Analytical methodology (e.g., CPM, PERT)
   - Number of tasks that can be handled (at least 50)
   - Number of resource types that can be accommodated (at least 10)
   - Help and error handling abilities
   - Milestone identification
   - Resource profiling and leveling
10. Hardware Requirements
    - Disk drive (single, dual, or fixed)
    - RAM requirement
    - Coprocessor or hardware board requirements
    - Input devices (mouse, joystick, keyboard, etc.)
    - Output devices (types of printers supported)
    - Display unit/adapter
    - WYSIWYG (What You See Is What You Get) screen capabilities
11. Vendor
    - Reputation
    - Sales volume

- Replacement support
- Product support
- Toll-free telephone line (for customer support)
- Cost of program updates
- Other supporting products

As mentioned earlier, some of these factors might be more important than others in specific project functions. As a result, you should make a careful overall analysis. With more and more new programs and updates to old software coming into the market, a crucial aspect of the project management function is keeping up with what is available and making a good judgment in selecting a program. The future directions for software applications in project management might be one or a combination of the following:

- A clearing house for software testing where users can preview specific software of interest
- Commercial software rental similar to video tapes
- Proliferation of shareware packages

2.5 ORGANIZING THE COMPUTER ENVIRONMENT

Project management applications have exploited recent developments in computer technology. The availability of powerful, reliable, and inexpensive personal computers has contributed considerably to the widespread use of project management software. As a result, project management techniques have become accessible not only to specialists such as network analysts and cost engineers, but also to business professionals, who can use them just like any other productivity tool, such as word processors or spreadsheets, to enhance their functions.

Personal computers can be used not only as stand-alone systems, but also as intelligent work stations connected to a host. With a personal computer setup, local data entry and processing are possible which leads to an increased user independence and satisfaction. Furthermore, communications are improved. Data can be transferred easily via diskettes that can be loaded or unloaded at local work stations, thereby avoiding the use of more complex and scarce resources such as tape units.

The general direction of organizing the computer environment for project management should cover system integration and communication. Project information will need to be shared in one or more of the following ways:

- Among projects in the same organization
- Among projects across organizations
- Among one internal project and several external projects
- Among several internal projects and one external project

In a large organization, the project management software environment might be set up in a way that takes advantage of the power of a mainframe system and the flexibility of personal computer system. For example, it can have the following:

- An intelligent workstation performing data entry, local numeric computations, reporting, and presentation
- A mainframe system performing department level analysis and reporting
- A network allowing communications and integration of intelligent workstations

2.6 DATA REQUIREMENTS

An important aspect of using computers for decision making is the determination of the data required. The fundamental steps involved in computer usage are:

- Input
- Process
- Output
- Storage

Data requirements fall in the input step and, as such, constitute a crucial point in the use of computers for decision making. The foundation of management is information and the basis for information is data. Effective management requires proper information management. *Information* can be broadly defined as data that facilitates effective decision making and action. Many organizations are now viewing information as one of their major resources. The emergence of the concept of ''information resources'' is a direct result of this awareness. Consequently, data and information management are becoming issues of concern to managers.

The idea of ''information processing'' is misleading. What is actually processed is data. The processing of data generates information. The processing of information generates decisions. Thus, good decisions are based on appropriate information, which in turn is based on reliable data. If you have a proper understanding of these concepts, then you should realize that data is your primary resource. A major challenge in the management of data and information will involve the following functions:

- How to capture computer-generated information and print it in a usable form for people and machines
- How to make diverse computers communicate in the same network
- How to use voice and pattern recognition to reduce paperwork
- How to achieve faster information systems response time

- How to incorporate flexibility and sharing options into information networks
- How to manage human's 100% reliance on systems that are less than 100% reliable

Data Pruning

Sophisticated data-processing and information-handling mechanisms are needed to govern the mass of information that currently inundates our society. An average manager now spends about 30 percent of his workday sorting through information. By the year 2000, the same manager will need to be reading ten times as much just to locate a piece of information needed for him to take action on crucial project issues. As the society becomes more information-driven, the problems of too much unwanted information or not enough information will be something that every manager will have to face. Too much irrelevant data is floating around. The capabilities of computers can be used to refine data so that much of the unwanted material can be eliminated before the data gets to the decision maker. A manager can wallow in data and still not be able to get to the information hidden inside.

Managing information will encompass the management of both the physical and logical components of an information system—the computer hardware, software, analysts, programmers, operators, operating systems, data communication links, information decision rules, organizational incentive structure, information clients, and information level of detail. Organizational effectiveness will depend on how well information is managed in order to generate good decisions. Good decisions are the blueprints for success. The route to making good decisions should pass through the following steps:

Choosing the Data. Data is comprised of the set of variables and associated values that adequately describe the system under consideration. Data categories should be selected on the basis of their relevance, the level of likelihood that they will be needed for future decisions, and their contribution to the enhancement of decisions. Intended users of the data should be identified.

Collecting the Data. A suitable method of collecting observations for the chosen data category should be identified. The source from which the data will be collected should be identified (e.g., organizational database). The collection method will depend on the particular operation being addressed. The common methods include manual tabulation, direct keyboard entry, optical character reader, magnetic coding, electronic scanner, and more recently, voice command. An input control can be used to confirm the accuracy of collected data. Such a control can be any of the following:

- Relevance check—Check the reasonableness of a datum by comparing it to a standard expected value.
- Limit check—Check whether the collected value exceeds a set limit for the particular data category.

- Critical Value—Identify the critical value of the elements contained in the dataset to check whether an input is within control limits or not.

Coding the Data. *Coding* is the technique of representing the collected data in a form usable for generating information. Coding should be done in a compact and yet meaningful format. The performance of information systems can be greatly improved if effective data formats and coding are designed into the system right from the beginning. Attention must be given to the conversion factors for measured quantities that must go through analog or digital data conversion processes.

Processing the Data. *Data processing* is the manipulation of data to generate useful information. Different types of information might be generated from a given set of data depending on how it is processed. The processing method should consider how the information will be used, who will be using it, and what caliber of system response time is desired. If possible, processing controls should be used. This might involve:

- Control Total—Check how complete the processing is by comparing accumulated output to a known total. An example is the comparison of machine throughput to standard production level or the comparison of cumulative project budget depletion to cost accounting standard.
- Consistency Check—Check if the processing is producing the same output for similar inputs. For example, an electronic inspection device that suddenly shows a measurement ten times higher than the norm warrants an investigation of both the input and the processing mechanisms.
- Scales of Measurement—For numeric scales, specify units of measurement, increments, zero point on the measurement scale, and range of values.

Using the Information. The process of decision making starts when information becomes available. Computers can collect data, manipulate data, and generate information; but the ultimate decision rests with the human. Intuition, training, interest, and ethics are just a few of the factors that determine how analysts use information. The same piece of information that is positively used in one instance might be fraudulently used in another instance. To ensure that data and information are used appropriately, computer-based security measures can be built into the information system.

Types of Data

We usually think of *measurement* as the assignment of numbers to objects or observations, for example, the measurement of the length of a piece of electrical wire. Such measurements, however, constitute just one in a range of measurement scales. Project managers often deal with different kinds of measurement scales depending on the particular task being considered. The use of computers for project management should be evaluated in the light of the kinds of data and measurement scales being used. The different kinds of data measurement scales follow:

- Nominal Scale—Nominal scale is the lowest level of measurement scales. It classifies items into categories. The categories are mutually exclusive and collectively exhaustive; that is, the categories do not overlap and they cover all possible categories of the characteristics being observed. For example, in the analysis of the critical path in a project network, each job is classified as either ''critical'' or ''not critical.'' Operator gender, type of automobile, job classification, and color are some examples of measurements on a nominal scale.
- Ordinal Scale—An ordinal scale is distinguished from a nominal scale by the property of order among the categories. An example is the process of prioritizing project tasks for resource allocation. We know that ''first'' is above ''second,'' but we do not know how far above. Similarly, we know that ''better'' is preferred to ''good,'' but we do not know by how much. In quality control, the ABC classification of items based on the Pareto distribution is an example of a measurement on an ordinal scale.
- Interval Scale—An interval scale is distinguished from an ordinal scale by having equal intervals between the units of measure. The assignment of criticality indices ranging from 0 to 100 for the tasks in a project is an example of a measurement on an interval scale. Even though a task might have a criticality index of zero, it does not mean that the task can have absolutely no influence on the completion time of the project. Similarly, scoring zero on an examination does not imply that you know absolutely nothing about the material covered by the examination. Temperature is a good example of an item measured on an interval scale. Even though there is a zero point on any temperature scale, the measurement is arbitrary. No one can touch an item and proclaim that ''it is 0° Fahrenheit cold!'' Other examples of interval scale are IQ measurements and aptitude ratings.
- Ratio Scale—A ratio scale has the property of an interval scale, but with a true zero point. For example, an estimate of zero time units for the duration of a task is a ratio scale measurement. Other examples of items measured on a ratio scale are age, length, height, and weight. Many of the items to be measured in a project management environment, such as cost and time, will be on a ratio scale.

When using computer tools for project management, the analyst will need to evaluate the capabilities of the tools in handling all the pertinent measurement scales that are expected to be encountered.

Another important aspect of the organization of project data is the classification scheme used. Most projects deal with both *quantitative* and *qualitative* data. Quantitative data require that we describe the characteristics of the items being studied numerically. Qualitative data, on the other hand, is associated with object attributes that are not numerically coded. Most items measured on the nominal and ordinal scales normally will be classified into the qualitative data category. Those items measured on the interval and ratio scales normally will be classified into the quantitative data category. The project data classification paths might follow those shown in FIG. 2-2.

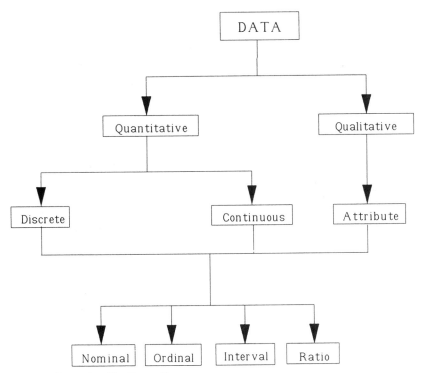

Fig. 2-2. Data classification paths.

Documenting Data Requirements

A comprehensive documentation of the data requirements should be developed. If data is properly documented, the chances for misuse, misinterpretation, mismanagement, or mishandling will be minimized. The components of the documentation should contain such things as the following:

- Data Summary—A general summary of the software for which the data is required, as well as the form in which the data should be prepared. Indicate the impact of the data requirements on the organizational goals.
- Processing Environment—Identification of the project for which the data is required, the user personnel, and the computer system to be used in

processing the data. Make reference to the project request or authorization and relationship to other projects. Specify expected data communication needs and mode of transmission.

- Data Handling Policies and Procedures—A description of the policies governing data handling, storage, and modification is needed. Describe the specific procedures for implementing changes to the data. Provide instructions for data collection and organization.
- Static Data Description—A description of the portion of the data that is used mainly for reference purposes and is rarely updated.
- Dynamic Data Description—A description of the portion of the data that is frequently updated based on the prevailing processing requirements.
- Frequency of Data Update—For the dynamic portion of the data, specify the expected frequency of data change. Describe this data change frequency in relation to the frequency of processing. For processing, if the input data arrives in a random fashion, specify the average frequency and a measure of the variance.
- Data Input Interface—A specification of the required input devices for the data. Identify active data inputs required interactively from the user and passive data inputs retrieved directly from a database.
- Data Constraints—A statement of the limitations on the data requirements. Specify if the constraint is procedural (e.g., based on corporate policy), technical (e.g., based on computer system limitation), or imposed (e.g., based on conflicting project requirements).

Data Security

An important factor to consider in data security is how an organization wants to manage its data security program. Some of the pertinent questions to evaluate include:

- Do departments or functional groups in the organization own their own computer systems and data?
- Are all computer systems within the organization viewed as the property of the Management Information Systems (MIS) department?
- Will the security administration be performed by a programmer or someone with less technical skill?
- How much technical time will be available to develop and maintain the security program?
- How large is the user base to be covered by the security program?
- Are PC-based tools interfaced with mainframe or minicomputer systems?

The exact security measures used will depend on the type and capability of the computer system to be protected. The three major access control software products for the IBM MVS operating system environment are RACF, ACF2, and Top Secret. All three have comparable features and functions.

ACF2. ACF2, now known as CA-ACF2, was developed by Computer Associates International of Garden City, New York, is a resource-oriented tool. It evaluates security based on which resource needs protection and then identifies the users who should have access to it. For example, if a project manager requests security to be placed on personnel files, ACF2 would start an identification of all personnel files. If the personnel files all start with the prefix PRO, ACF2 identifies PRO as the key that shows it where to look in the database. It also develops the access rules that are associated with the control of all PRO files.

After ACF2 has identified the PRO ruleset, it provides each user with an identifier (UID). The UID is a collection of data fields that have been defined for security purposes. It generally represents the hierarchy of the company as it relates to who needs what information. ACF2 builds an access rule for all requests for data within each qualifier of the dataset or resource name.

Top Secret. Top Secret, on the other hand, looks at access security by starting with controls over a user or group of users. It maintains information about a user group and calls that collection of information an *accessorid* or *acid*. For example, technicians in a project environment might have a defined grouping or acid named TECHNI. The profile for this acid would then list all of the access privileges specifically associated with all users in the TECHNI group by identifying the different files that they need to perform their functions.

RACF. RACF facilitates a bit of both ACF2 and Top Secret. It provides resource-oriented protection by maintaining profiles that list who should have what access. It also maintains user and group profiles, which allow a manager to structure access privileges on either an individual or group basis. The user or group name is then identified in the resource profile. The resource profile can be either *discrete* or *generic*. A discrete profile pertains to a specific address space exclusively; A generic profile pertains to a generalized group or resources that follow a defined naming structure.

The same mode of security structures available on larger computers also can be implemented for the smaller stand-alone systems such as desktop PCs. You can find a list of some data security products in Appendix A.

Information Filtering

The problem of getting the right information to the right target in a timely manner has been addressed by the development of the following communication aids:

- Electronic mail
- Distribution lists
- Teleconferences

However, the problem of information management has only been partially solved. More information than is needed is still getting to the users. With the increasing proliferation of new products and services, the cost of generating distributing, storing, or sorting irrelevant information is becoming prohibitive.

Information filtering seems to be the next wave of attempts to streamline information. Information filtering can be achieved by using information categorization rules to restrict the size and flow of information. The same procedures used in data security measures can be employed in directing or restricting the flow of information for effective project management.

An example of a PC-based tool for data and information filtering is the ViewLink program recently introduced by Traveling Software, Inc. of Bothell, Washington. ViewLink is an applications management utility designed to let PC users organize and work with applications and data according to their needs, rather than their computers' needs. It allows users to bypass an operating system's hierarchical framework of directories and subdirectories to manipulate and extract data without using file names or directory paths to locate it. With ViewLink, users can access data stored on floppy disks, hard disks, and multiple network file servers.

ViewLink integrates several information management characteristics similar to those found in personal-information managers, hard-disk managers, shells, search utilities, indexing programs, and applications bridges. It categorizes a user's various types of applications and files, and establishes "views" based on user-defined criteria such as file content, date, name, formula, or any combination of criteria. Individual files inside a view are called *items*. For example, a project-information view presented in a word processing file format can have the following as its related items:

- A graphics file of project schedules
- A spreadsheet file of estimated project costs
- A database file of project tasks
- An electronic mail file containing a memo from the project manager

Any of these items can be linked to other views. The relationship between the views and items can be set up and changed either by the user or through an *associative linking* feature that automatically enters a file into all appropriate predefined views.

ViewLink is targeted for middle-management business users who want multidimensional access to different applications and their files. But at a price about of $149, the product should quickly make a strong showing at all levels of management. Managers involved particularly with multiple projects will find ViewLink to be a valuable software tool for managing the interactions between project tasks. For example, spreadsheet, database, and word processing files that refer to a particular project can be linked as items within the same view. These items can be mixed and matched in views regardless of the applications or projects under which they were generated.

2.7 USER INTERFACE

In order for computer tools to succeed in any management environment, proper user interface must be incorporated into computer systems. User interface should be designed based on the needs and levels of use of the users. Despite all the claims about "user-friendliness," many user interfaces are still seriously deficient in satisfying user needs. A good interface should not only be a simple avenue for interacting with the computer, it also should be an unambiguous channel for data entry and retrieval. In addition to being "friendly," a good user interface should be versatile for such things as data certification, access control, and internal audit. Data certification involves designing a system so only the right people have access to its contents, so the data is correct, and so you can keep track of who made what changes to the data.

Strong password capabilities needed for ensuring data integrity and audit trails have been available on mainframe systems for a long time, but those capabilities are just beginning to emerge in the PC environment. When you use structured windowing procedures and careful path protection, your users are presented only what they need to see to perform their relevant functions. The user interface needs to be designed to control the display of information to the user and the entry of data by the user. For example, an order-entry clerk will have no need to be presented with vendor performance rating information.

In addition to ensuring that only the right personnel are in the right application file, the interface also should contain a means of preventing the personnel from entering the wrong data. For example, internal edits can be used to limit the choices of the person entering data into the computer system. For a given project environment, a smart user interface can, for example, prevent a project analyst from entering data about a task that is not relevant to the prevailing project scenario. Thus, mistakes at the data-entry level can be fixed instantly before hard-to-rectify paper reports are generated.

Features needed to enhance the user-friendliness and versatility of a computer software tool for project management include the following:

- Menus—A menu is simply a listing of the available options. A menu provides a user an organized means of having access to the various program functions without the need to memorize the software command structure.
- Mouse Devices—A mouse is a remote device that controls the movement of the cursor and permits the selection of certain functions with little strain on the user.
- Help Function—A help function allows the user to seek clarification of any of the functions of the software. Help functions are usually designed to be *context-sensitive*, which means they provide prompt on-line help for the current function being used by the user.
- Tutorial—Tutorials offer on-line training for a user. A tutorial is the quickest way to become familiar with the major features of the software.

It leads the user through all the steps involved in using the available functions. A tutorial is normally divided into lessons so the user can select the lesson suitable for his or her level of competence with the software.

- Windows and Screen Switching—Well-designed user interfaces contain windowing capability that enables users to open multiple work windows at the same time. For example, one window might be opened for project resource allocation while another is opened for project tasks definitions. A user can switch from one window to another to perform relevant functions. Windows can be opened in the *split-screen format*, in which case multiple windows are seen simultaneously on the screen. They also can be opened in the *zoom format*, in which case one of the windows is displayed on the screen at a time.

- Screen Previewing—Screen previewing permits the user to get an on-line preview of what the software output might look like when printed on paper. Some previews offer capabilities to handle both text and graphics at once. The enhanced capabilities of the present generation of display units (EGAs and VGAs) should facilitate better previewing capabilities for future generations of software tools.

- Color Coding—Color coding can be used to call the user's attention to key items on the display screen. Because of the variety of color preferences by different users, the software interface should allow users to set desired color combinations.

- Error Messages—Error messages are the means through which the software informs the user of the validity of inputs or requested processes. In many cases, the cursor returns to the inadmissible data element, and the software requires that the data be corrected or deleted before the user can proceed. Error messages help prevent the corruption of your database or project report. The interactive availability of error messages in the PC environment is a major advantage over mainframe systems. Users get immediate notification of a problem, rather than waiting for processing to come back with errors from the batch execution in a mainframe system.

- Sound Effects—In addition to color coding and other visual cues that guide the user through the use of the software, sound effects can be added to further emphasize what the user needs to be aware of. However, the use of sound effects should not be overdone. Some sound effects become very annoying after repeated invocation, particularly by novice users.

- Escape Routes—For those unfortunate cases when a user finds himself or herself in hostile spots within the software, there should be an escape route. The ESC key is often used to enable the user to return to the previous level of the software process. Therefore, an undesired step in the process can be easily aborted without the need to completely break out of the program.

2.8 USER RESPONSIBILITY

The user has a tremendous amount of responsibility as far as the proper use of computer tools is concerned. The organization should provide written recommendations for preparing data inputs. The user must be aware of the source and the required format for data requirements. No matter how well designed a computer tool is, the user still has the responsibility of ensuring the tool is used appropriately.

2.9 MANAGEMENT RESPONSIBILITY

Management has a great deal of responsibility in ensuring that resources needed for project management functions are available. Computer tools should be made available where appropriate. Management must carefully evaluate the output of computers before using the outputs for decision-making purposes. Management must create a personnel environment conducive to the use of computers to enhance project functions. Management itself must strive to become computer literate to better appreciate the role of computers in management decision making.

2.10 MONITORING PROGRESS

The computerized implementation of project management facilitates real-time monitoring of projects. Progress can be quickly monitored, recorded, and evaluated for better management decisions. Measurements can be taken on each of the three components of project constraints: time, performance, and cost. Project progress with respect to time might cover items including missed milestones, reliability of time estimates, and changes of due dates. Progress with respect to performance might cover quality of work or product, functional conflicts, and resource utilization levels. Progress evaluation based on cost might relate to cost overruns, budget revisions, cost reporting inconsistencies, and high resource costs.

2.11 SCHEDULE CONTROL

The Gantt charts developed in the scheduling phase of a project can serve as the yardstick for measuring project progress. Project status should be monitored frequently. Symbols can be used to mark actual activity positions on the Gantt chart. A record should be maintained of the difference between where the activity should be and where it actually is. This information is then conveyed to the appropriate personnel. The more milestones or control points in the project, the better. The larger number allows for more frequent and distinct avenues for monitoring the schedule so problems can be identified and controlled before they accumulate into a major problem.

Schedule variance magnitudes can be plotted on a time scale (e.g., on a daily basis). If the variance continues to get worse, drastic actions might be necessitated. Temporary deviations without a lasting effect on the project should not be a cause for concern. Some corrective actions that can be taken for project schedule delays are:

- Expediting of activities
- Elimination of unnecessary activities
- Productive improvement of tasks
- Reevaluation of milestones or due dates
- Revision of project master plan
- Revision of time estimates for pending activities
- Recomputation of activity network data

2.12 PERFORMANCE CONTROL

Most project performance problems will not surface until after the project is completed, making performance control very difficult. However, every effort should be made to measure all the interim factors of the project. But this means that a lot of time will be needed to collect and evaluate project data. The amount of effort required usually discourages analysts from doing a proper job of performance control. However, with a computer, the monitoring and controlling functions become effortless and can even be fun. Some performance problems might be indicated by time and cost deviations. Careful evaluation of the performance basis throughout the life cycle of a project should help identify problems early enough so that managerial actions can be taken to forestall greater problems later in the project.

2.13 COST CONTROL

The topic of cost control is very expansive. Numerous accounting and reporting systems have been developed for project cost monitoring and control. The complete cost management involves a good control of each of the following:

- Cost estimating
- Cost accounting
- Project cash flow
- Company cash flow
- Direct labor costing
- Overhead rate costing
- Incentives, penalties, and bonuses
- Overtime pays

The process of controlling cost covers several key issues that management must address:

- Proper planning of the project to justify the basis for cost elements
- Reliable estimation of time, resources, and cost
- Clear communication of project requirements, constraints, and available resources
- Sustained cooperation of project personnel
- Good coordination of project functions
- Strict policy of expenditure authorization
- Timely recording and reporting of project consumptions: time, materials, labor, and budget
- Frequent review of the project's progress
- Periodic revision of the schedule to account for prevailing project scenario
- Periodic evaluation of the reasonableness of budget depletion vs. the actual progress

These items must be evaluated as an integrated control effort, rather than as individual functions. The interactions between the various actions needed might be so unpredictable that the success achieved on one side might be masked by failure on another side, thereby making cost performance tracking even more elusive. Computer tools are the only means by which a complete analysis of all aspects of cost control can be performed quickly for prompt managerial decisions.

2.14 GENERATING REPORTS

Computers offer a convenient environment for generating the various kinds of reports that are used in project management. Many computer tools, models, and techniques are available to quickly generate reports such as:

- Financial reports
- Updated network plans
- Graphic schedules (e.g., Gantt charts)
- Time performance plots (e.g., expected versus actual)
- Cost performance plots (e.g., budgeted versus actual)
- Performance requirements
- Project progress reports
- Vendor supply schedule
- Client delivery schedule
- Miscellaneous project records

There is a good basis for taking advantage of the power of computers for project decision making. All the functions found within the project management environment can be enhanced with the aid of computer tools. Conversely, all the presently available computer tools can be applied somewhere within the project management environment. Subsequent chapters of this book discuss some specific computer tools and models and ways they can be used to advance the practice of project management.

3

Spreadsheets and Project Analysis

This chapter presents examples of how an electronic spreadsheet can be used for enhancing many of the numeric analyses that are often encountered in project management. Such analyses might include budgeting, resource allocation, cost estimating, development of presentation graphics, and many more. Because there is a limit to what can be included in the presentations, we have used only a selected number of topics and analyses for discussion in this chapter. However, the use to which a reader can put a spreadsheet program is limited only by his or her own imagination and the level of proficiency of the software.

It is assumed that the reader already has some proficiency in using spreadsheets. This chapter does not attempt to teach how to use a particular spreadsheet program because there are numerous tutorial books available. Instead, it illustrates how basic spreadsheet functions and procedures can be used to perform analyses useful for project management. Even though Lotus 1-2-3 is used as the basis for discussing most of the examples presented, we do not promote the use of any particular spreadsheet program. The presentations and discussions are generic enough that the reader can use any spreadsheet program with which he or she is currently familiar in performing the analyses presented. Appendix A presents a guide to some of the available spreadsheet software packages.

3.1 SPREADSHEET CONCEPTS

With appropriate data input and instructions, an electronic spreadsheet offers a powerful, integrated program that combines three major functions: spreadsheet (or worksheet), graphics, and database. You can conveniently put all these functions to use for project management purposes. A spreadsheet program electronically duplicates an accountant's or bookkeeper's tools such as a ledger pad, pencil, eraser, and calculator. With the spreadsheet, you enter and correct figures by typing on a keyboard, rather than writing with a pencil, and you view your work on a computer screen, or monitor, rather than read a ledger pad. Although the capabilities of an electronic spreadsheet are traditionally associated with the tools of an accountant, you can find widespread applications in various areas not related to accounting.

Once data is entered on the spreadsheet, you can apply a variety of calculations ranging from simple addition, subtraction, multiplication, and division to trigonometric, statistical, and business calculations. With a spreadsheet program, analyses related to project management can be easily performed. Examples of project management analyses are:

- Budget Analysis
- Reporting
- Project Planning
- Cost Estimating
- Market Analysis
- Forecasting
- Resource Planning
- Schedule Development and Tracking
- Project Presentation Graphics
- Performance Evaluation

Electronic spreadsheet models have greatly decreased the amount of computer expertise required to use a computer for decision making. Personal computer based spreadsheets are much more attractive and easy-to-use for the decision maker than those available on most mainframe computer systems. It is easy to transport small project-decision models on a personal computer from one location to another. This transportability facilitates the flexibility of making timely project decisions.

3.2 SPREADSHEET CAPABILITIES

Spreadsheet products available today range from the industry giants to little-known packages with great power and shareware programs with surprising capabilities (Bryan 1989). For example, the Smart Spreadsheet with Graphics, a free-standing module of the SmartWare system sold by Innovative Software Inc., an Informix subsidiary in Lenexa, Kansas, has high-speed processing, a data matrix of 999 by 9,999 columns, formula-locking and file-linking capabilities, a programming language, and no RAM limitations because of support for virtual memory. Users can work with as many as 50 spreadsheets in memory and on-screen at the same time.

There are spreadsheet programs that serve specialized functions. IFPS/ Personal, from Execucom Systems Corp. in Austin, Texas, is an established, highly regarded financial modeling package. Ming Telecomputing of Lincoln, Mass. offers ySTAT which is a complete statistical analysis program in the form of a spreadsheet.

Lotus 1-2-3 from Lotus Development Corporation is undoubtedly the leader in the spreadsheet software market. However, other software vendors have been gaining on Lotus in the past few years. Notable among these competing vendors is Microsoft Corporation, Computer Associates International Inc., and Borland International Inc. The spreadsheet products from these vendors offer functions that compete with and sometimes surpass those available in Lotus 1-2-3. The new release of SuperCalc5 from Computer Associates International contains new features such as 3-D worksheets, the ability to link dissimilar SuperCalc or 1-2-3 worksheets, a comprehensive auditing and debugging module, more than 100 variations of presentation-quality graphs, and enhanced printing.

The minimum hardware required by SuperCalc5 is an XT with 512K of memory. This is a modest requirement compared to products like Microsoft's Excel, which requires at least an 80286 microprocessor. Release 3 of Lotus 1-2-3 includes file linking, links to databases, 3-D worksheets, and graph printing from within 1-2-3 instead of through a separate PrintGraph utility. The 1-2-3 release 3, which was originally scheduled for shipment in June 1988, was available in summer 1989. TABLE 3-1 presents a comparison of the advanced capabilities of some selected spreadsheets.

Table 3-1. Advanced Spreadsheet Capabilities.

Capabilities	1-2-3 Rel 3	Quattro	SuperCalc5	Excel
Links to Databases	*			
3-D Worksheets	*		*	*
Sophisticated Graphics	*	*	*	*
Three Worksheet Windows	*			
Enhanced Printing	*		*	*
Auditing and Debugging	*		*	*

The most recent upgrade of Excel appeared in October 1988. It contains a run-time version of Windows/286, network capabilities, and improved support for expanded memory. An upcoming version of Excel will have visual or drawing enhancements in the form of an added layer on a spreadsheet where artwork can be superimposed. It will also provide contact with external databases through Structured Query Language (SQL) commands embedded in cells and it will have 3-D spreadsheets. To win users over to Excel, Microsoft is offering a scaled-down version of the product free to anyone. Users can obtain free copies of Excel by calling (800) 541-1261 in the U.S.A. or (416) 673-7638 in Canada. The free version of Excel is a complete functional version. However, the spreadsheet is limited in size to 16 columns by 64 rows, there are no help screens, and very limited documentation is provided. To run Excel, users must have an 80286 computer with a mouse and EGA.

Quattro, from Borland International of Scotts Valley, California, continues to enjoy wide user acceptance. File compatibility is a major strong point of Quattro. The program can read and write in the formats of a variety of spreadsheets. Data can be pulled in by merely specifying a named range for the import. It does not matter which program created the specified range. This allows each user in an organization to use whichever spreadsheet program he or she is most comfortable with. A future version of Quattro will incorporate sophisticated file-linking capabilities and have extensive capabilities for creating professional-quality printouts.

VP-Planner Plus, the spreadsheet from Paperback Software International of Berkeley, California, is rated as one of the fastest spreadsheets on the market. It incorporates its own five-dimensional database module and is expected to have a LAN version in the future.

By using the multidimensional (3-D) capability of some spreadsheet programs, budgeting and financial analysis in a project management environment can be simplified. The annual budget of an entire company involving several different profit centers and divisions can be prepared in a matter of hours compared to a number of days required by conventional spreadsheets. The 3-D capability can be used to replicate the format of an original income-statement worksheet onto a series of other pages for each subsidiary business entity. Financial information for each subsidiary can be entered into individual pages in the file. A single @SUM function can be used to consolidate the totals of all the pages by means of the third dimension. Pages can be grouped instantly for specific analysis.

A finance department can perform "what if" analysis with the figures by issuing single commands to alter the numbers on the pages instead of individually changing many separate 2-D spreadsheets. Specific factors can be compared across different operations or departments arranged along the third dimension of a 3-D spreadsheet. For example, resources utilization levels can be graphed over a range of multiple projects. FIGURE 3-1 shows a conceptual layout of a 3-D spreadsheet for analyzing financial data for multiple projects.

	Unit Cost	Cost Basis	Days Worked	Cost
Labor				
Design Engineer	$ 200	Day	34	$ 6,800
Carpenter	150	Day	27	4,050
Plumber	175	Day	2	350
Electrician	175	Day	82	14,350
IS Engineer	200	Day	81	16,200
Labor Subtotal				$ 41,750
Contractor				
Air conditioning	10,000	Fixed	5	$ 10,000
Access Flooring	5,000	Fixed	5	5,000
Fire Suppression	7,000	Fixed	5	7,000
AT&T	1,000	Fixed	50	1,000
DEC Deinstall	4,000	Fixed	2	4,000
DEC Install	8,000	Fixed	7	8,000
VAX Mover	1,100	Fixed	7	1,100
Transformer Mover	300	Fixed	7	300
Contractor Subtotal				$ 36,400
Materials				
Site Preparation	$ 2,500	Fixed	--	$ 2,500
Hardware	31,900	Fixed	--	31,900
Software	42,290	Fixed	--	42,290
Other	10,860	Fixed	--	10,860
Materials Subtotal				$ 87,550
GRAND TOTAL				$165,700

Projects: Project A, Project B, Project C, Project D. Comments:

Fig. 3-1. Multiple projects data in 3-D spreadsheet.

Several add-in products are available to address most of the shortcomings that have been identified in Lotus 1-2-3. Add-ins also provide enhancements such as word processing and a relational database. For example, Allways, from Funk Software Inc. of Cambridge, Massachusetts, and Look & Link, from Personics Corp. of Maynard, Massachusetts are two popular add-in products. Look & Link lets you see two separate worksheets on-screen simultaneously and permits dynamic linking and automatic consolidations with Lotus 1-2-3 release 2.01. Allways has enjoyed mass distribution because it is offered free to buyers of Lotus 1-2-3.

Forthcoming tools from Lotus Development Corporation are expected to help the company maintain its grip on the spreadsheet market. Blueprint will let database vendors connect their products to Lotus 1-2-3. Lotus/DBMS will be a product family running under the Presentation Manager version of OS/2. It will include a local database server that will be able to access mainframe databases through SQL. Both tools are expected to be available soon.

3.3 DEVELOPING PROJECT PLANS

Spreadsheets can play significant roles in the development of project plans. Project planning provides the basis for the initiation, implementation, and termination of a project. It sets guidelines for specific project objectives, project structure, tasks, milestones, personnel, cost, equipment, performance, and problem resolution. An analysis of what is needed and what is available is conducted in the planning phase of a project. The availability of technical expertise within the organization and outside the organization is reviewed during project planning. The "make," "buy," "lease," or "do nothing" alternatives can be mutually compared during the planning phase. In the initial stage of project planning, the internal and external factors that influence the project can be determined and given priority weights. This information can be tabulated as shown (weight of 1.0 = highest priority; weight of 0.0 = lowest priority):

Factors Affecting Project Plans

Internal Factors	Weights
Management Policy	0.80
Organizational Goal	1.00
Labor Relations	0.95
Company Size	0.52
Technical Manpower	0.92
Resource Availability	1.00
Location	0.00

External Factors	Weights
Market Needs	0.92
Industry Movement	0.78
Technology Status	0.80
Public Demand	0.95
Government Regulations	0.20
Infrastructure	0.11
Competition	0.95

In general, project planning covers the following elements:

- Summary of Project Plan—The summary gives a brief description of what is planned. Project scope and objectives are enumerated in this summary. Organizational goals, budget size, and important milestones also are included.

- Objectives—Objectives outline what the project is expected to achieve and how the expected achievements will contribute to overall goals of the organization.
- Approach—The managerial and technical methodologies of implementing the project are embodied in the project approach. The managerial approach might relate to project organization, communication network, approval hierarchy, responsibility, and accountability. The technical approach might relate to company experience on previous projects and currently available technology.
- Contractual Requirements—Contractual requirements outline reporting requirements, communication links, customer specifications, performance specification, deadlines, review processes, project deliverables, delivery schedules, internal and external contacts, data security, policies, and procedures.
- Project Schedule—The project schedule signifies the commitment of resources against time in pursuit of the project objectives. The schedule is based on reliable time estimates for project tasks. The estimates might come from knowledgeable personnel, past records, elemental specificity, or statistical extrapolation. Spreadsheet analysis can be used in generating the required time estimates.
- Resources—Project resources, budget, and costs are documented in this section of the project plan. Capital requirements are specified by tasks. Resources might include personnel and equipment. Special personnel skills, hiring, and training should be explained. TABLE 3-2 shows an example of a spreadsheet detailing the data and resource requirements of a planned project.
- Performance Measures—Measures of evaluating project progress are incorporated into the project plan. Measures can be based on standard practices or customized needs. The method of monitoring, collecting, and analyzing the measures also is specified.
- Contingency Plans—Courses of actions to be taken in the case of undesirable events are predetermined and recorded as a component of the project plan.

The feasibility of a project can be ascertained in terms of technical factors, economic factors, or both. A feasibility study is documented with a report showing all the ramifications of the project. Elements of project feasibility normally include:

- Need Analysis—Is the need significant enough to warrant action? Will the need still exist by the time the project is finished? What are the alternate means of satisfying the need? What is the economic impact of the need? If the end result of the proposed project is a consumer product, then market analysis will be a vital component of the need analysis.

- Process Work—Process work is the preliminary analysis done to determine what will be required to satisfy the need.
- Engineering and Design—Engineering and design is a detailed technical study of the proposed project. Written quotations are obtained from suppliers and subcontractors and can be recorded in a spreadsheet format.
- Cost Estimate—Estimating project cost to an acceptable level of accuracy. Both the initial and operating costs are included in the cost estimation.
- Financial Analysis—Financial analysis is an analysis of the cash flow profile of the project. The analysis should consider rates of return, inflation, sources of capital, payback periods, breakeven point, residual values, and sensitivity. This is a crucial analysis because it determines if and when funds will be available to the project. The project cash-flow profile, in effect, determines the economic feasibility of the project. The financial analysis is one major area that can benefit from the use of spreadsheets.

For the do-it-yourself home owners, a spreadsheet program offers a tool for personal project planning. TABLE 3-3 shows a home improvement project plan for a single family dwelling. A column is included in the spreadsheet to indicate if a given improvement task is contracted out or not. Similarly, a purchasing plan can be developed with the aid of a spreadsheet as shown in TABLE 3-4. A

Table 3-2. Spreadsheet of Project Data.

Activity	Predecessor	PERT Time			Resource Units	
		a	m	b	Type 1	Type 2
A	-	1	2	4	3	0
B	-	5	6	7	5	4
C	-	2	4	5	4	1
D	A	1	3	4	2	0
E	C	4	5	7	4	3
F	A	3	4	5	2	7
G	B,D,E	1	2	3	6	2

Table 3-3. Home Improvement Project Plan.

PROJECT	Next 3 Months	4 to 6 Months	7 to 12 Months	Check If Contracted Out
Heating/AC	[ ]	[ ]	[ ]	[ ]
Security System	[ ]	[ ]	[ ]	[ ]
Room Additions	[ ]	[ ]	[ ]	[ ]
Solarium	[ ]	[ ]	[ ]	[ ]
Siding/Gutters	[ ]	[ ]	[ ]	[ ]
Roofing	[ ]	[ ]	[ ]	[ ]
Remodeling	[ ]	[ ]	[ ]	[ ]
Kitchen Cabinets	[ ]	[ ]	[ ]	[ ]
Swimming Pool	[ ]	[ ]	[ ]	[ ]
Sliding Doors	[ ]	[ ]	[ ]	[ ]
Windows/Skylights	[ ]	[ ]	[ ]	[ ]
Storm Windows	[ ]	[ ]	[ ]	[ ]
Painting	[ ]	[ ]	[ ]	[ ]
Carpeting	[ ]	[ ]	[ ]	[ ]
Basement/Attic	[ ]	[ ]	[ ]	[ ]
Wood Flooring	[ ]	[ ]	[ ]	[ ]
Tile Flooring	[ ]	[ ]	[ ]	[ ]
Vinyl Flooring	[ ]	[ ]	[ ]	[ ]
Bath Remodeling	[ ]	[ ]	[ ]	[ ]
Insulation	[ ]	[ ]	[ ]	[ ]
Sprinkler System	[ ]	[ ]	[ ]	[ ]

Table 3-4. Purchasing Plan Spreadsheet.

ITEM	Next 3 Months	4 to 6 Months	7 to 12 Months	Check If Financed
Major Appliances	[ ]	[ ]	[ ]	[ ]
TV/VCR/Stereo	[ ]	[ ]	[ ]	[ ]
Kitchen Appliances	[ ]	[ ]	[ ]	[ ]
Living Room Furn.	[ ]	[ ]	[ ]	[ ]
Dining Room Furn.	[ ]	[ ]	[ ]	[ ]
Bedroom Furniture	[ ]	[ ]	[ ]	[ ]
Mattress	[ ]	[ ]	[ ]	[ ]
Patio Furniture	[ ]	[ ]	[ ]	[ ]
Ceiling Fan	[ ]	[ ]	[ ]	[ ]
Power Tools	[ ]	[ ]	[ ]	[ ]
Garden Tools	[ ]	[ ]	[ ]	[ ]
Bath Accessories	[ ]	[ ]	[ ]	[ ]
Automobile	[ ]	[ ]	[ ]	[ ]

column in the spreadsheet indicates whether or not a given item is to be financed or not. Spreadsheet layouts similar to those presented can be developed for any project based in the home, business, or industry.

3.4 PROJECT CASHFLOW ANALYSIS

Cashflow analysis for project management purposes is another potential candidate for spreadsheet application. TABLE 3-5 shows an example of an income statement spreadsheet analysis for a planned project. By using built-in functions of a spreadsheet program, you can make quick recalculations in the income statement. If the formulas are set up properly, the whole spreadsheet will be updated automatically whenever a single cell is changed. These built-in functions are a major advantage over conventional accounting procedures where you would have to manually update all the cells that are affected by the single change.

Table 3-5. Sample Project Income Statement.

Statement of Income	(In thousands, except per share amounts)	
Two years ended December 31:	**1988**	**1987**
Net Sales	**1,918,265**	**1,515,861**
Costs and expenses:		
Cost of sales	$ 1,057,849	$ 878,571
Research and development	72,511	71,121
Marketing and distribution	470,573	392,851
General and administrative	110,062	81,825
	1,710,995	**1,424,268**
Operating income	207,270	91,493
Consolidation of operations	(36,981)	
Interest and other income, net	9,771	17,722
Income before taxes	180,060	109,215
Provision for income taxes	58,807	45,115
Net Income	**$ 121,253**	**$ 64,100**
Equivalent shares	61,880	60,872
Earnings per common share	**$ 1.96**	**$ 1.05**

3.5 GENERATING PROJECT CHARTS AND GRAPHICS

A spreadsheet is very useful when you want to organize and analyze data for project decision making purposes. By developing a series of spreadsheet graphs, a project analyst can quickly spot important trends in the available data. The data presented in FIG. 3-2 is used to show how you can use the five graph types available in Lotus 1-2-3 to analyze multiple project cash flows. The data contains monthly budget expenditures for four projects. A data box showing the settings for the data ranges is presented for each of the example plots. In addition to analyzing cash flows, the graphs also can be used to evaluate resource allocation and utilization, schedule slippage, project milestones, time estimates, and so on.

```
B11:  (C2) [W15] @SUM(B6..B9)                                    READY

        A           B            C            D            E
 1                                        1989
 2                              Multiple Projects Data
 3                            ABCS Corporation, Norman, Oklahoma
 4
 5                     Jan          Feb          Mar          Apr
 6    Project A   $300,000.00  $320,000.00  $340,000.00  $280,000.00
 7    Project B   $120,000.00  $190,000.00  $250,000.00  $240,000.00
 8    Project C   $450,000.00  $340,000.00  $460,000.00  $420,000.00
 9    Project D   $200,000.00  $250,000.00  $320,000.00  $260,000.00
10
11    Total     $1,070,000.00 $1,100,000.00 $1,370,000.00 $1,200,000.00
12
13
14
15
16
17
18
19
20
18-Mar-89  01:11 PM
```

Fig. 3-2. Cash flow data for multiple projects.

FIGURE 3-3 shows the graph menu for Lotus 1-2-3 release 2.01. By using your Lotus 1-2-3 user's manual, you can explore each choice on the graph menu. Begin by arranging the multiple projects data in contiguous cells in appropriate row and column combinations. For ease of analysis, do not leave any blank cells in between data ranges unless the entries for the cells are actually missing. It is also helpful to keep the sizes of the data ranges identical.

You can specify data ranges X and A through F. The X range can contain values or labels. In all graphs, except the pie graph, the X range contains the data that appears on a graph's X axis. In the pie graph, the X range contains labels that appear adjacent to each piece of the pie. The X range of XY graphs always contains values. Every graph type except the pie can plot up to six data ranges (A through F data ranges). Pie graphs are limited to only one data range.

63

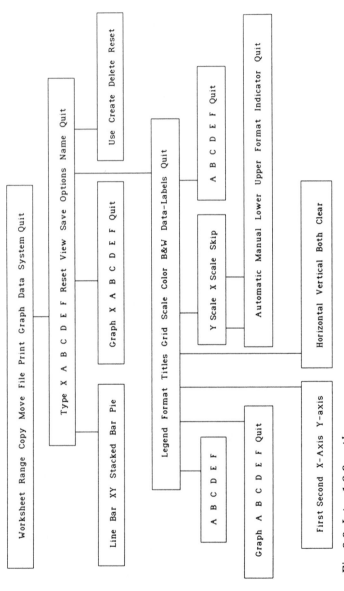

Fig. 3-3. Lotus 1-2-3 graph menu.

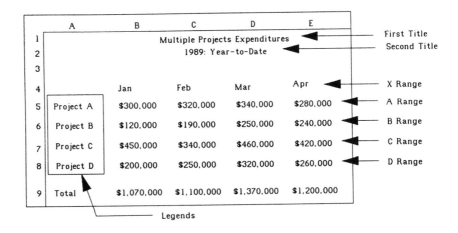

	A	B	C	D	E	
1			Multiple Projects Expenditures			← First Title
2			1989: Year-to-Date			← Second Title
3						
4		Jan	Feb	Mar	Apr	← X Range
5	Project A	$300,000	$320,000	$340,000	$280,000	← A Range
6	Project B	$120,000	$190,000	$250,000	$240,000	← B Range
7	Project C	$450,000	$340,000	$460,000	$420,000	← C Range
8	Project D	$200,000	$250,000	$320,000	$260,000	← D Range
9	Total	$1,070,000	$1,100,000	$1,370,000	$1,200,000	

Legends

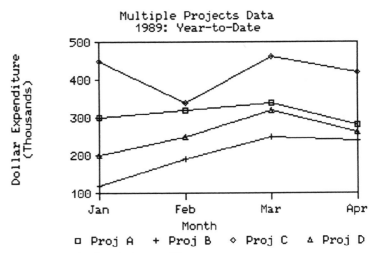

Fig. 3-4. Line graph of projects expenditures.

Line Graph

A line graph is useful when you want to show changes in data over time. For example, a line graph can quickly indicate that Projects A, B, and D show similar trends in expenditures as shown in FIG. 3-4. The data you specify as the X range appears as labels on the X axis of the line graph and identifies each data point. By specifying data for graph data ranges A through F, you can plot up to six lines on a single graph. Thus, you can simultaneously compare up to six projects on one line graph. Lotus 1-2-3 automatically assigns a different symbol to each line and displays the values as symbols connected by lines. If you are using a color monitor, you can select /Graph Options Color Quit View to display each line on the graph in a different color.

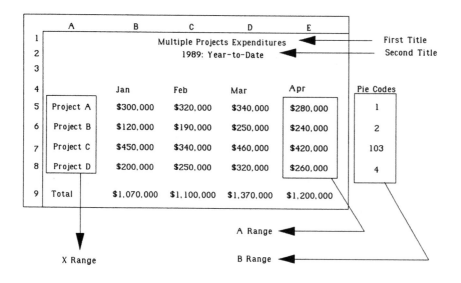

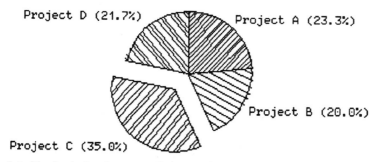

Fig. 3-5. Pie chart of projects expenditures.

Pie Chart

A pie chart compares the relative proportions of parts in a data set. In FIG. 3-5, we can see the relationship that each project's expenditure in April had to total April budget expenditure. Lotus 1-2-3 automatically calculates and displays percentages. In a pie chart, the X range contains labels to identify each wedge of the pie. The A range contains the values to be graphed, the B range contains codes for the shading or color of the wedges. The shading codes are numbered 0 through 7. An exploded wedge, such as Project C in FIG. 3-5, emphasizes a particular aspect of the presentation graphics. To explode a wedge in Lotus 1-2-3 release 2.01, add 100 to the shading code.

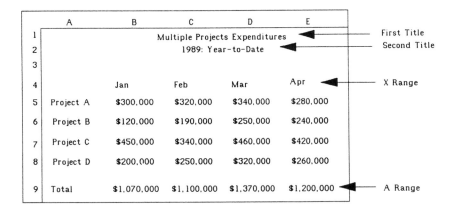

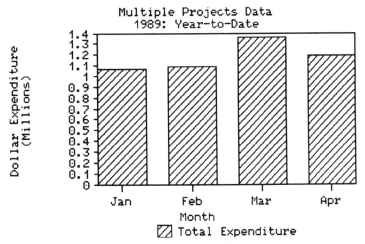

Fig. 3-6. Single-range bar graph of projects expenditures.

Bar Graph

The bar graph comes in two varieties, single-range graph and multiple-range graph. A single-range bar graph, like the one shown in FIG. 3-6, highlights the differences between values in one set of data. In this case, we are comparing total project expenditures by month. Looking at the graph, we quickly see that total expenditures shot up in March, while expenditures in January and February remained level. April showed a decline from the March expenditure level. Visual information such as these can be very valuable for prompt project-control decisions.

A bar graph always displays labels along the X axis. In a single-range bar graph, you specify data for only the A range. The data for bars can be positive or negative. Even though Lotus 1-2-3 automatically scales the Y axis based on graph values, you can scale the upper limit of the Y axis manually. You cannot

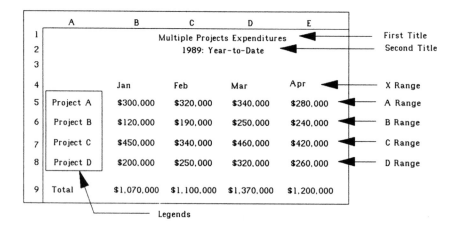

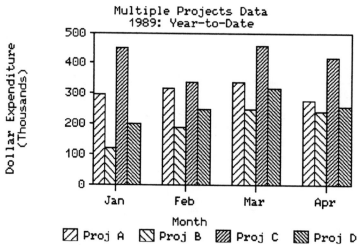

Fig. 3-7. Multiple-range bar graph of projects expenditures.

scale the lower limit manually. Bars in a bar graph automatically appear shaded with different cross-hatch patterns. If you are using a color monitor, you can select the Color option and display bars as solid colors. For each bar, you can specify a data label, which appears centered above a positive bar and below a negative bar.

A multiple-range bar graph is useful when you want to make comparisons between corresponding values in data sets. In FIG. 3-7, the total monthly expenditure for each project is shown, whereas the single-range bar in FIG. 3-6 represents total monthly expenditures for all the projects. Instead of specifying data for only the A range, you specify data for the B, C, and D ranges as well. And instead of one large bar representing each month, there are groups of four

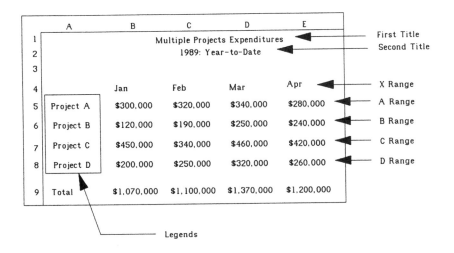

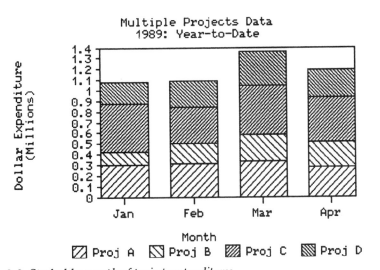

Fig. 3-8. Stacked-bar graph of projects expenditures.

bars. Each group represents one month, while each single bar represents one project's expenditure for that month.

In a stacked-bar graph, each segment of a bar represents a corresponding value from each data range. In FIG. 3-8, the segments are stacked on top of each other to show each project's individual monthly expenditures as a part of total monthly expenditures. The height of each bar indicates that month's total expenditure. Lotus 1-2-3 automatically creates different cross-hatch patterns for each segment of the stacked bar. Each stacked bar can contain up to six bar

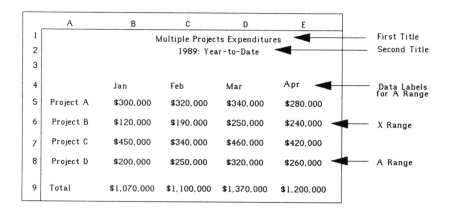

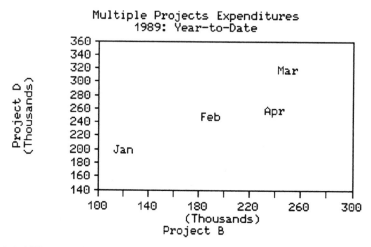

Fig. 3-9. XY graph of projects expenditures.

segments. A bar on a stacked-bar graph can plot negative data only if all its segments are negative.

XY Graph

An XY graph pairs each value from the X range with the corresponding value from each of the A through F ranges to plot points on the graph. FIGURE 3-9 shows an XY graph correlating expenditures for Project D and Project B. An XY graph differs from a line graph in that its X axis displays numbers, not labels. Lotus 1-2-3 automatically scales the X and Y axes and assigns both lines and symbols as the format for the graphed data. Depending on the data plotted, the lines connecting data points might zigzag across the graph, thereby confusing the presentation. If this occurs, specify Symbols as the format for each data range. This will prevent lines from appearing on the graph. All graphing options apply to the XY graph. To set Symbols for the data range, select /Graph Options Format (relevant range, e.g. A) Symbols.

3.6 PROJECT BUDGET ALLOCATION ANALYSIS

After the planning for a project has been completed, the next step is the allocation of the resources required to implement the project plan. This is referred to as budgeting or capital rationing. Budgeting is the process of allocating scarce resources to the various endeavors of an organization. It involves the selection of a preferred subset from a set of acceptable projects due to overall budget constraints. Budget constraints might result from restrictions on capital expenditures, shortage of skilled manpower, or shortage of materials. The budget analysis serves many useful purposes including:

- A plan of how resources are expended
- A project selection of criterion
- A projection of organizational policy
- A basis for control by managers
- A performance measure
- A standardization of operations within a given horizon
- An incentive for efficiency

The preliminary effort in the preparation of a budget is the collection and proper organization of appropriate data. A spreadsheet program can play a very important role in this aspect. The preparation of a budget for a project is more difficult than the preparation of budgets for standard elemental times. Recurring endeavors usually generate historical data which serves as input to subsequent estimating functions. Such estimation based on historical data can be performed by a spreadsheet program. Most projects are one-time undertakings without the benefits of prior data. The input data for the budgeting process typically includes inflationary trends, cost of capital, standard cost guides, past records, and quantitative projections. All this data involves extensive numeric calculations that can benefit from the capability of a spreadsheet.

Top-Down Budgeting

This involves collecting data from upper level sources such as top and middle managers. The figures applied by the managers might come from their judgments, past experiences, or past data on similar project activities. The cost estimates are passed to lower-level managers, who then break the estimates down into specific work components within the project. These estimates can, in turn, be given to line managers, supervisors, and others to continue the process. Finally, individual activity costs emerge. The top management provides the global budget while the functional level employee provides specific budget requirements for project items.

Bottom-Up Budgeting

This approach is the converse of top-down budgeting. In bottom-up budgeting, elemental activities; schedules, descriptions, and labor skill requirements are used to construct detailed budget requests. The line workers that are actually performing the activities are requested to furnish cost estimates. Estimates are made for each activity in terms of labor time, materials, and machine time. The estimates are then converted to dollar values. The dollar estimates are combined into composite budgets at each successive level up the budgeting hierarchy. If estimate discrepancies develop, they can be resolved through the intervention of senior management, junior management, functional managers, project manager, accountants, or standard cost consultants.

Analytical tools, such as learning curve analysis, work sampling, and statistical estimation can be coupled with spreadsheet analysis to improve the quality of cost estimates. FIGURE 3-10 shows an enhanced pie chart of budget allocation in a manufacturing enterprise. The original pie was prepared with Lotus 1-2-3. The picture file was then exported to the Lotus Freelance Plus graphics program where graphical enhancements were made.

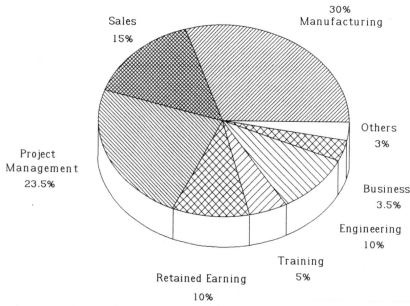

Fig. 3-10. Pie chart of budget allocation.

3.7 LEARNING CURVE ANALYSIS

Learning refers to the improved efficiency obtained from repetition of a procedure, process, task, or operation. Learning is time dependent and studies have shown that human performance improves with reinforcement or frequent repetitions. Reductions in operation times directly translate to cost savings. Thus, the effect of learning is important in project management functions. The cost of an operation is sometimes determined by variables that are within the control of the organization. As production runs increase, the effects of learning cause a reduction in operation time requirements. However, with the passage of time, the rate of decrease becomes smaller.

If the learning effect is not considered, costs might be overestimated and result in waste and inefficiency. Consider the so-called "80 percent learning effect" as an example. Under this concept, a process is subject to 20 percent unit cost reduction or 20 percent productivity improvement (i.e., 80 percent learning rate) each time the production quantity doubles. This phenomenon is shown in the spreadsheet in FIG. 3-11. In the spreadsheet, the unit cost reduced from $100 to $26 due to the effect of learning. The standard cost deviation of minus $5 in the second batch might be permissible if management is cognizant of the fact that the learning effect is just beginning to work. You can see a 20 percent reduction in unit costs between successive production batches. In actual practice, cost reduction relationships might not be as proportional as indicated by the spreadsheet data. You might be able to realize even larger reductions in the early stages than in the later stages when learning levels off. You should realize that a new learning curve does not necessarily commence each time a new operation is started because workers can sometimes transfer previous skill to new operations.

A1: [W15]   R

	A	B	C	D	E	F
1		The 80 Percent Learning Curve Effect				
2		██				
3						
4	Cumulative	Cumulative	Standard		Standard	
5	Production	Average Cost	Cost Per	Percent	Cost	
6	Units	Per Unit	Unit	Learning	Deviation	
7						
8	1	$100	$75	–	$+25	
9	2	80	75	80%	+5	
10	4	64	75	80%	-11	
11	8	51	75	80%	-24	
12	16	41	75	80%	-34	
13	32	33	75	80%	-42	
14	64	26	75	80%	-49	
15						
16						
17						

Fig. 3-11. Spreadsheet data for learning percentage.

The point at which the learning curve begins to flatten depends on the degree of similarity of the new operation to previously performed operations. Typical learning rates that have been encountered in practice range from 70 percent to 95 percent. The percent learning is computed as 100 times the cumulative average-cost-per-unit at a given total production divided by the cumulative average-cost-per-unit at the production level that is half of the given level.

When linear graph paper is used, the learning curve is a hyperbola of the form:

$$C_x = C_1 X^m$$

On log-log paper, the learning curve is represented by:

$$\log C_x = \log C_1 + m \log X$$

where

C_x =   cumulative average cost of X units
C_1 =   cost of the first unit
X =   number of cumulative units to be produced
m =   exponent representing slope of the learning curve on log-log scale
   =   learning rate

By definition, the learning percent is given by

$$p = 2^m$$

where

$$m = \frac{\log p}{\log 2}$$

Thus, given the slope m, you can solve for p. Alternately, if p is given, then you can find the slope. For example, assume that 50 units are produced at a cumulative average cost of $20 per unit. You want to compute the learning percentage when 100 units are produced at a cumulative average cost of $15 per unit. That is:

At first production level: units = 50 ; cost = $20
At second production level: units = 100 ; cost = $15.

Using the log relationship, you can obtain the following simultaneous equations:

$$\log 20 = \log C_1 + m \log 50$$
$$\log 15 = \log C_1 + m \log 100$$

Subtracting the second equation from the first yields:

$$\log 20 - \log 15 = m \log 50 - m \log 100$$

That is,

$$m = \frac{\log 20 - \log 15}{\log 50 - \log 100}$$

$$= \frac{\log (20/15)}{\log (50/100)}$$

$$= -0.415$$

Therefore:

$$p = (2)^{-0.415}$$
$$= 0.75$$
$$= 75\% \text{ learning}$$

In general:

$$m = \frac{\log C_1 - \log C_2}{\log X_1 - \log X_2}$$

where:

C_1 = average cumulative cost per unit at the first production level
X_1 = production volume (units) at the first production level
C_2 = average cumulative cost per unit at the second production level
X_2 = production volume (units) at the second production level

For project operations, the effect of learning should be considered in developing activity time estimates. The formulas just presented might be evaluated in terms of time, or some other measure of worth, instead of cost. Simply replace each cost variable with the corresponding time variable. Standard tables that give learning percentages for various values of learning curve slopes are widely available. These tables can be stored as spreadsheet data and then retrieved for analysis as needed. Alternately, spreadsheet macro programs can be developed to perform the mathematical calculations whenever needed.

As an example, suppose an observation of the cumulative hours required to produce a unit of an item was made by a project management analyst. His recorded observations are presented in TABLE 3-6.

The project analyst would like to perform the following computational analyses:

Table 3-6. Learning Curve Observations.

Cumulative Units Produced (X)	Cumulative Average Hours (C_x)
10	92.5
15	71.2
25	50.0
40	35.0
50	26.2
60	20.0
85	11.3
115	10.0
165	7.5
190	6.25

- Calculate the learning curve percentage when cumulative production doubles from 10 units to 20 units.
- Calculate the learning curve percentage when cumulative production doubles from 20 units to 40 units.
- Calculate the learning curve percentage when cumulative production doubles from 40 units to 80 units.
- Calculate the learning curve percentage when cumulative production doubles from 80 units to 160 units.
- Compute average learning percentage rate for the given operation.
- Estimate a standard time for performing the given operation if steady production-level-per-cycle is 200 units.

A learning curve fitting the above data was developed with the aid of the line graph option of Lotus 1-2-3. If the spreadsheet line graph does not give a smooth enough curve for interpolation and estimation purposes, you can export the data into a statistical software program such as STATGRAPHICS. The curve shown in FIG. 3-12 was developed by STATGRAPHICS.

The computational procedure for learning percentage requires an estimate of the cost of the first unit. The best estimate of this cost, in the absence of further information, is the cumulative average hours from the first ten units, that is, 92.5 hours.

Following the computational procedures, the analyst obtained the results shown in TABLE 3-7. From the curve in FIG. 3-12, an estimate of the time standard required per unit at a steady production level is five hours. Interpolation formulas can be set up easily with spreadsheet math functions and macros to estimate time requirements for the operation at different production levels.

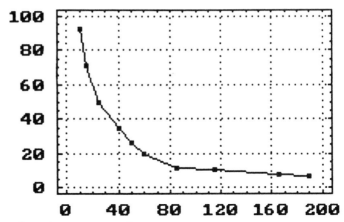

Fig. 3-12. Learning curve example.

Table 3-7. Learning Curve Percentage Analysis.

Initial Production Level	Final Production Level	Learning Percentage
10	20	64.87%
20	40	58.33%
40	80	37.14%
80	160	61.54%
Average Learning Percentage		55.47%

3.8 PROJECT BREAKEVEN AND SENSITIVITY ANALYSIS

Sensitivity is the relative magnitude of the change in one or more elements of a data set required to cause a change in a project decision. An analysis of the sensitivity of a decision to the various parameters emphasize the important and significant aspects of a project. *Project sensitivity analysis* is the investigation of the effect of changing some parameters due to the outcome of a project decision analysis. Sensitivity analysis coupled with computer simulation can be very useful for evaluating R & D projects particularly at the conceptual stages.

For example, you might be concerned that the estimates for annual maintenance and future salvage value in a particular project could vary substantially

```
A4: PR [W4]                                                    READY


        A       B          C        D        E       F      G       H
 4
 5    DATA
 6       First Cost                        740000
 7       Taxes on sale ,...               50000
 8       Mortgage rate              9.5% nominal compounded monthly
 9       Down payment                     10%
10       Rent                             4750 per month
11       Operating costs
12          Property taxes              12000 per year
13          Fire insurance              1240 per year
14          Repairs maintenance         6000 per year
15          Rental agents comision at 9%  5130 per year
16       Vacancy rate                     5%
17       Investment period                   8 years
18       Opportunity cost of capital     15%
19       Property appreciation           10%  per year
20       Operating costs rise            5%  per year
21       Tax rate                       32.5%
22       Commission on property sale     1%
23       50% of capital gains be taxed as ordinary income
19-Mar-89  10:54 AM                                           CAPS
```

Fig. 3-13. Sensitivity analysis data.

based on changes in some project parameters. Sensitivity analysis might indicate that a decision is insensitive to the salvage value estimate over the full range of possible values. However, you might find that the decision is sensitive to changes in the annual maintenance estimate. With this information, you could place a greater emphasis on improving the estimate of annual maintenance costs and less emphasis on the estimation of salvage value.

Breakeven analysis is performed to determine the conditions under which project alternatives are equivalent. Once the breakeven conditions are determined, sensitivity analysis can be performed to examine the range of parameter values that could cause changes in the decision to select one alternative over another. Breakeven and sensitivity analyses offer management a powerful tool for decision making in a project environment.

Steiner (1988) presents a simple Lotus 1-2-3 spreadsheet program for performing multi-variable sensitivity analysis. As an example, Steiner uses the program to examine the parameters involved in the evaluation of a commercial building as a real estate venture. The conditions considered include cost, taxes, legal fees, escrow fees, mortgage rate, potential rent, property taxes, insurance, maintenance, vacancy rate, investment period, and cost of capital.

The input data, as contained in the spreadsheet program, is presented in FIG. 3-13. A projection of what is expected to happen if the property is purchased include:

- 10 percent appreciation on the property value
- 5 percent annual increase on the operating costs due to inflation
- Rent income from the property will increase by 5 percent per year

- 32.5 percent tax bracket
- 1 percent real estate commission on sale of the property at the end of the investment
- 50 percent of capital gains will be taxed as ordinary income

Some pertinent questions addressed by Steiner in the evaluation of this investment property are:

- What after-tax rate of return will be realized on the venture?
- To which input variables is the rate of return most sensitive?
- How sensitive is the rate of return to the input values?

FIGURE 3-14 shows the tabulated analysis of the problem as presented by the spreadsheet program while FIG. 3-15 presents the variables that can be altered to study the sensitivity of the decision. The three variables of interest (as shown in FIG. 3-15) are:

1. Loan period: 30 years
2. Appreciation rate: 10 percent
3. Taxable portion of capital gains: 50 percent

Any or all of the variables can be changed to determine the *Internal Rate of Return* (IROR) for the investment project. For the particular combination of variable values presented above, the IROR is 18.74 percent (see FIG. 3-15). You can try different combinations of variable values and examine the resulting IROR. FIGURE 3-16 presents another combination of variable values with a

```
A51: PR [W4] 'Taxes on Capital Gain are:                          READY


       A        B        C        D        E        F        G        H
32    YEAR     COSTS    REVENUE  -------MORTGAGE ANALYSIS----------  DEPRE-
33                                                                  CIATION
34                               PAYM-    INTER-   PRINC- REMAINING
35                               ENTS     EST      IPAL   BALANCE
36    ------------------------------------------------------------------
37     0      -124000                                   666000
38     1       -24370   54150   -70178   -66067   -4111  661889  -20000
39     2       -25590   56860   -70178   -65659   -4518  657371  -20000
40     3       -26870   59700   -70178   -65211   -4967  652405  -20000
41     4       -28210   62690   -70178   -64719   -5459  646945  -20000
42     5       -29620   65820   -70178   -64177   -6001  640945  -20000
43     6       -31100   69110   -70178   -63582   -6596  634349  -20000
44     7       -32660   72570   -70178   -62927   -7250  627098  -20000
45     8       -34290   76190   -70178   -62208   -7970  619129  -20000
46     8
47
48
49    The Taxable Capital Gain is:          470198
50
51    Taxes on Capital Gain are:            152814
19-Mar-89  10:55 AM                                        CAPS
```

Fig. 3-14. Tabulated sensitivity analysis.

```
A73: PR [W4]                                                        READY

       A       B        C        D      E      F       G        H
54
55    VARIABLES TO BE INVESTIGATED           INTERNAL RATE OF RETURN
56
57    1)  Loan Period          30.00          !----------------!
58    2)  Appreciation Rate     0.10          !     0.187399    !
59    3)  Taxable Portion                      !----------------!
60        of Capital Gain       0.50
61
62
63    Item changed                           IROR (%)
64    --------------------------------
65    None                                   18.74%
66    Appreciation rate = 5%                  6.00%
67    Appreciation rate = 0%                -20.86%
68    Loan Period = 25 years                 18.39%
69    Loan Period = 20 years                 17.81%
70    Taxable portion of capital gains = 30%  20.05%
71    Taxable portion of capital gains = 40%  19.41%
72    Taxable portion of capital gains =100%  14.99%
73
19-Mar-89  10:56 AM                                          CAPS
```

Fig. 3-15. Parameter variables for sensitivity analysis.

```
D58: U [W8] 0.1                                                    READY

       A       B        C        D      E      F       G        H
54
55    VARIABLES TO BE INVESTIGATED           INTERNAL RATE OF RETURN
56
57    1)  Loan Period          15.00          !----------------!
58    2)  Appreciation Rate     0.10          !     0.168314    !
59    3)  Taxable Portion                      !----------------!
60        of Capital Gain       0.50
61
62
63    Item changed                           IROR (%)
64    --------------------------------
65    None                                   18.74%
66    Appreciation rate = 5%                  6.00%
67    Appreciation rate = 0%                -20.86%
68    Loan Period = 25 years                 18.39%
69    Loan Period = 20 years                 17.81%
70    Taxable portion of capital gains = 30%  20.05%
71    Taxable portion of capital gains = 40%  19.41%
72    Taxable portion of capital gains =100%  14.99%
73
19-Mar-89  10:58 AM                                          CAPS
```

Fig. 3-16. Sensitivity to loan period.

resulting value of 16.83 percent for the IROR. A further analysis where all three variables are changed is presented in FIG. 3-17. If a minimum acceptable rate of return (MARR) has been set for the venture, then you can quickly perform iterative evaluations and come to a final decision.

```
 D60: U [W8] 0.4                                              READY


      A        B        C        D        E       F      G        H
 54
 55  VARIABLES TO BE INVESTIGATED                  INTERNAL RATE OF RETURN
 56
 57  1)  Loan Period              15.00           !----------------!
 58  2)  Appreciation Rate         0.08           !   0.134122     !
 59  3)  Taxable Portion                          !----------------!
 60      of Capital Gain           0.40
 61
 62
 63  Item changed                                 IROR (%)
 64  ---------------------------------
 65  None                                         18.74%
 66  Appreciation rate = 5%                        6.00%
 67  Appreciation rate = 0%                      -20.86%
 68  Loan Period = 25 years                       18.39%
 69  Loan Period = 20 years                       17.81%
 70  Taxable portion of capital gains = 30%       20.05%
 71  Taxable portion of capital gains = 40%       19.41%
 72  Taxable portion of capital gains =100%       14.99%
 73
 19-Mar-89  10:59 AM                                          CAPS
```

Fig. 3-17. Alternate combination of sensitivity parameters.

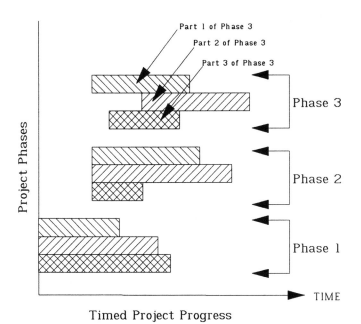

Fig. 3-18. Progress of project phases.

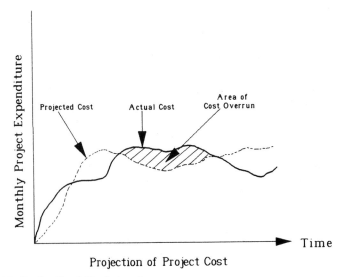

Fig. 3-19. Evaluation of project costs.

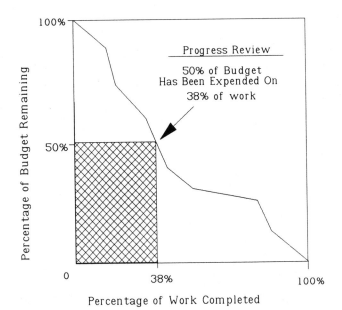

Fig. 3-20. Evaluation of work completed versus budget depletion.

3.9 PROJECT STATUS REPORT

The computational and graphical capabilities of spreadsheet programs also can be used for tracking the progress of projects. The most useful method of monitoring the progress of a project is the use of graphical presentations. Progress can be monitored and reported in terms of schedule, budget depletion, resource utilization, or any other parameter of interest. A tabulation of information in a spreadsheet format also can be used to convey a visual assessment of the progress of a project.

The basic graphs provided by a spreadsheet program (e.g., Lotus 1-2-3), might be exported to a graphics software package (e.g., Lotus freelance Plus or Harvard Graphics) where it can be enhanced for more effective presentations. Examples of such presentations are shown in FIGS. 3-18, 3-19, and 3-20.

4

Project Database Management

This chapter presents basic database management concepts for project management applications. As with the spreadsheet discussions in the preceding chapter, no particular database program is recommended here. The presentations are generic enough to illustrate how you can utilize a present database management program for project management applications. However, to provide a uniform basis for our discussions, the capabilities of dBASE III Plus are used as examples whenever specific examples are called for. Word processing programs are designed to manipulate character strings (words): spreadsheet programs are designed to manipulate numbers; and database programs are designed to manipulate data. Appendix A presents a guide to some of the available database management packages.

4.1 DATABASE ORGANIZATION

A database has the capability to store, retrieve, and manage large amounts of data. Pieces of data can be quickly retrieved and processed as appropriate to generate information needed for decision making. In a project management environment, large amounts of data are dealt with on a day-to-day basis. For example, data is maintained about tasks, personnel, equipment, due dates, and project organization. In order to make timely and effective decisions, you need to have access to relevant data promptly. The traditional paper and pencil record-keeping system is definitely not adequate for the high-paced multidimensional projects of today.

An example of the use of a database to track data is the 1987 celebrated trial of Michael K. Deaver, former assistant to President Reagan. Deaver was convicted on charges that he lied to a U.S. House of Representatives subcommittee and to a federal grand jury investigating his lobbying activities after he left the Reagan Administration. During the trial, the staff of Independent Counsel Whitney North Seymour, Jr. used the Inmagic Text Database software from Inmagic, Inc. to keep track of about 100,000 documents, 8,000 pages of grand jury testimony, FBI interviews, nearly 4,000 pages of trial transcripts, and the testimony of 110 witnesses. A key aspect of the ability of computers to manage such large amounts of data with ease is the manner in which data is organized for computer processing.

The hierarchy of data organization for computer manipulation goes from bits, characters, data elements, records, and files to database. Characters are combined to form data elements or fields in a data set (e.g., David). Related data elements are grouped to form records (e.g., David Goodman, 1234 Homebase Street, Norman, Oklahoma 73007). Records with identical files are grouped to form a file (e.g., personnel file). Finally, different files are stored together to form a database (e.g., corporate database).

A database is a collection of facts organized for a specific purpose. A computerized database is a collection of facts stored in a form that can be accessed and manipulated by a computer. A database management system is a structured methodology for accessing and manipulating the data. TABLE 4-1 shows what the personnel file for a project team might look like.

Table 4-1. Contents of a Project Personnel File.

Last Name	First Name	Dept.	Function	Employee No.	Date Assigned
Badrian	David	E2	Engineer	001B023	03/21/89
Winski	Gary	C1	Manager	124W459	12/03/88
Arears	Ben	J2	Technician	100A111	03/25/89
Alquiston	John	A1	Maintenance	423A010	11/02/78
Lator	Calcu	E2	Analyst	999L001	04/01/87
Druthers	Bill	F9	Drafting	321D052	02/25/89
Moniski	Cathy	J5	Accountant	786M019	09/23/88

The entire table constitutes the personnel file for this particular project. The first row of the table identifies the fields or data elements in the file. Thus, the first column of the table is the field containing the last name of each person in the project team. There are six fields in the files: last name, first name, department, function, employee no., and date assigned. There are seven records in the file. The second row in the table contains the record of one of the project team members. That record consists of six record-specific data items: Badrian, David, E2, Engineer, 001B023, 03/21/89. Several files related to the same project can be collated to form a database for the project information. Some files that can be included in the project database are:

- Personnel file
- Resource file
- Budget file
- Responsibility assignment file
- Task list file
- Cost estimates file
- Management correspondence file
- Purchase orders files
- Milestones file
- Delivery dates files

The related files of a database must be stored in a manner that allows them to be simultaneously accessed. A data management program that can manipulate the related files of a database is called a *database management system* (DBMS). A DBMS allows the project analyst to use the file in a database to update and retrieve data, answer questions, and prepare project reports. New data files can be added while the structure of existing ones can be changed with the DBMS. The DBMS provides a common basis for organizing project data. Without this standard data format, each department or application would require its own program and files making it impossible for one department to access and use files developed by another department because the departments would have incompatible file formats. There are three major kinds of database management systems: relational, hierarchial, and network database.

Relational Database Model

A relational database is a collection of related data files in which the files are connected by means of linking columns. You will understand the structure of a relational database if you consider a data file as a table with a column for each field. Each field has a title and each row of the table represents a single record in the file. A collection of such tables constitutes a database. Some of the tables in the database might contain field names that are the same. Common field names indicate that the tables contain common information. In other words, they are related (i.e., relational database). Many popular commercial database management programs, including dBASE III Plus and R:BASE 5000, use the relational system. TABLES 4-2 and 4-3 are two examples of what can be found in a relational database in a project management office.

Table 4-2. Task List File in a Relational Database.

Task Code	Description	Personnel Name	Duration	Cost

Table 4-3. Personnel Resource File in a Relational Database.

Personnel Name	Department	Availability Code	Gender	Pay

TABLE 4-2 contains the list of tasks involved in the project. The record of each task contains the task code, description, name of the personnel in charge, duration, and cost. TABLE 4-3 contains the list of project personnel. The record of each person contains the person's name, department, availability code, gender, and pay. The two tables have a common column labelled PERSONNEL NAME. This column is called a linking column. It provides a link between the two tables or files. You can use a *linking column* to relate information in one file to information in another file.

Suppose that you want to obtain a list of the departments of all personnel that are currently assigned to project tasks. You could look in the task file to get a list of the currently assigned personnel. Then, you could look in the personnel file for the corresponding names and be able to determine the relevant departments. In some cases, to prevent ambiguities, more than one linking column is necessary to connect the data items in related files. For example, if two people have the same last name, a field labelled LAST will not be sufficient to uniquely identify each person. In such a case, a second field labelled FIRST also can be used as a linking column.

The relational model is often called a *flat file structure* because there is no hierarchy of data sets. There is no complex network of data to navigate through.

Instead, there is a series of data element relationships that are established in table-like form. Data elements that are related are called *tuples*. For example, there might be a tuple called "project member" that consists of the following related data elements:

- Member name (the key data item)
- Department
- Availability code
- Gender
- Pay
- Task assigned

In the relational system, many files are created for specific needs and linked as appropriate for various data access needs. You might wonder why you need to create two different files for a task list and a personnel list in the previous example. Even though a relational database causes duplication of fields, there are obvious advantages. Some of the disadvantages of employing only one file instead of the multiple files used by a relational database need to be discussed.

- If the personnel department, availability code, gender, and pay were included in the task list file, records would become unreasonably long.
- If more than one person is assigned to a task, then it would be necessary to create a separate record and repeat the task name for each person assigned. Imagine what the task list would look like in cases where up to ten people are assigned to each task.
- If a single file is used, the job of updating a single large file will be complicated. If there is one change to be made in a task, it might be necessary to make many corrections in the file because of that one change. On the other hand, if different files are maintained for different collections of information, then only the affected files will need to be retrieved and updated.
- The personnel resource file is an important file that might need to be accessed for a variety of uses that have nothing to do with task lists. If the task list file is mixed with the personnel file, then the job of accessing only the personnel information will become difficult.

As you can see, very careful thought should be given to the organization of data within a project management database. The best strategy is to use a large number of simple data files, rather than a few large and complex files. With the appropriate choices of linking columns, several files can be connected to provide an overall collection of information for decision-making purposes.

Hierarchical Database Model

A hierarchical database management system is like a decision tree or the directory structure of a computer operating system with branches of data structured in multiple levels. The units farther down the tree structure are subordinate to the ones above. Finding a record usually requires starting at the top of the hierarchy and proceeding through the appropriate paths in the data hierarchy. This search means that data stored at the lower level nodes in the hierarchy can be accessed only through the parent node. This relationship among data records is commonly called a set or *parent-to-child* relationship, with one record called the *owner*, or parent, record and the others called *member*, or child, records.

A drawback of the hierarchical model is that deleting a branch deletes all the subordinate branches associated with that branch. Also, a subordinate data branch cannot be added to the database without a superior branch. A member always has only one owner, whereas an owner can have many members. It might be necessary to duplicate some records if two owners need to be superordinate to the same member record information. FIGURE 4-1 presents a graphical illustration of the structure of a hierarchical data organization.

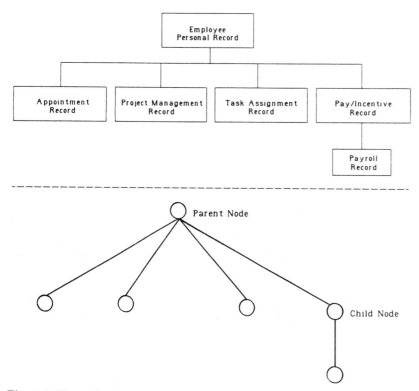

Fig. 4-1. Hierarchical data organization.

Network Database Model

A network database has records in hierarchical arrangements, but the records are also linked in several relationships. In the network data model, each subordinate can have more than one superior. Thus, information can be extracted by starting with any record. For example, given access to the task list record, we can access the payroll record or any other record associated with the task list record. Because of its capacity for accessing multiple records, the network model generally creates less duplication. So data redundancy is minimized. However, as the complexity of the possible interrelationships increases, the programming logic required to implement the design becomes more complicated. The complexity can become even more problematic when data access security measures need to be incorporated into the logic. FIGURE 4-2 shows a graphical method of the network database system.

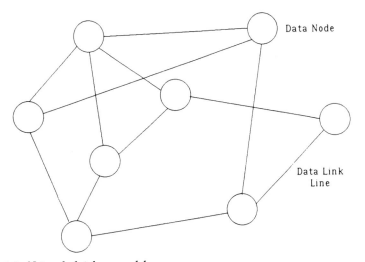

Fig. 4-2. Network database model.

4.2 DATABASE CAPABILITIES

Software developers are packing their database products with more and more functional capabilities. Many features are now available to facilitate effective management of project management databases. Listed below are some of the generic capabilities available in many of the recently updated database management systems such as dBASE IV, R:BASE, and FOXBASE+.

- Speed—Heuristic query optimization techniques enable some database programs to choose the fastest method executing a command based on such things as how much RAM is available, how much data needs to be processed, and where the destination of the data is. These techniques permit operations like sorting, view processing, and CROSSTAB to execute much faster than the older generations of database programs.

- Powerful Programming—Newer database programs offer programming environments that emulate conventional programming languages. Mathematical, statistical, financial, string manipulation, logic, trigonometric, and data type functions are available in some programs. This programming provides a comprehensive calculation capability for rapid and complex data anlaysis.
- User Interface—Pleasing menu-driven interfaces are available to aid both beginning and experienced users. For example, Prompt By Example (PBE), used by R:BASE, is a menu-driven, interactive user interface that provides capabilities to structure, enter, update, query, and retrieve data without programming. Users are guided through DBMS command creation without having to remember commands or syntax.
- Embedded Query Language—Many of the commands of the popular structured query language (SQL) are now embedded in the newest of the DBMS packages. SQL will be discussed in the next section.
- Connectivity—Data exchange is becoming more important in these days of limited resources. Managers are finding out that data need not be regenerated in its original form at each application site. Each information system can be accessed in a central repository. Data file import and export capabilities have become a major objective of many data management programs. Connectivity in the form of PC-to-PC or PC-to-mainframe is essential for project management functions. For example, project analysis can access corporate databases for cost estimating purposes.
- Multiuser Configuration—In these days of shared resources, database systems now have capabilities for simultaneous data entry and editing with concurrency control. Multiple users can safely edit and update informatoin in the same database. Protection procedures are incorporated into the programs so that databases and application files are not accidentally destroyed in the multi user environment. An example is the "automatic time lock release" used by R:BASE to provide protection against the lock-up of a database when two users attempt to lock the same set of tables at the same time.
- Data Security—Passwords can be assigned to databases, tables, and views. Individual users can be given selective access privileges through special commands. For example, in dBASE IV memo fields in a database can be encrypted for confidentiality either explicitly by using the PROTECT command or automatically when the associated database is encrypted.

4.3 STRUCTURED QUERY LANGUAGE

For small databases, you can locate a record by browsing through the contents of the database. However, for large databases, browsing through the records can be very slow and inefficient. A more efficient way is to retrieve only the needed files or records, rather than searching through all of them.

The *Structured Query Language* (SQL) is a way for you to easily retrieve the pertinent records from a file. With simple English-like words, you can query the database about the desired data. The query is composed of clauses such as FROM, SELECT, WHERE, and ORDER. The clauses are used to specify search parameters. For example:

FROM identifies the file(s) with the proper records
SELECT identifies the field(s) to be retrieved
WHERE sets specific conditions that the field(s) data must meet
ORDER sorts the records by a key field alphabetically or numerically

The FROM clause is mandatory because it specifies the name of the file to be searched. The other clauses are optional. Their use depends on the data being requested. All the clauses do not have to be used at once, but if they are, they must follow the order of FROM, SELECT, WHERE, and ORDER. Both relational operators and logical operators can be used in the query. The permissible operators are:

Relational Operators
    Greater than ($>$)
    Less than ($<$)
    Greater than or equal to ($<=$)
    Less than or equal to ($<=$)
    Equal to ($=$)
    Not equal to ($<>$)

Logical Operators
    AND
    OR
    NOT

The AND operator requires that all the stated conditions must be met before a record can be retrieved. The OR operator requires that any one of the conditions can be satisfied in order to retrieve the record. The NOT operator requires that the record be retrieved only if the stated condition(s) are not satisfied. The use of SQL to retrieve a record is illustrated with the example below:

```
FROM PROJECT
SELECT TASK,DURATION,DUE_DATE
```

```
WHERE DURATION > 5 AND DUE_DATE < 10
ORDER DUE_DATE
```

The above query retrieves records from the PROJECT file. The data fields of interest are TASK, DURATION, and DUE_DATE. The selected records must have durations greater than 5 time units and due dates less than 10 time units. After the records are selected, they are arranged in numeric order by due dates. This example might be a case where you need a list of projects tasks that have imminent due dates but are likely to exceed the due dates because of their long durations.

SQL has been the standard for accessing mainframe database systems. It has just recently begun to make its appearance on microcomputers. SQL makes the powerful data professional now view SQL as the database interface of the future. The move to SQL is driven by the growing prevalence of microcomputers as a database management tool. Thousands of small businesses now employ mircrocomputers to track and manage their important data. The growing awareness that stand-alone databases would, in the future, need to share information with other systems has prompted the move towards SQL as the standard for database interactions. IBM has given credence to this move by providing the basis for speculations that its successful DB2 mainframe database, which uses SQL, will soon be ported to the mirocomputer level.

Ashton-Tate, the developer of the dBASE series, is also moving in the SQL direction. The latest addition to the dBASE series, dBASE IV, has an SQL facility. Informix Software, Inc. of Menlo Park, California, now has its own version of SQL called Informix-SQL. Informix also has a fourth-generation language called Informix-4GL and a product called ESQL/C, which allows C programmers to incorporate SQL into their user-written programs. SQL also can be embedded into popular m ainframe languages such as COBOL and PL/1. SQL is supported as a general standard by the American National Standards Institute (ANSI). The forthcoming OS/2 Extended Edition is expected to include an SQL-based database module. SQL has the major advantage of bringing the distributed computing and data integrity of mainframes to the PC level.

An alternative to the SQL facility is OS/2 Extended Edition is the SQL Server to be jointly marketed by Ashton-Tate and Microsoft. The SQL-Server is an operating-system software package that is designed to allow multiuser SQL database programs to run on OS/2-based networks. For users of database programs that do not offer SQL, add-on packages could be the answer. An example is dQuery from QuadBase Systems, Inc. The add-on package is a low-cost enhancement tool that alows dBASE and Lotus 1-2-3 users to access their local data files with SQL commands. Because SQL is implemented across a wide variety of hardware and software units, SQL-based database software running on one type of system can often exchange data with SQL databases on another system.

Despite its advantages and unavoidable emergence as a standard, SQL does have its faults. A survey (Jenkins 1988) indicates that those who are adapting to SQL are doing so reluctantly, mainly because of the difficulty associated with learning the language. However, enhancements to the language that can improve its user-friendliness and interface are possible. Such enhancements are expected in the next few years.

For project managemant, SQL, even with its present PC-level limitations, can be very beneficial. Project management decisions often require evaluation of data based on management heuristics. SQL already has the rudiments for implementing such heuristics for prompt decisions. For example, information about due dates can be retrieved and evaluated on the basis of established milestones and prevailing resource availability so that project control actions can be taken.

4.4 ORGANIZING A PROJECT DATABASE

Data is the basis for information and information is the basis for decision. Good decisions are based on good information. Timely decisions are based on timely information. Project management is information intensive. Consequently, effective project management depends on proper data management. The capabilities of database management programs can significantly facilitate the managing of data for project management purposes.

The first step in organizing a project database is to carefully study the project scenario and then design the structures of files that will need to be maintained. FIGURE 4-3 shows an example of file structures and kinds that you might need. You must study the present data management system (manual or automated) before deciding to implement a new one.

- Study the present data management system to determine its strengths and weaknesses. Is it providing all the data needed? Is the data properly organized? Is the necessary data easy to locate for prompt decision?
- If the present system is deficient, find out why.
- Develop a conceptual model of what the project data files should look like. If possible, use a manual design to develop the model. By manually tackling the data organization problem, you will gain a better understanding of what the data needs are. If your data is not properly organized in a manual implementation before you computerize, you will simply end with a disorganized computer model of your data and it will be more difficult to get things straightened out.
- Decide what kind of output and what format you need from the database system. Identify the questions you need to have answered by the output.
- Do not try to obtain only what the system can offer you, rather specify what you want the system to do for you.

- Establish the data input requirements. Relate the source of input to the input capabilities of the system. Identify what data items are available for input and what data items should be generated by the database system.
- Organize the data items and the resulting files in a logical fashion.
- List the procedures for accessing information contained in the data files.

Once the structure of the database has been developed, you will need to give management instructions to the database management system. Managing

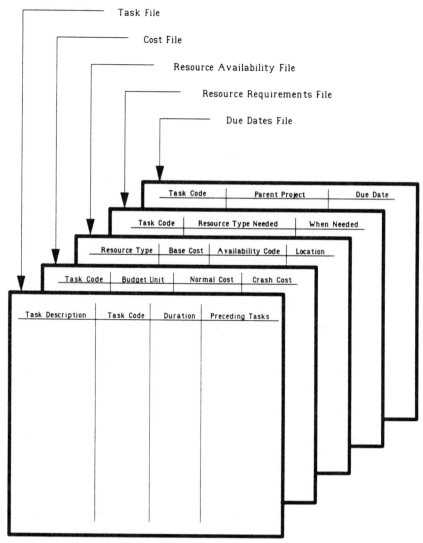

Fig. 4-3. Project file structures.

project database will primarily involve the following:

- Adding new data to the database
- Sorting the database into some meaningful order
- Searching the database for specific information
- Printing selected data onto formatted reports
- Editing data in the database
- Deleting data from the database

FIGURE 4-4 shows an example of the organization of a database for project management. Data entry and update can be performed at the functional department level. Information generated at that level can be used for routine project decisions or be routed to a centralized database system where comprehensive maintenance and security are performed. The centralized information can be accessed by authorized levels of management for decision making purposes. FIGURE 4-5 offers an alternative view of how information can be shared or exchanged in the project management environment.

4.5 STORAGE AND RETRIEVAL CONSIDERATIONS

The level of data-management performance that can be achieved depends on effective selection and configuration of the computing devices and the intended uses. Project-database management has some important consider-

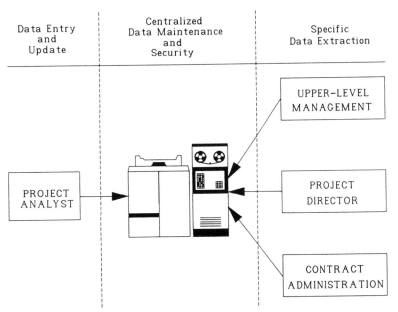

Fig. 4-4. Organization of project management database.

97

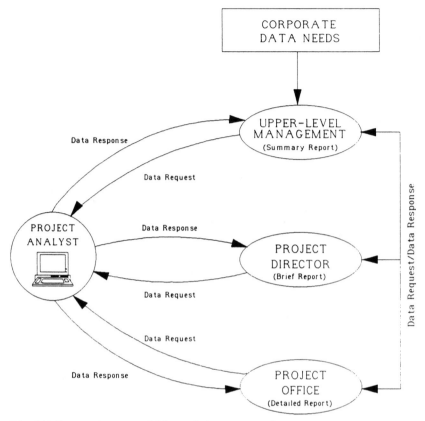

Fig. 4-5. Data exchange model for project management.

ations that need to be carefully evaluated. It is not necessary to dump every bit of data into a database simply because the database facility is available. Each data set should be scrutinized for storage and retrieval needs.

Transient Data

There is a class of data which has been classified as *transient data*. This data is defined as volatile data that passes through the project manager's desk for one-time decision-making and then is not needed again. An example might be the number of technicians that show up at a job site on a given day. Unless there is some correlation between the day-to-day attendance records of electricians, this piece of information will have relevance for only that given day. The project manager can make his decision for that day on the basis of that day's attendance record. Transient data need not be stored in a permanent database record unless it is needed for future analysis or use (e.g., forecasting and incentive programs).

Recurring Data

Recurring data is encountered frequently enough to necessitate storage on a permanent basis. An example is a file containing contract due dates. This file will need to be kept at least through the project life cycle. Recurring data can be further categorized into static data and dynamic data. Recurring data that is static will retain its original parameters and values each time it is retrieved and used. Recurring data that is dynamic has the potential for taking on different parameters and values each time it is retrieved and used.

Storage and retrieval considerations for project management database should cover the following questions:

1. What is the origin of the data?
2. How long will the data be maintained?
3. Who needs access to the data?
4. What will the data used for?
5. How often will the data be accessed?
6. Is the data for "loop-up" purposes only (i.e., no printouts)?
7. Is the data for "reporting" purposes (i.e., generate reports)?
8. In what format is the data needed?
9. How fast will the data need to be accessed?
10. What security measures are needed for the data?

Answers to these questions will help determine what kind of storage mechanisms to use and what kind of retrieval procedures to employ. The method of organizing the records in a file is referred to as the *file structure*. The method of searching the file in order to retrieve data is called the *access mode*. There are three common methods of file organization, namely:

1. Sequential access
2. Random access (or direct access)
3. Indexed sequential access

These methods are based on a "key" which is used as the pointer for both storage and retrieval data. The key uniquely identifies each record in a file.

Sequential Access Files. Sequential files offer the simplest file structure. A sequential file simply stores records in linear fashion, one after the other. Records in a sequential file are accessed in the same order in which they are stored. Intermediate records cannot be skipped in order to retrieve a record. It is a first-come-first-serve situation or a first-saved-first-retrieved access system. Sequential files are normally associated with magnetic tape storage devices. Because of its inflexibility in data access, sequential access is seldom used for database storage when the database must be frequently accessed. Sequential access is typically used to produce reports for which every record must be processed. A project task list file is an example of a file every record must be processed. A project task list file is an example of a file that might be suitable for sequential storage and retrieval because all the tasks making up the project must be listed whenever the file is processed. Because project tasks are usually listed in numerical order (e.g., 1,2,3, . . .), it is logical to always print the list sequentially in its inherent order. A major advantage of sequential file processing is its simplicity and low cost.

Random Access Files. In random access storage, a magnetic disk stores the data so that any record can be accessed directly as needed. Random access is often referrred to as *direct access*. This method permits selective access to desired records. Any record chosen at "random" can be accessed in the same amount of time as any other record. The physical location of the record on the storage device has no effect on the retrieval time. This is not the case in sequential access where the last record in the file will certainly take longer to locate than the record at the top of the file. The advantage of random access file processing is its speed and flexibility in data access. An example of a project file that might be suitable for random access processing is the project personnel file. There are many instances where we would like to retrieve only the records of certain personnel who meet a specified set of criteria. In such instances, direct access to the desired record(s) is the most logical method.

The computer has an "address" of each record so that it can locate it on the disk. One method of finding a record's address is to start with the *primary key*. The primary key is one field or a combination of fields that uniquely identifies a record from all other records. In the personnel file shown in TABLE 4-1, the employee number is a reasonable primary key for locating a particular person. Employee's last names might or might not be unique so they should not be used as a primary key. The secondary key offers an auxiliary key for identifying subsets of the records identified by the primary key. For example, if we wanted a list of all employees in the personnel file who belong to a given department, we could use the employee number as a primary key and the last name as a secondary key.

Indexed Sequential Access Files. Indexed sequential access combines the direct and sequential access methods. In this method, the primary key field is used to locate the area on the disk where the sequential search begins. Indexed sequential access works fine as long as there is a limited number of additions and deletions in the files being processed. Deletions are not actually removed from the disk; they are simply marked for permanent removal when the entire disk is rewritten as a later time. Additions to the disk are simply added onto the end of the records already present in the appropriate area. When this area is full, an overflow area is used to store the new records. If a record cannot be retrieved from the appropriate search area, a sequential search of the overflow area is performed.

The problem with sequential files is that they have long search times. Random access files reduce the search time but the drawback is the records are not presorted in any sequence (e.g., alphabetically). While indexed sequential files have a longer search time than random access files, the records of indexed sequential files are already in sequential order. This order facilitates easy printing of such things as alphabetical lists. Random access files, by contrast, must be explicitly processed to sort records into a desired order.

An indexed sequential file is a combination of at least two files. A data file and an index file make up an indexed sequential file. The data file contains the actual data items. The index file contains pointers that direct a search to the correct block of data for any item you are retrieving. The database for a very large project is an example of a data set suitable for indexed sequential access. The size of each record and the size of the entire file would prohibit bringing the entire file into the main memory of the computer at once. The access to the main memory is faster than the access to auxiliary storage devices, which house the database. As a result, you should have the index file in many memory while the entire database remains in auxiliary storage. Because the index file is normally a smaller file, keeping it in main memory does not pose any unreasonable load on the computing system. The index file can be quickly accessed in main memory to provide the pointer or key to any desired record in the large database. Thus, records in the database are brought into main memory only when they are needed. This indexing facilitates better utilization of our computing resources.

4.6 DATABASE SORTS

Traditional data processing is associated with computational analysis of data sets that are primarily numeric. Recently, however, the concept of text processing has invaded the realm of data processing. The increasing prominence of word processors, text editors, and text formatters continues to suggest new capabilities for data processing. Sorting and text formatting are now among them major aspects of data processing. These relate to the following two needs:

1. The extraction of useful meaning from text stored in a database
2. The physical presentation of database text in an informative format

Perhaps the simplest method of processing database data is by sorting. Sorting implies physically rearranging the records in a database in some meaningful order. For example, the project management file containing due dates can be sorted according to the order of the due dates it contains. The major reason for sorting data is to aid the decision maker. Sorted due dates, for example, can quickly identify imminent project deadlines so the project manager can take appropriate actions to ensure the deadlines are met. Another advantage of sorting is that meaningful reports can be generated more quickly.

FIGURE 4-6 shows the dBASE III Plus screen dump of a task list that illustrates a database sort. The list file contains records of six tasks with data fields labelled Activity, Activity Code, Description, Due Date, and Project. All the

Activity	Activity Code	Description	Due Date	Project
AA1	B89015	Develop Specs	04/15/89	A
FJ2	G12578	Write Program	04/29/89	A
PL2	M45454	Test & Debug	05/17/89	A
WY3	GH0010	Collect System Data	05/10/89	A
D23	DP2390	Document Program	06/01/89	A
E44	EASY12	Run Program	07/12/89	A

Fig. 4-6. Task list to be sorted.

tasks belong to Project A. For decision making purposes, the project manager might want to obtain this list in some sorted form. For example, he might want the tasks listed in ascending order of due dates. The result of using dBASE III Plus to sort the file by due date is shown in FIG. 4-7. You can see in the figure that activities PL2 and WY3 have been interchanged based on the due date criterion.

In a large project, presenting a task list that is sorted by due date can be valuable to the project manager. He can easily identify a subset of the project that should get the most immediate attention. Other important fields that can be used for sorting the project task list include duration, cost, criticality index, resource units, and number of immediate predecessors. As an alternative, FIG. 4-8 shows the task list after it has been sorted by Activity Code. If a large database of activities in a multiple project environment is maintained, sorting by project code (e.g., A, B, and C) can offer a way to categorize the set of all activities into project groups.

Page No.   1
03/25/89

Activity	Activity Code	Description	Due Date	Project
AA1	B89015	Develop Specs	04/15/89	A
FJ2	G12578	Write Program	04/29/89	A
WY3	GH0010	Collect System Data	05/10/89	A
PL2	M45454	Test & Debug	05/17/89	A
D23	DP2390	Document Program	06/01/89	A
E44	EASY12	Run Program	07/12/89	A

Fig. 4-7. Task list sorted by due date.

Activity	Activity Code	Description	Due Date	Project
AA1	B89015	Develop Specs	04/15/89	A
D23	DP2390	Document Program	06/01/89	A
E44	EASY12	Run Program	07/12/89	A
FJ2	G12578	Write Program	04/29/89	A
WY3	GH0010	Collect System Data	05/10/89	A
PL2	M45454	Test & Debug	05/17/89	A

Fig. 4-8. Task list sorted by activity code.

4.7 MULTIDIMENSIONAL DATABASES

Multidimensional spreadsheets have been gaining popularity lately. But what is really available on the market are 3-D spreadsheets, which offer just one step towards multidimensionality. Among database products, VP-Planner Plus offers a level of multidimensionality not yet available in many spreadsheet programs. For users who have more dimensions for their data needs, the multidimensional capability of VP-Planner Plus can provide some relief.

The difference between a 3-D product and a multidimensional one is the number of dimensions available. Paperback Software International (1989) provides examples to illustrate the differences between "different dimensions" in data management.

One-Dimensional

A one-dimensional group of data is simply a list. For example, the list of products sold by a computer store is one-dimensional.

Two-Dimensional

Typical spreadsheets have horizontal and vertical dimensions—They are organized in a two-dimensional layout. For example, our project task list is organized in a two-dimensional layout because we have rows of activities and columns of specific characteristics associated with the activities.

Three-Dimensional

Adding depth to two-dimensional spreadsheets by stacking them creates a third dimension. For example, we can stack the task lists from various projects one after the other to create a 3-D data group for multiple projects.

Computer displays do not have any depth. Therefore, the third dimension in a 3-D spreadsheet is usually invisible. You can view only one of the stacks or pages at once and then use commands like PgUp and PgDn to move from stack to stack.

A problem appears when you try to refer to the various cells in each of the various spreadsheet stacks in a 3-D layout. You will need to supply a third piece of information to the cell address to indicate which stack is desired. Adding this address is often done by adding more letters to the typical column letter and row number sequence. For example, B:E5 might refer to cell E5 in the second (B) spreadsheet of a stack. This convention can become very cumbersome for large dimensions.

Multidimensional addressing in a database is handled by VP-Planner by referring to each item by its name. For example, if a multidimensional database keeps track of sales figures for various products by month and year, you can easily refer to the Total Sales for Product A in March. This referring style significantly simplifies the addressing problem. It also enhances understanding by conveying a logical idea about the data items being processed.

Four-Dimensional

For more complex data sets, the simplification of cell address is even more desired. A 4-D database would be analogous to having several stacks of spreadsheets placed side-by-side. Conventional addressing would require a 4-part address for each item of data: the stack number, the worksheet letter within that stack, and column and row coordinates of the specific cell. As an example, consider our stack of task lists for the multiple projects. Now suppose that you need to develop another stack consisting of the resource files associated with the multiple projects. Then you would have the situation depicted in FIG. 4-9.

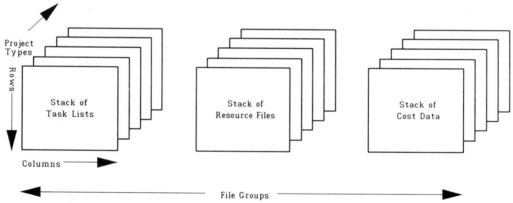

Fig. 4-9. 4-D project data layout.

Five-Dimensional

A 5-D data layout is shown in FIG. 4-10. This layout is similar to having vertical layers (up and down) of a 4-D data layout. You can use this layout if you want to organize project data for various divisions of an organization. The first division might be represented by the top layer, the second division by the second layer down, and so on. In the VP-Planner multidimensional database address, you can refer to a data cell, for example, as Income from Projects in Oklahoma during March of 1989.

Obviously, memory capacity and execution speed will be of concern in managing multidimensional databases. The approach taken by VP-Planner is to keep all of the data on disk. Only the specific items referred to are loaded into memory, therefore, very little memory is used at any given time and recalculations occur at a much faster rate.

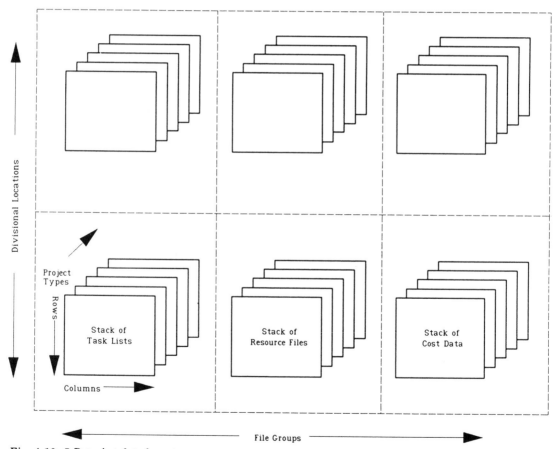

Fig. 4-10. 5-D project data layout.

4.8 DATA INTEGRATION

Linking data for project management purposes will give you the flexibility you need to make more effective decisions. No decision can be complete these days without considering the various factors likely to be encountered during the project life cycle. Software can be used to provide an integration of the various data sets you need for decisions. There must be integrated access to such things as cost data, communication matrix, resource data, corporate database of technical manpower, and design data.

ABT Project Workbench by Applied Business Technology Corp., for example, has data links to other project management packages and a presentation graphics program. There is a link utility that lets Project Workbench users import data from Symantec Corp.'s Time Line project management system. One other utility permits data imports from SofTrak System Inc.'s PlotTrak graphics package. A data link also is available for file imports from the mainframe programs PAC II and III developed by AGS Management Systems, Inc. Consulting project analysts using one type of project management software can use a data link to upload data directly from the database of a client who uses different software.

This flexibility is transferring and integrating project data from different sources should help eliminate the traditional confinement to a single software package. For example, Time Line can be used effectively for smaller independent projects. When such small projects become a part of other larger projects, the more sophisticated capabilities of packages such as Workbench can be invoked by transferring the Time Line data to the higher level environment and integrating it with other data sets.

Project Workbench's link to PlotTrak allows you to plot large network diagrams showing the sequence of tasks in a project. If you have always agonized over the slow printing speed of some project management packages such as Harvard Total Project Manager, now you have some graphics allies. The poor performance of many project management packages is due to the design primarily for computational analysis of project data rather than graphical representation of data.

Packages that operate on mainframes have traditionally offered their tremendous capabilities only to corporate users who have required computing resources. With the emerging sophistication of project data links and integration, ordinary users now can have their project data collected and organized in local computing environments, such as the PC level and then transferred to the higher computing platforms for more sophisticated analyses.

Alpha Software Corp. of Burlington, Mass., introduced Alpha Four that serves as a good example of data integration. The product merges the power of relational database with the ease of use of a menu-driven file manager. The software, which was originally designed as a file manager, now incorporates unique features that let nonprogrammers build sophisticated applications such as accounting, inventory-control, and invoicing systems. These are all applications that have valid places in project management environments. The product is file-compatible with dBASE, allowing it to share data with any other dBASE program. The new "set" technique employed by Alpha Four allows as many as 10 related databases to be linked in a set. This file set can then be queried as if it were a single database. Thus, information can be pulled from multiple databases into one report.

A data link also has been developed to transfer files to and from Time Line and Artemis software (Metier Management Systems). The link, called Exporter, allows Time Line project information to be uploaded to an Artemis series of programs which runs on high-end PCs, DEC Vaxes, HP minicomputers, and IBM mainframes. The link is designed for companies that need to integrate data from PCs to mainframe files, to produce summary reports for management, and to take advantage of the extra speed, capacity, and sophisticated graphics provided by mainframes. The exporter can directly transmit both Time Line and resource assignments and task sequences to Artemis.

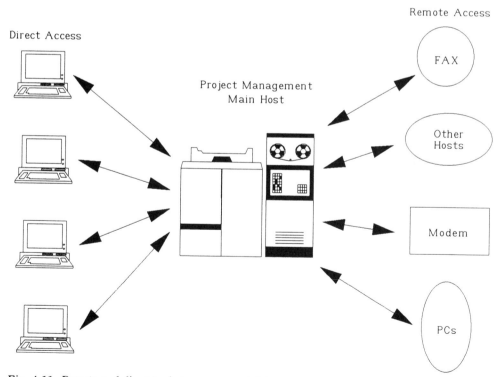

Fig. 4-11. Remote and direct project management data access.

4.9 REMOTE AND DIRECT DATA ACCESS

For large projects, using the Work Breakdown Structure can help break a project into its component parts. These component parts can be handled as small projects. If you have responsibilities for the components, you will have the option of logging into a mainframe computer directly for project analysis or uploading your data through remote access. The overall project work can be packaged to several analysts. Each analyst will use a low-end project management software package to schedule a part of the large project and then upload the data to the mainframe for overall comprehensive project management. A conceptual model of the data access options is shown in FIG. 4-11.

5

Analytical Tools
for Project Analysis

This chapter presents some special analytical tools for project management analysis. Topics covered include computer simulation as a project planning tool, engineering economic analysis for project cost versus income evaluation, and basic statistical techniques for evaluating decision parameters involved in project management. A BASIC computer program is used to illustrate the effectiveness of computer simulation for project planning. Other BASIC programs are used to illustrate the economic analysis aspect of project management. The commercial STATGRAPHICS software is used to illustrate some of the statistical analyses available for use in project management.

5.1 SIMULATION AS A PROJECT PLANNING TOOL

The interest in computer simulation has been growing steadily over the past several years. Several businesses and industries now use simulation on a routine basis as a planning tool. Many academic institutions now offer formal courses in simulation. Simulation has been effectively used for decisions in areas ranging from marketing to production facility design. The benefits of simulation that have been experienced in these various areas can also be realized in a project management environment.

What is computer simulation? Computer simulation is the process of experimenting with a computer model of a real system. Simulation permits you to study the real system without actually building it (if it is a proposed system), without disturbing it (if it is an existing operational system), or without dismantling or destroying it (if it is a system in a delicate state of operation). Most project management actions are taken for the sake of future operations. Thus, simulation offers a tool for making decisions about future project events without actually having a setup of those future events.

The project management software market has become a multimillion dollar giant. In addition to offering capabilities for basic project management analyses, many packages also offer some unique functions. Simulation is one function that can be incorporated into computer analysis of projects. STARC (Badiru and Whitehouse 1987) is a BASIC computer program that offers simulation capability to the project analyst.

5.2 USING STARC PROJECT SIMULATION PROGRAM

STARC is a project planning aid. It was developed to simulate project networks and perform what-if analysis of projects involving probabilistic activity times and resource constraints. The program is useful as a training tool for project management analysis and students.

The simulated schedules generated by the program are designed to serve as decision aids for project planners. The effects of different activity time estimates and resource allocation options can be easily studied with STARC prior to operational implementations in an actual project.

STARC is a menu-driven program written in the BASIC programming language for the IBM PC and true compatibles. The program is easy to run and provides a quick view of the effects of variabilities in the project environment. This section presents a brief illustration of the type of pre project analysis that can be performed with STARC. Further details on the simulation methodology, input requirements, and output analysis of STARC are presented by Badiru (1988a).

The simulation run time for large networks will typically be very long. To expedite the analysis of large networks, you can break the network up into small subprojects which can be quickly analyzed. The results for the subprojects can then be integrated to obtain a composite project profile.

Running STARC from Floppy Disk

STARC is written in nine segments named STARC1, STARC2, STARC3, STARC4, ..., STARC9. The appropriate segments are loaded or chained automatically as needed by the program after STARC1 is started. All segments must be on the same floppy disk in the default floppy drive or in the same hard disk directory so automatic loading and chaining can be effected.

To run STARC from a floppy drive at the BASIC level, do the following:

1. Change to the desired default floppy drive (e.g., A>)
2. Load BASIC
3. Type RUN STARC1.BAS

The program can also be started from the DOS level by typing: BASIC STARC-1.BAS at the default DOS prompt.

Running STARC from Hard Disk

All nine segments of STARC can be copied onto a hard disk to facilitate easy access and faster execution. You simply need to create a subdirectory named \ STARC and copy all STARC files and the BASIC programming language file into the subdirectory. To start running STARC from the hard disk, do the following.

1. Change to the STARC directory by typing CD \ STARC
2. Load the BASIC language
3. Type RUN STARC1.BAS

Alternately, the program can be started at the DOS level within the \ STARC subdirectory by typing BASIC STARC1.BAS.

Main Menu

The main menu for STARC is shown in FIG. 5-1. The following input items are needed to run a simulation of a project from option 1 in the main menu.

- Data filename. Specify the data file in which the project data is stored.
- Number of simulation runs desired. 10 is usually adequate. But a large number like 50 can give a better histogram of the distribution of the projcet duration in the printed output. For large projects, memory requirement limitations and long simulation times might prevent using large numbers of simulation runs.
- The number of project completion deadlines to be evaluated. STARC calculates the probability of completing a project within a given deadline. Up to 10 deadlines can be evaluated during 1 simulation run.

```
                      MAIN MENU
* * * * * * * * * * * * * * * * * * * * * * * * * * * * * * * * * * * * * * * * * * * * * * * * * * * * * *
*    1.  RUN STARC SIMULATION USING DISK DATAFILE         *
*    2.  CREATE NEW DATAFILE                               *
*    3.  EDIT A DATAFILE                                   *
*    4.  PRINT A DATAFILE                                  *
*    5.  PRINT AN OUTPUT FILE                              *
*    6.  TERMINATE PROGRAM                                 *
* * * * * * * * * * * * * * * * * * * * * * * * * * * * * * * * * * * * * * * * * * * * * * * * * * * * * *


                   ENTER OPTION NUMBER:  _
```

Fig. 5-1. Risk coverage adjustment for PERT time estimates.

- Resource allocation weighting factor. This is between 0.0 and 1.0. The weighting factor is used in calculating the resource allocation priority measure for each project activity. The priority measure used by STARC is the *Composite Allocation Factor* (CAF) [Badiru 1988a]. The measure takes into consideration both the resource requirements of an activity and the time duration variability of the activity. The weighing factor is used to give relative weights to these two components of CAF.
- Duration risk coverage factor. This factor is a percentage factor for simulating the duration of each activity in the project. It provides a risk coverage for the imprecision in the three PERT time estimates (a, m, and b) for each activity. A risk factor of 10 percent, for example, extends the simulation range [a,b] for an activity's duration by 10 percent over the specified PERT time interval. An example of the dilation of the activity duration interval is shown in FIG. 5-2.

Creating a Datafile

STARC automatically appends the extension .DAT to datafiles it creates. The file creation program segment asks for the following information:

1. Data filename
2. Project ID—an optional description for the project data
3. Number of activities
4. Number of different resource types
5. Units of each resource type available
6. Data for each activity

Editing a Data File

The file edit option is shown in FIG. 5-3. If option number 4 is selected for resource changes, FIG. 5-4 sub-submenu is displayed.

If the data file print option is selected, the following two printing choices are available:

1. Print data file on screen
2. Print data file on printer

With the above data editing facilities, changes can quickly be made in the project data and the effects of the changes can be studied by repeating the simulation of the project network.

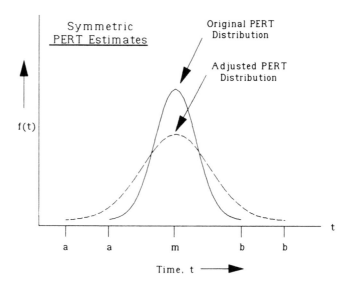

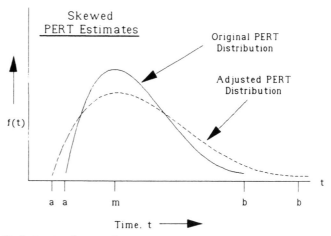

Fig. 5-2. Project network example.

Output Menu

The output menu for STARC can be seen in FIG. 5-5. The output is presented in a simple and organized format with the appropriate level of detail for quick managerial decisions.

```
        +======== EDITING MENU ========+
+++++++++++++++++++++++++++++++++++++++++++++++++++++++
        1.  Add New Activities(up to 25 at a time)
        2.  Delete Activity
        3.  Change Individual Activity Data
        4.  Change Resource Availability
        5.  Change Project Name(Identification)
        6.  Print The File Being Edited
        7.  End Editing and Save Datafile
        8.  Return to Main Menu
+++++++++++++++++++++++++++++++++++++++++++++++++++++++
              ENTER OPTION NO.: _
```

Fig. 5-3. *Initial project data.*

```
            ++++ OPTIONS ++++

        1.   Change Units Available
        2.   Add New Resource Type
        3.   Delete Resource Type
        4.   Return to Editing Menu
        +++++++++++++++++++++++++++++

            Enter Your Choice: _
```

Fig. 5-4. *STARC main menu.*

```
        STARC OUTPUT MENU
**********************************************************
*       1. PRINT CURRENT OUTPUT ON SCREEN                *
*       2. PRINT CURRENT OUTPUT ON LINE PRINTER          *
*       3. STORE CURRENT OUTPUT IN AN OUTPUT FILE        *
*       4. RETURN TO MAIN MENU(Output Will Be Cleared)   *
**********************************************************



        ENTER THE DESIRED NUMBER : _
```

Fig. 5-5. *Data file edit menu.*

STARC Simulation Assumptions

STARC simulates a project schedule based on the following assumptions:

- Resource availability is in whole units
- No partial assignment of resources
- No splitting of activities
- Activity preemption is not allowed
- Total resource units required must be available before an activity can start
- All predecessors must be finished before an activity can start

5.3 EXAMPLE OF STARC ANALYSIS

The small project presented in TABLE 5-1 is used to illustrate a project network simulation analysis using STARC. The project network is shown in FIG. 5-6. PERT's three time estimates (optimistic time, most likely time, and pessimistic time) for each activity are shown below the activity label in the network. The sample project contains seven activities and one resource type (say machine operator). There are ten units of the resource available at the beginning of the project.

Table 5-1. Sample Project Data with Resource Constraint.

Activity	Act. No.	Predecessor	(DAYS)			Resource Units Required
			a	m	b	
A	1	-	1	2	4	3
B	2	-	5	6	7	5
C	3	-	2	4	5	4
D	4	A	1	3	4	2
E	5	C	4	5	7	4
F	6	A	3	4	5	2
G	7	B,D,E	1	2	3	6

Total resource units available initially = 10 units

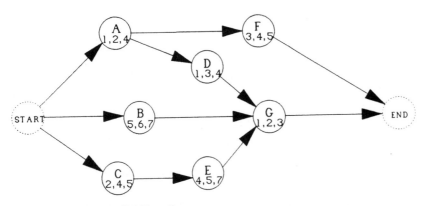

Fig. 5-6. Resource availability edit menu.

Sample Simulation Output

FIGURE 5-7 shows the initial project data as formatted by STARC. The network activities originally labelled A, B, C, D, and so on, have been renamed as activities 1, 2, 3, 4, and so on in the data file to facilitate computational manipulations. If an analyst wishes to make changes in the resource data, the resource menu in FIG. 5-4 will be needed. This menu offers various options for conducting "what-if" analysis of resource availability. FIGURE 5-5 shows the options available for the simulation output.

The data shown earlier in FIG. 5-7 was simulated with a sample size of 100. As a part of the input, a request was made to analyze 10 potential deadlines for the project. The resulting simulation output is shown in a series of screen dumps presented in the following figures.

FIGURE 5-8 shows the output heading indicating the project name, number of activities, number of resources, resource allocation weighting factor, risk coverage factor, and initial resource availability.

```
Datafile name:- example
Project Name(identification):- Example
Number of Activities:-  7
Number of Resource Types:-  1
Resource Units Available: R1= 10
```

ACT.	PERT			IMMEDIATE			RESOURCES REQD.		
NO.	a	m	b	PRECEDING ACTIVITIES			1	2	3 ....
---	---	---	---	---	---	---	---	---	---
1	1.0	2.0	4.0				3		
2	5.0	6.0	7.0				5		
3	2.0	4.0	5.0				4		
4	1.0	3.0	4.0	1			2		
5	4.0	5.0	7.0	3			4		
6	3.0	4.0	5.0	1			2		
7	1.0	2.0	3.0	2	4	5	6		

Fig. 5-7. STARC output menu.

116

```
STARC PROJECT SCHEDULING SIMULATION OUTPUT
- - - - - - - - - - - - - - - - - - - - - - - - - - - - - - - - - - - - - - - -

              PROJECT NAME:- Example
              NUMBER OF ACTIVITIES = 7
              NUMBER OF RESOURCES = 1
              CAF weighting factor, w = .5
              Duration risk coverage factor, q = .15

              RESOURCE AVAILABILITY
        RESOURCE #        UNITS AVAILABLE
        - - - - - - - - - - - - - - - - - - - - - - - - - - - -

              1                 10
```

Fig. 5-8. STARC output heading.

FIGURE 5-9 shows the output of the conventional PERT analysis without resource limitation. The expected duration (DUR), earliest start (ES), earliest completion (EC), latest start (LS), latest completion (LC), total slack (TS), free slack (FS), and the indicator for criticality (CRIT) are presented for each activity. The output shows that the PERT time without resource constraint is 11 days. It is seen that activities 3, 5, and 7 are on the critical path.

```
                  UNCONSTRAINED PERT SCHEDULE
  ACT.   DUR.    ES     EC     LS      LC     TS     FS    CRIT
  - - - - - - - - - - - - - - - - - - - - - - - - - - - - - - - - - -
   1     2.17   0.00   2.17   4.00    6.17   4.00   0.00  0.000
   2     6.00   0.00   6.00   3.00    9.00   3.00   3.00  0.000
   3     3.83   0.00   3.83   0.00    3.83   0.00   0.00  1.000
   4     2.83   2.17   5.00   6.17    9.00   4.00   4.00  0.000
   5     5.17   3.83   9.00   3.83    9.00   0.00   0.00  1.000
   6     4.00   2.17   6.17   7.00   11.00   4.83   0.00  0.000
   7     2.00   9.00  11.00   9.00   11.00   0.00   0.00  1.000
  UNCONSTRAINED PERT PROJECT COMPLETION TIME = 11
```

Fig. 5-9. Conventional PERT analysis.

FIGURE 5-10 shows the simulated sample averages of the variables associated with each activity. The average project duration in 100 simulation runs is 12.96 days. With the resource constraints, the criticality indices are 0.96, 0.0, 0.04, 0.74, 0.04, 0.22, and 0.78, respectively for activities 1 through 7. The criticality index of an activity is the probability that the activity will fall on the critical path. In other words, the criticality index indicates the long-run tendencies of an activity. You can see in the simulation result that Activity 1 is critical most of the time (probability of 0.96) and Activity 2 is never on the critical path. The average observed durations of the activities are also presented in the Figure.

You should note that the ES, EC, LS, LC, TS, and FS values in the sample average output will not necessarily match conventional PERT network calcula-

```
                       SIMULATED SAMPLE AVERAGES
     ACT.   MEAN   MEAN   MEAN    MEAN   MEAN    MEAN    MEAN   CRIT.
      #     DUR.    ES     EC      LS     LC      TS      FS    INDEX
     -------------------------------------------------------------------
      1     2.16   6.01   8.17    6.01   8.18    0.06    0.00   0.960
      2     6.01   0.00   6.01    4.94  10.95    4.94    4.86   0.000
      3     3.87   0.00   3.87    1.86   5.73    1.86    0.00   0.040
      4     2.67   8.17  10.85    8.28  10.95    0.16    0.08   0.740
      5     5.22   3.87   9.09    5.73  10.95    1.86    1.78   0.040
      6     4.00   8.17  12.17    8.96  12.96    0.79    0.00   0.220
      7     2.00  10.89  12.89   10.96  12.96    0.08    0.00   0.780
     AVERAGE PROJECT DURATION = 12.96228
```

Fig. 5-10. Simulated sample averages.

tions. In other words, you cannot draw a PERT network based on the output in FIG. 5-10 because each average value (e.g., MEAN EC) is computed from the results from the 100 independent simulation runs. However, for each given simulation run, all the values observed will conform to the conventional PERT computational procedure.

FIGURE 5-11 shows an aspiration level analysis of a set of project deadlines. The second column in the figure presents the probabilities calculated analytically based on the Central Limit Theorum. The third column presents the sample probabilities based on the observations in the simulated sample. The analytical probabilities in the second column are presented as a validation measure for the observed probabilities. The two columns agree fairly closely.

Suppose you are considering a contract deadline of 14 days and you want to know the probability of finishing the project in that time frame. The simulation output indicates a calculated probability of 0.8858 and a simulated probability of 0.9100. So, there seems to be a good chance of finishing the project in 14 days. Now you can proceed with the contract. Even though the conventional PERT duration for the project is 11 days, you can see that there is a very low probability (0.0114 calculated, 0.0 observed) of finishing the project in 11 days when you consider resource limitations.

```
                   PROJECT DEADLINE ANALYSIS
     DEADLINE    CALCULATED PROBABILITY    OBSERVED PROBABILITY
     -------------------------------------------------------------
       10.00           0.0003                   0.0000
       11.00           0.0114                   0.0000
       12.00           0.1321                   0.1300
       13.00           0.5174                   0.5600
       14.00           0.8858                   0.9100
       15.00           0.9910                   0.9900
       16.00           1.0000                   1.0000
       17.00           1.0000                   1.0000
       18.00           1.0000                   1.0000
       19.00           1.0000                   1.0000
```

Fig. 5-11. Project deadline analysis.

FIGURE 5-12 shows the shortest simulated schedule for the example. The shortest observed project duration in a sample of 100 simulation runs is 11.01 days. This schedule can serve as an operational schedule for planning purposes. In this schedule, only two activities (1 and 6) are on the critical path.

FIGURES 5-13 and 5-14 present the sample variances and ranges for the activities in the project. The variances might be needed for statistical analysis such as control charts for activity durations and resource loading diagrams.

SHORTEST SIMULATED SCHEDULED

ACT.	DUR.	ES	EC	LS	LC	TS	FS	CRIT
1	1.83	5.16	6.99	5.16	6.99	-0.00	0.00	1.000
2	5.16	0.00	5.16	3.74	8.89	3.74	3.64	0.000
3	3.11	0.00	3.11	0.10	3.21	0.10	0.00	0.000
4	1.14	6.99	8.13	7.75	8.89	0.76	0.66	0.000
5	5.68	3.11	8.79	3.21	8.89	0.10	0.00	0.000
6	4.03	6.99	11.01	6.99	11.01	0.00	0.00	1.000
7	2.12	8.79	10.92	8.89	11.01	0.10	0.00	0.000

SHORTEST SIMULATED PROJECT DURATION = 11.01316

Fig. 5-12. Best simulated project schedule.

SAMPLE VARIANCES

ACT. #	VAR. (DUR)	VAR. (ES)	VAR. (EC)	VAR. (LS)	VAR. (LC)	VAR. (TS)	VAR. (FS)
1	0.28	0.15	0.41	0.19	0.40	0.17	0.00
2	0.15	0.00	0.15	0.59	0.67	0.59	0.64
3	0.30	0.00	0.30	1.00	0.91	1.00	0.00
4	0.39	0.41	0.84	0.39	0.67	0.22	0.19
5	0.35	0.30	0.60	0.91	0.67	1.00	1.07
6	0.16	0.41	0.53	0.86	0.74	0.47	0.00
7	0.13	0.70	0.86	0.63	0.74	0.03	0.00

SAMPLE VARIANCE OF PROJECT DURATION = .7420697

Fig. 5-13. Simulated sample variances.

SAMPLE RANGES

ACT. #	RANGE (DUR)	RANGE (ES)	RANGE (EC)	RANGE (LS)	RANGE (LC)	RANGE (TS)	RANGE (FS)
1	2.44	1.65	2.87	2.70	3.42	4.00	0.00
2	1.65	0.00	1.65	4.25	4.23	4.25	4.25
3	2.45	0.00	2.45	4.80	5.10	4.80	0.00
4	2.74	2.87	4.99	3.53	4.23	4.00	4.00
5	2.95	2.45	3.71	5.10	4.23	4.80	4.80
6	1.73	2.87	3.43	4.71	4.44	2.38	0.00
7	1.54	4.33	4.94	4.23	4.44	1.02	0.00

SAMPLE RANGE OF PROJECT DURATION = 4.442803

Fig. 5-14. Simulated sample ranges.

```
                 PROJECT ACTIVITIES DATA
  ACTIVITY        A    M    B    MEAN  VAR.  RANGE  CAF
  ------------------------------------------------------
     1           1.0  2.0  4.0   2.2   0.3   3.0    55.4
     2           5.0  6.0  7.0   6.0   0.1   2.0   100.0
     3           2.0  4.0  5.0   3.8   0.3   3.0    72.6
     4           1.0  3.0  4.0   2.8   0.3   3.0    54.0
     5           4.0  5.0  7.0   5.2   0.3   3.0    88.0
     6           3.0  4.0  5.0   4.0   0.1   2.0    66.6
     7           1.0  2.0  3.0   2.0   0.1   2.0    75.3
```

Fig. 5-15. Echo of project data.

An echo of the initial PERT data for the project is shown in FIG. 5-15. The scaled priority measure (CAF) for allocating resources to competing activities are presented for each activity in the last column in the figure. You can see that Activity 2 has the highest priority for resource allocation when activities compete for units of the available resources.

5.4 SAMPLING OF ACTIVITY TIMES

STARC uses a mathematical procedure to fit a beta distribution for each activity time. Activity durations are sampled from this distribution. The parameters for each activity's distribution are presented in FIG. 5-16. Refer to Badiru (1988a) for the mathematical procedure for fitting the beta distributions if you are interested in this distribution.

A frequency distribution histogram for the project duration based on the simulated sample is presented in FIG. 5-17. Also, the 95 percent confidence interval for the project duration is computed by STARC. For the illustrative example, the interval is from 12.79 to 13.13 days, meaning there is a 95 percent confidence that the project can be completed between 12.79 and 13.13 days.

```
                FITTED BETA PARAMETERS
   ACT.    ALPHA    BETA     MU    VAR.    MODE
   ---------------------------------------------
      1     2.94    4.62    2.19   0.33    2.05
      2     4.00    4.00    6.00   0.15    6.00
      3     4.62    2.94    3.81   0.33    3.95
      4     4.62    2.94    2.81   0.33    2.95
      5     2.94    4.62    5.19   0.33    5.05
      6     4.00    4.00    4.00   0.15    4.00
      7     4.00    4.00    2.00   0.15    2.00
```

Fig. 5-16. Parameters of fitted distributions for activity times.

FREQUENCY DISTRIBUTION HISTOGRAM FOR PROJECT DURATION

CLASS	INTERVAL	ELEMENTS
1	11.01 to 11.24	3 *********
2	11.24 to 11.46	0
3	11.46 to 11.68	5 ***************
4	11.68 to 11.90	4 ************
5	11.90 to 12.12	3 *********
6	12.12 to 12.35	7 *********************
7	12.35 to 12.57	9 ***************************
8	12.57 to 12.79	11 *********************************
9	12.79 to 13.01	14 **
10	13.01 to 13.23	7 *********************
11	13.23 to 13.46	11 *********************************
12	13.46 to 13.68	8 ************************
13	13.68 to 13.90	6 ******************
14	13.90 to 14.12	4 ************
15	14.12 to 14.35	1 ***
16	14.35 to 14.57	2 ******
17	14.57 to 14.79	2 ******
18	14.79 to 15.01	2 ******
19	15.01 to 15.23	0
20	15.23 to 15.46	1 ***

Fig. 5-17. Histogram of project duration.

5.5 RISK COVERAGE FOR PERT ACTIVITY TIME ESTIMATES

Finding a knowledgeable person on the project management team to provide reliable time estimates for the PERT procedure is often possible. Even though the estimates are reliable, they are subjective and probabilistic and are never perfect. To provide a risk coverage for the imperfect estimates (a,m,b), STARC uses a procedure where the estimated PERT range for an activity duration is extended to allow for simulated durations that might fall below the optimistic estimate or above the pessimistic estimate (FIG. 5-2). The magnitude of the interval extension, called the *risk coverage factor*, is specified interactively in percentage by the projection analyst.

To provide a risk coverage for a and b, the interval $[a,b]$ is dilated by a specific percentage denoted by q (Risk Coverage Factor). An example of the dilated interval $[a', b']$ is given in FIG. 5-2. The magnitude of the dilation, $(b' - a') - (b - a)$, is apportioned to either end of the original interval based on the skewness of the PERT estimates. Thus:

$$(b' - a') = (b - a) + q(b - a)$$
$$= (1 + q)(b - a)$$

where q is expressed in decimals. The values of a' and b' are computed, respectively as:

$$a' = a - q(b-a)[(m-a)/(b-a)]$$
$$= a - q(m - a)$$

$$b' = b + q(b-a)[(b-m)/(b-a)]$$
$$= b + q(b-m)$$

Consequently, the values a', m and b' are used to fit a beta density function for each "risk-covered" activity. As a result, there are chances of generating activity durations between a and a' or b and b'. Such extraneous observations help to simulate the duration "outliers" that occur in a real project.

If a risk coverage of 0 percent is specified, there is no interval dilation and no adjustments are made to any of the PERT estimates. On the other hand, a coverage of 100 percent will yield a dilated interval that is twice as long as the original PERT interval. While a large coverage can be desirable for more effects of the interval dilation on the mean and variance of the original PERT estimates are evaluated as follows. The original mean and adjusted mean are given respectively by:

$$t_e' = (a + 4m + b)/6$$

$$t_e = (a' + 4m + b')/6$$
$$= \{[a-q(m-a)] + 4m + [b + q(b-m)]\}/6$$
$$= (a + 4m + b)/6 + q(a-2m + b)/6$$

Thus, the original mean of the activity duration is changed by the quantity qd; where d is a constant defined as:

$$d = (a-2m + b)/6.$$

That is,

$$t_e' = t_e + qd$$

The magnitude and sign of d depends on the skewness of the PERT estimates such that:

$$d < 0, \text{ if } (m-a) > (b-m); \text{ negatively skewed}$$
$$d = 0, \text{ if } (m-a) = (b-m); \text{ symmetric}$$
$$d > 0, \text{ if } (m-a) < (b-m); \text{ positively skewed}$$

In the case of the variance, the original value is given by:

$$s_e^2 = (b-a)^2/36$$

and the adjusted variance is given by:

$$s_e^{2'} = (b' - a')^2/36$$
$$= \{[b + q(b-m)] - [a - q(m-a)]\}^2/36$$
$$= (1 + q)^2 \{(b-a)^2/36\}.$$

That is, the original variance is increased by a factor of $(1 + q)^2$. For example, a risk coverage factor of 10 percent implies that $q = 0.10$, leading to a sampled variance that is $(1 + 0.10)^2 = 1.21$ times the original PERT variance.

5.6 ACTIVITY PRIORITIZING RULES

STARC uses the composite allocation factor (CAF) to select activities for resource allocation. The resource allocation process takes into account both the resource requirements and the variabilities in activity times. For each activity i, CAF is computed as a weighted and scaled sum of two priority measures: Resource Allocation Factor (RAF) and Stochastic Activity Duration Factor (SAF). The computations proceed as presented below:

$$\text{CAF}_i = (w)\text{RAF}_i + (1 - w)\text{SAF}_i$$

where w is a weighting factor between 0 and 1. RAF is defined for each activity i as:

$$\text{RAF}_i = \frac{1}{t_i}\left(\sum_{j=1}^{R}\frac{x_{ij}}{y_j}\right)$$

where:

x_{ij} = number of resource type j units required by activity i
y_j = maximum units of resource type j required by any activity in the project
t_i = the expected duration of activity i
R = the number of resource types involved

RAF is a measure of the expected resource consumption per unit of time. A scaling procedure is used in such a way that the differences among the units of resource types are eliminated to obtain real numbers that are complaisant to ordinary addition. The set of RAF values is itself scaled from 0 to 100 as follows:

$$\text{Scaled RAF}_i = \left(\frac{\text{Unscaled RAF}_i}{\text{Max}\{\text{RAF}_i\}}\right)(100)$$

123

This scaling helps to eliminate the time-based unit, thus, the RAF measure is reduced to a dimensionless real number. Resource-intensive activities have larger magnitudes of RAF and require a greater attention in the scheduling process. To incorporate the stochastic nature of activity times in a project schedule, SAF is defined for each activity i as:

$$SAF_i = t_i + \frac{s_i}{t_i}$$

where:

t_i = expected duration for activity i
s_i = standard deviation of duration for activity i
s_i/t_i = coefficient of variation of the duration of activity i

In order to eliminate the discrepancy in the units of the terms in the expression for SAF, the expected activity duration (in time units) is scaled to a dimensionless value between 0 and 50 to obtain the following:

$$scaled\ t_i = \left(\frac{unscaled\ t_i}{Max\{\ t_i\ \}} \right) (50)$$

The coefficient of variation is scaled from 0 to 50. Thus, SAF ranges from 0 to 100. Because RAF and SAF are both on a scale of 0 to 100, CAF also is scaled from 0 to 100. An activity is assigned a priority for resource allocation in the project schedule on the basis of the magnitudes of CAF. An activity that lasts longer, consumes more resources, and varies more in duration will have a larger magnitude of CAF. Such an activity is given priority for resources during the scheduling process.

The weighting factor, w, is used to vary the relative weights assigned to the RAF and SAF priority measures in the resource allocation process. Consequently, STARC gives you the option of assigning more weight to the resource requirement aspects of a project and less to the probabilistic time aspects and vice versa. A simulation experiment can be conducted to find out the best value of w for a given project and is described in section 5.8.

5.7 MANAGERIAL DECISION ANALYSIS

A review of the output of STARC might indicate what type of what-if analysis can be performed. For example, a revision of the project data (resource availability, time estimates, predecessors, and resource requirements) was effected in the example presented earlier. As shown in FIG. 5-18, the number of available units of resource has been increased from 10 to 15.

```
Datafile name:- sample-2
Project Name(identification):- Example
Number of Activities:- 7
Number of Resource Types:- 1
Resource Units Available: R1= 15
```

ACT.		PERT		IMMEDIATE	RESOURCES REQD.			
NO.	a	m	b	PRECEDING ACTIVITIES	1	2	3	....
1	1.0	2.0	3.0		3			
2	4.5	5.0	6.0		4			
3	3.0	4.0	4.5		3			
4	1.0	3.0	4.0	1	2			
5	4.0	5.0	7.0	3	4			
6	3.0	4.0	5.0	1	2			
7	1.0	2.0	3.0	4 5	5			

Fig. 5-18. Revised project data.

A partial listing of the simulation output for this revised data is shown in FIGS. 5-19 and 5-20. With the additional resource allocation and the other data changes, the average project duration was reduced from 12.96 days (as shown earlier in FIG. 5-10) to 11.09 days. FIGURE 5-19 shows the output of the deadline analysis. You can see that the probability of finishing the project in 14 days increased to 1.0 both by analytical calculation and sample estimate. Now there is guarantee that the contract of 14 days can be satisfied. Even a duration of 13 days has a high probability of being achieved. So, management can make decisions accordingly. FIGURE 5-20 shows the histogram of the distribution of the project duration. The histogram shows that most of the observed project durations in the simulation fall below 11.53. In fact, the 95 percent confidence interval for the project duration is [10.86, 11.32].

A second revision of the original project data was also analyzed. In this revision, the resource availability was changed from 10 units to 7 units. It turns out that decreasing the initial resource availability by 3 units caused the average project duration to increase from 12.96 to 17.56 days. A partial listing of the output of this new ''what-if'' simulation is presented in FIGURES 5-21 and 5-22. FIGURE 5-21 shows the revised deadline analysis. Now, even a generous deadline of 17 days has a low probability of being accomplished (0.28 calculated and 0.32

```
                    PROJECT DEADLINE ANALYSIS
     DEADLINE   CALCULATED PROBABILITY   OBSERVED PROBABILITY
     ------------------------------------------------------------
        10.00        0.0915                  0.0800
        11.00        0.4561                  0.4800
        12.00        0.8666                  0.8400
        13.00        0.9901                  1.0000
        14.00        1.0000                  1.0000
        15.00        1.0000                  1.0000
        16.00        1.0000                  1.0000
        17.00        1.0000                  1.0000
        18.00        1.0000                  1.0000
        19.00        1.0000                  1.0000
```

Fig. 5-19. Partial output of second simulation: Deadline analysis.

```
FREQUENCY DISTRIBUTION HISTOGRAM
    FOR PROJECT DURATION
---------------------------------
CLASS       INTERVAL        ELEMENTS
---------------------------------
   1      9.65 to    9.92     4 *********************
   2      9.92 to   10.19     4 *********************
   3     10.19 to   10.46     6 ********************************
   4     10.46 to   10.73     3 ***************
   5     10.73 to   10.99     7 *************************************
   6     10.99 to   11.26     3 ***************
   7     11.26 to   11.53     8 ******************************************
   8     11.53 to   11.80     5 **************************
   9     11.80 to   12.07     3 ***************
  10     12.07 to   12.34     3 ***************
  11     12.34 to   12.61     4 *********************

TOTAL SIMULATION SAMPLE = 50

95% CONFIDENCE INTERVAL FOR PROJECT DURATION:
     10.86347 <= ACTUAL MEAN <= 11.31733
```

Fig. 5-20. Partial output of second simulation: Duration histogram.

PROJECT DEADLINE ANALYSIS

DEADLINE	CALCULATED PROBABILITY	OBSERVED PROBABILITY
10.00	0.0000	0.0000
11.00	0.0000	0.0000
12.00	0.0000	0.0000
13.00	0.0000	0.0000
14.00	0.0000	0.0000
15.00	0.0038	0.0000
16.00	0.0522	0.0200
17.00	0.2806	0.3200
18.00	0.6778	0.6800
19.00	0.9338	0.9200

Fig. 5-21. Partial output of third simulation: Deadline analysis.

```
FREQUENCY DISTRIBUTION HISTOGRAM
    FOR PROJECT DURATION
---------------------------------
CLASS       INTERVAL        ELEMENTS
---------------------------------
   1     15.99 to   16.29     4 ************************
   2     16.29 to   16.59     4 ************************
   3     16.59 to   16.89     7 ******************************************
   4     16.89 to   17.19     5 ******************************
   5     17.19 to   17.48     7 ******************************************
   6     17.48 to   17.78     5 ******************************
   7     17.78 to   18.08     2 ************
   8     18.08 to   18.38     2 ************
   9     18.38 to   18.68     5 ******************************
  10     18.68 to   18.98     5 ******************************
  11     18.98 to   19.28     4 ************************

TOTAL SIMULATION SAMPLE = 50

95% CONFIDENCE INTERVAL FOR PROJECT DURATION:
     17.29164 <= ACTUAL MEAN <= 17.82309
```

Fig. 5-22. Partial output of third simulation: Duration histogram.

observed). With this kind of analysis, a project analyst can study the sensitivity of project completion times to change in resource availability. FIGURE 5-22 shows the histogram of the project duration based on the third simulation trial. The analysis shows that the 95 percent confidence interval for the project duration has changed to [17.29, 17.82].

5.8 FURTHER STATISTICAL ANALYSIS

With "what-if" analysis similar to those presented in the preceeding sections, you can study the potential effects of decisions prior to making actual resource and time commitments. STARC can help you determine appropriate project inputs in the "safe environment" of simulation. The information acquired with the aid of simulation can then serve as the input for developing operational project schedules. If desired, the simulation output can be used to conduct additional statistical analyses that can further enhance project decisions. Such analyses are discussed in this section.

The STATGRAPHICS software package was used to perform a series of statistical analyses for the sample project in TABLE 5-1. An additional resource type was added to the project data to obtain the revised project data shown in TABLE 5-2. Several simulation experiments were conducted on the sample

Table 5-2. Project Data With One Additional Resource Type.

Activity	Predecessor	a	m	b	Resource Units Type 1	Resource Units Type 2
A	-	1	2	4	3	0
B	-	5	6	7	5	4
C	-	2	4	5	4	1
D	A	1	3	4	2	0
E	C	4	5	7	4	3
F	A	3	4	5	2	7
G	B,D,E	1	2	3	6	2

Units of resource type 1 available initially = 10

Units of resource type 2 available initially = 15

project. The weighting factor, w, and risk coverage factor, q, were used as decision variables in the simulation trials. Several combinations of w and q were
used and the average project durations were recorded for simulation sample
sizes of 10. The simulation outputs were tabulated as shown in TABLE 5-3. Values of w range from 0.0 to 1.0 while values of q are 0, 0.1, 0.15, and 0.2. The
observed average project durations are given inside the body of TABLE 5-3.

A multiple X-Y scatter plot of the data in TABLE 5-3 was developed using the
STATGRAPHICS software package. The plot is shown in FIG. 5-23. You can
observe that three is not much difference between the simulation results for
risk coverage levels (q) of 0%, 10%, 15%, and 20%. So, for the particular project involved in this experiment, you can infer that the project duration is insensitive to risk coverage levels less than or equal to 20%. This preliminary
conclusion was later confirmed by a formal statistical test.

Based on the plot in FIG. 5-23, there seems to be differences between the
simulation results for different weighting levels (w) between 0.0 and 1.0. In fact,
the increase in the project durations for values of w greater than 0.9 seems to
be particularly pronounced. So, the project duration appears to be sensitive to
changes in w. This observation was later confirmed by a formal statistical test.

Table 5-3. Output of Simulation Experiments.

w	Average Project Duration			
	q=0.0	q=0.1	q=0.15	q=0.2
0.0	12.98	13.06	13.12	12.60
0.1	13.56	12.88	13.33	13.05
0.2	13.56	12.96	13.03	13.30
0.3	13.48	13.18	12.90	13.03
0.4	13.33	13.08	13.13	13.02
0.5	12.69	13.34	12.51	13.63
0.6	12.76	13.12	13.11	12.91
0.7	13.33	12.10	12.65	12.50
0.8	13.01	13.09	13.45	13.19
0.9	13.25	13.42	13.04	13.23
1.0	16.89	16.77	16.71	17.03

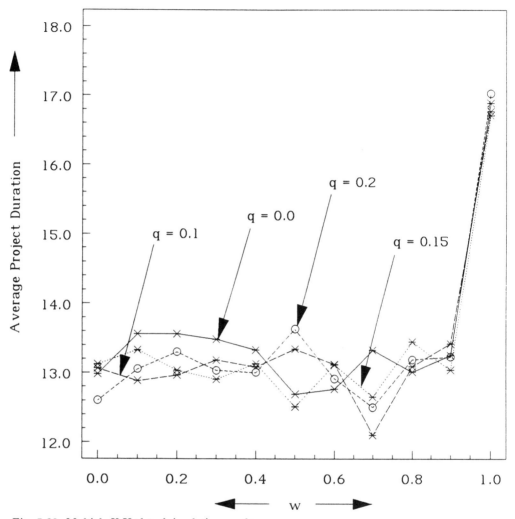

Fig. 5-23. Multiple X-Y plot of simulation results.

However, a prudent project analyst might want to conduct follow-up detailed simulation experiments for values of *w* between 0.9 and 1.0.

A multifactor analysis of variance (ANOVA) of the simulation results was conducted with STATGRAPHICS. Two replicates of the simulation experiment were used in the analysis. The data shown in TABLE 5-3 is for the first replicate. A screen dump of the resulting ANOVA table is presented in FIG. 5-24. The significance level (last column) of the ANOVA table shows that the effect of *w* on the project duration is significant at the 95 percent confidence level ($a = 0.05$) while the effect of *q* is not significant. This confirms the earlier observation based on the scatter plot in FIG. 5-23. You can also note that the interaction

Analysis of Variance for STARC.dur

Source of variation	Sum of Squares	d.f.	Mean square	F-ratio	Sig. level
MAIN EFFECTS	107.56827	13	8.274483	167.434	.0000
STARC.w	107.36331	10	10.736331	217.250	.0000
STARC.q	.20497	3	.068322	1.383	.2606
2-FACTOR INTERACTIONS	5.2261205	30	.1742040	3.525	.0001
STARC.w STARC.q	5.2261205	30	.1742040	3.525	.0001
RESIDUAL	2.1744500	44	.0494193		
TOTAL (CORR.)	114.96884	87			

0 missing values have been excluded.

Fig. 5-24. Multifactor ANOVA table.

effect of w and q is significant at the 95 percent confidence level. Even though q does not seem to have a direct effect on the project duration, it interacts with w to contribute to the observed differences in the project duration.

To further analyze the differences in the levels of the factors involved in the experimental study of the project duration, the multiple range analysis was conducted. FIGURE 5-25 shows the result for q and FIG. 5-26 shows the result for w. You can see that all four levels of q fall in the same homogeneous group at the 95 percent confidence level. You can conclude that there is no significant difference between the levels of q. This analysis also agrees with the earlier observation in the scatter plot. Based on the result in FIG. 5-26, you can conclude that there are significant differences between the levels of w in the experiment for this particular project.

The results above indicate that discriminating attention should be given to resource and time variability aspects of scheduling this project. Thus, you can determine where to direct most of his or her control actions. Because $w = 1.0$ yielded the longest average project duration, the priority measure defined as:

$$CAF = (w)RAF + (1-w)SAF$$

Multiple range analysis for STARC.dur by STARC.q

Method: 95 Percent Confidence Intervals

Level	Count	Average	Homogeneous Groups
0.15	22	13.345455	*
0.2	22	13.415455	*
0.1	22	13.432273	*
0	22	13.480000	*

Fig. 5-25. Multiple range test for levels of q.

Multiple range analysis for STARC.dur by STARC.w

Method: 95 Percent Confidence Intervals			
Level	Count	Average	Homogeneous Groups
0.7	8	12.563750	*
0	8	12.895000	*
0.4	8	13.050000	**
0.8	8	13.052500	**
0.5	8	13.078750	**
0.6	8	13.125000	***
0.3	8	13.131250	***
0.1	8	13.176250	***
0.2	8	13.251250	**
0.9	8	13.427500	*
1	8	16.850000	*

Fig. 5-26. Multiple range test for levels of w.

suggests that this particular project duration elongates when total emphasis is placed on the resource aspects alone.

You might want to study the regression relationship between the project duration and w. Because there are 11 levels of w in the experiment, a regression model could be attempted. The simulation result for q of 15 percent was selected from TABLE 5-3 as the data for the regression modeling process. STATGRAPHICS was used to fit a linear regression function for the selected data. The result is shown in FIG. 5-27. The fitted model is:

Duration $= 12.565 + 1.5936w$

This model does not represent a good fit because R-squared is only 21.40 percent and the ANOVA result indicates that the model does not significantly account for variability in the project duration. Other regression models that were investigated include exponential, reciprocal, and multiplicative models. None of these faired any better than the simple linear model. For other project configurations, you might be able to develop a reliable regression model that can be used for prediction purposes. In the absence of any other tool for predicting the project duration, the fitted model above, even with its noted deficiencies, can still be useful for effective project management decisions. As long as the decision maker exercises caution in invoking the model, a dim glimpse at the future of a project should be better than no glimpse at all.

Regression Analysis - Linear model: Y = a+bX

Dependent variable: STARC.average				Independent variable: STARC.weight
Parameter	Estimate	Standard Error	T Value	Prob. Level
Intercept	12.565	0.602278	20.8625	.00000
Slope	1.59364	1.01804	1.5654	.15193

Analysis of Variance

Source	Sum of Squares	Df	Mean Square	F-Ratio	Prob. Level
Model	2.7936445	1	2.7936445	2.450489	.15193
Error	10.260319	9	1.140035		
Total (Corr.)	13.053964	10			

Correlation Coefficient = 0.462609   R-squared = 21.40 percent
Stnd. Error of Est. = 1.06772

Fig. 5-27. Simple linear regression model for project duration.

5.9 PROJECT CAPABILITY ANALYSIS

The computational procedure of process capability analysis can be applied to projects that are composed of recurring processes. For example, if each cycle in a manufacturing operation is viewed as a project, then process capability analysis can be conducted to infer the overall capability of the project to manufacture a given product. As another example, if mixing concrete is a recurring operation in a construction project, then you might want to conduct an analysis of the capability of the concrete mixing process. The analysis can be done, for instance, by taking several samples of concrete and measuring the strength or another property of interest. These samples can then be analyzed in accordance with the process capability procedure. A simple computer program such as the one developed by Badiru (1985) can be used for the analysis.

Process capability analysis involves the determination of the tolerance that a process must operate within if it is to remain statistically in control. A process represents a unique combination of such things as resources, materials, and methods engaged in a given function. Process capability analysis is based on the short-run variability of the process that is being studied. The variability becomes evident whenever a quality characteristic of the product in the process is measured. By using the control chart method, the results of a process capability analysis should indicate when it is necessary to conduct an investigation to locate the sources of variability. For example, the sudden jump in the average project duration discussed earlier might instigate a hunt for the sources of such a large variation.

If you conclude that the process does not meet specifications, the specifications can be adjusted, if possible, or an enhancement of the process can be instituted. The data for the analysis should be collected in at least 10 Shewhart subgroups, with each subgroup containing at least 6 sample points (Duncan, 1965). The steps in the process capability analysis procedure are presented below:

Step 1: Test the product quality characteristic of interest (e.g., concrete strength) for lack of statistical control by means of X-bar and R charts. If there is no evidence of lack of control, proceed to Step 2. If there is an evidence of lack of control, discard the data, locate and eliminate the cause of the lack of control, and repeat step 1.

Step 2: Compute the process capability measure as:

$$p = 6s$$

$$= \frac{6R}{d_2}$$

where

s = process sample standard deviation
R = average range of subgroup measurements
d_2 = conversion factor from control chart tables

Step 3: Compare the computed process capability (p) to the specification spread (spec):

If $p < = $ spec, then the process is capable.
If $p > $ spec, then the process is not capable.

If the component processes that make up a project are found to be incapable of satisfying its stated goals, then the project itself can be said to be incapable of satisfying its stated goals. Thus, process capability analysis can be extended to project capability analysis.

As an illustrative example of process capability analysis, the data in TABLE 5-4 was analyzed by the computer program mentioned earlier. The data represents the outside diameters (in inches) of the end plates of an oil-filter product. The data has been truncated for illustrative purposes. The complete data was collected over several production runs and included 10 subgroups and 6 production rates. There are 2 replicates used in each observation cell. The upper and lower specification limits for the product are 3.645 inches and 3.635 inches, respectively.

Based on the standard X-bar and R control charts, the computer program found that the process producing the end plates was statistically in control. The

Table 5-4. Process Capability Analysis Data.

Production	Subgroups				
Rate	1	2	3	4	5
1	3.636	3.633	3.636	3.637	3.635
	3.636	3.636	3.634	3.637	3.632
2	3.642	3.634	3.636	3.634	3.633
	3.639	3.632	3.635	3.635	3.633
3	3.634	3.636	3.634	3.633	3.634
	3.634	3.637	3.632	3.633	3.632

process capability was calculated to be 0.011 inch while the specification spread was 0.01 inch. You can conclude that the process was not capable of handling the product specifications.

5.10 PROJECT DEBT ANALYSIS

Many capital investment projects are financed with external funds. To get a good grasp of what a project would cost in terms of borrowing money, a computer program might be used. Badiru (1988b) presents such a program named GAMPS (Graphical Evaluation of Amortizing Payments). The program analyzes the periodic payments on the finance arrangement, the unpaid balance, principal amounts paid per period, total periodic payment, and current cummulative equity. It also calculates the *equity break-even point* for the debt being analyzed. The equity break-even point is that point in time when the unpaid balance is equal to the cummulative equity. With the output of this program, the cost of servicing the project debt can quickly and more correctly be evaluated. A part of the output of the program presents the percentage of the periodic debt payment going into equity and interest charge respectively.

Computational Procedure

The computational procedure for analyzing project debt proceeds following the steps specified below:

1. Given a principal amount, P, a periodic interest rate, i (in decimals), and a discrete time span of n periods, the uniform series of equal end-of-

period payments needed to amortize P is computed as:

$$A = \frac{P[i(1 + i)^n]}{(1 + i)^n - 1}$$

2. The unpaid balance after making t installment payments is given by:

$$U(t) = \frac{A[1 - (1 + i)^{t-n}]}{i}$$

3. The amount of equity or principal amount paid with installment payment number t is given by:

$$E(t) = A(1 + i)^{t-n-1}$$

4. The amount of interest charge contained in installment payment number t is derived to be:

$$I(t) = A[1 - (1 + i)^{t-n-1}]$$

where

$$A = E(t) + I(t)$$

5. The cumulative total payment made after t periods is denoted by:

$$C(t) = (t)(A)$$

6. The cumulative interest payment after t periods is given by:

$$Q(t) = \sum_{x=1}^{t} I(x)$$

7. The cumulative principal payment after t periods is computed as:

$$S(t) = \sum_{x=1}^{t} E(x)$$

8. The percentage of interest charge contained in installment payment number t is:

$$W(t) = \frac{I(t)}{A}(100\%)$$

9. The percentage of cumulative interest charge contained in cumulative total payment up to and including payment number t is:

$$F(t) = \frac{Q(t)}{C(t)} (100\%)$$

Example

A construction project will be used to illustrate the procedure for project debt analysis. Suppose a construction project with an initial cost of $500,000 is totally financed at an annual nominal interest rate of 10 percent over a period of 15 years. The installment payments on the project loan will be paid on a monthly schedule. The first payment on the loan is to be made exactly one month after financing is approved. If you desire to perform a detailed analysis of the loan schedule, the GAMPS computer program can be used to analyze this problem. FIGURES 5-28 and 5-29 show portions of the output of the program. FIG-URE 5-28 shows the beginning of the output. The tabulated result shows a monthly payment of $5,373.04 on the loan. Considering the situation after 10 months (i.e., $t = 10$), it is seen that:

U(10)	=	$487,473.80 (Unpaid balance)
A(10)	=	$5,373.04 (Monthly payment)
E(10)	=	$1,299.92 (Equity portion of the tenth payment)
I(10)	=	$4,073.11 (Interest charge contained in the tenth payment)
C(10)	=	$53,730.36 (Total payment to date)
S(10)	=	$12,526.28 (Total equity to date)
W(10)	=	75.81% (Percentage of the tenth payment going into interest charge)
F(10)	=	76.69% (Percentage of the total payment going into interest charge)

Over 76 percent of the sum of the first ten installment payments goes into interest charges.

FIGURE 5-29 shows the end of the tabulated output. You can see that by time $t = 180$, the unpaid balance has been reduced to 0 [U(180) = 0.0]. The total payment made on the loan is $967,148.40. Thus, the total interest charge on the loan is $967,148.40 – $500,000 = $467,148.40. So, 48.30 percent of the total payment goes into interest charges. The information about interest charges might be very useful for tax purposes. Looking at the tabulated values, you can see that equity builds up slowly while unpaid balance decreases slowly.

This scenario is depicted in FIG. 5-30. The rate at which the unpaid balance decreases is shown by the descending curve while the rate at which equity builds up is shown by the ascending curve. Note that very little equity is accumulated during the first few months of the loan schedule.

P= 500000   RATE= 9.999999 %/Year   MONTHS= 180 (15 Years)

Month #	U(t)	A(t)	E(t)	I(t)	C(t)	S(t)	W(t)%	F(t)%
1	498793.70	5373.04	1206.37	4166.67	5373.04	1206.37	77.55	77.55
2	497577.20	5373.04	1216.42	4156.61	10746.07	2422.79	77.36	77.45
3	496350.70	5373.04	1226.56	4146.48	16119.11	3649.35	77.17	77.36
4	495113.90	5373.04	1236.78	4136.26	21492.14	4886.13	76.98	77.27
5	493866.80	5373.04	1247.09	4125.95	26865.18	6133.22	76.79	77.17
6	492609.40	5373.04	1257.48	4115.56	32238.21	7390.70	76.60	77.07
7	491341.40	5373.04	1267.96	4105.08	37611.25	8658.65	76.40	76.98
8	490062.90	5373.04	1278.52	4094.51	42984.29	9937.18	76.20	76.88
9	488773.70	5373.04	1289.18	4083.86	48357.32	11226.36	76.01	76.78
10	487473.80	5373.04	1299.92	4073.11	53730.36	12526.28	75.81	76.69
11	486163.10	5373.04	1310.75	4062.28	59103.39	13837.04	75.60	76.59
12	484841.40	5373.04	1321.68	4051.36	64476.43	15158.71	75.40	76.49
13	483508.70	5373.04	1332.69	4040.34	69849.46	16491.40	75.20	76.39
14	482164.90	5373.04	1343.80	4029.24	75222.50	17835.20	74.99	76.29
15	480809.90	5373.04	1355.00	4018.04	80595.54	19190.20	74.78	76.19

Fig. 5-28. Partial output of GAMPS (top portion).

Month #	U(t)	A(t)	E(t)	I(t)	C(t)	S(t)	W(t)%	F(t)%
166	70722.59	5373.04	4744.15	628.89	891925.50	429281.10	11.70	51.87
167	65938.94	5373.04	4783.68	589.35	897298.60	434064.80	10.97	51.63
168	61115.39	5373.04	4823.54	549.49	902671.60	438888.30	10.23	51.38
169	56251.73	5373.04	4863.74	509.29	908044.70	443752.10	9.48	51.13
170	51347.44	5373.04	4904.27	468.76	913417.80	448656.40	8.72	50.88
171	46402.37	5373.04	4945.14	427.90	918790.80	453601.60	7.96	50.63
172	41416.00	5373.04	4986.35	386.69	924163.90	458588.00	7.20	50.38
173	36388.11	5373.04	5027.90	345.13	929536.90	463615.90	6.42	50.12
174	31318.30	5373.04	5069.80	303.23	934910.00	468685.70	5.64	49.87
175	26206.30	5373.04	5112.05	260.99	940283.10	473797.80	4.86	49.61
176	21051.67	5373.04	5154.65	218.39	945656.10	478952.50	4.06	49.35
177	15854.07	5373.04	5197.61	175.43	951029.20	484150.10	3.27	49.09
178	10613.17	5373.04	5240.92	132.12	956402.20	489391.10	2.46	48.83
179	5328.64	5373.04	5284.59	88.44	961775.30	494675.70	1.65	48.57
180	0.00	5373.04	5328.63	44.41	967148.40	500004.30	0.83	48.30

Fig. 5-29. Partial output of GAMPS (bottom portion).

The point at which both curves intersect is the equity break-even point. It indicates when the unpaid balance is exactly equal to the accumulated equity. Any equity accumulated after that point can be viewed as true equity with no loan claim against it. The equity break-even point is also printed as a part of the output of GAMPS. For the illustrative example, the equity break-even point is 120.9 months (over 10 years). The effects of inflation, depreciation, property appreciation, and other economic factors are not included in the analysis presented. You are to include such factors whenever pertinent to the prevailing project situation.

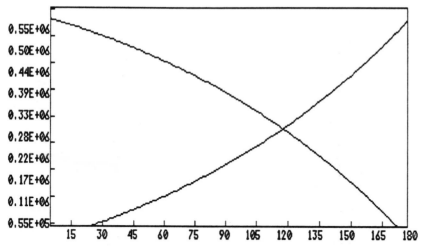

Fig. 5-30. Rate of change of equity and unpaid balance.

5.11 PROJECT REVENUE REQUIREMENT ANALYSIS

Companies evaluating capital expenditures for proposed projects must weigh the expected benefits against the initial and expected costs over the life of the project. One method often used is the Minimum Annual Revenue Requirements analysis (MARR). Using the information about costs, interest payments, recurring expenditures, and other project-related financial obligations, MARR needed by a project can be calculated. Badiru and Russel (1987) present a computer program to perform annual MARR analysis. Using basic principles of engineering economic analysis, the computer program computes the break-even point of a project. The break-even point is then used to determine the level of revenue that must be produced by the project in order for it to be a profitable venture. The program is written in BASIC for IBM PC and compatibles. The program will accomodate either the flow-through or normalizing methods (Stevens 1979) of the MARR analysis.

The factors included in the analysis by the program include: initial investment cost, book salvage value, tax salvage value, annual project costs, useful life for book purpose, book depreciation method, tax depreciation method, useful life for tax purpose, rate of return on equity, rate of return on debt, capital interest rate, debt ratio, and investment tax credit.

6

Project Networking and Communication Tools

This chapter discusses computer networking and communication links to coordinate and enhance project management functions performed at different locations. Networking and remote communication links make it possible to share information on a timely basis for prompt decision. Some of the available communication technologies are discussed to inform you what tools are available and how the tools can be used in the project management environment. Specific local area network (LAN) terms can be found in the glossary.

6.1 PROJECT MANAGEMENT INFORMATION SYSTEM

As the complexity of systems increases, the information requirements increase. Project management is taking on added significance in many organizations because it offers a systematic approach to information exchange and use. Complex projects require a well-coordinated communication system that can quickly reveal the status of each activity. Reports on individual project elements must be tied together in a logical manner to facilitate managerial control. Project management must have quick access not only to individual activity status, but also to the overall state of the project. A crucial aspect of this function is the prevailing level of communication, cooperation, and coordination in the project system. The project management information system (PMIS) has evolved as the solution to the problem of monitoring, organizing, storing, and disseminating project information. Many commercial computer programs have been developed for the implementation of PMIS. Many more are being introduced as modules in integrated software packages. The basic reporting elements in a PMIS include:

- Financial reports
- Up-to-date network plan

- Graphical Schedule (e.g., Gantt Chart)
- Time performance plots (plan versus actual)
- Cost performance plots (expected versus actual)
- Performance requirements evaluation plots
- Project progress reports
- Vendor supply schedule
- Client delivery schedule
- Subcontractor schedule and performance status
- Project conference schedule and records

Many standard forms have been developed to facilitate the reporting processes in project management. But with the availability of computerized systems, manual project information systems are no longer desirable. Many of the currently available communications technologies can be effectively utilized for project management needs.

6.2 PROJECT MANAGEMENT LAN

Local area networking is now making a direct appearance in project management software packages. High-end project management software packages on mainframes have been taking advantage of LAN technology for quite some time. However, networking for low-end project management has just begun to emerge. Low-end project management has traditionally been limited to one project analyst or manager performing independent analysis without the need to connect to other analysts or managers. The increasing push for LAN in many companies is now driving a push for the networking of project management software.

LAN capability is a relatively new idea in low-end project management software. Single-user project management software typically has been used for individual, simple, and localized projects. LAN project management software is directed at complex projects that require multiple users and data sharing. Symantec Corp. of Torrance, California has been one of the leaders in the incorporation of LAN capability into low-end project management packages. The company has introduced a LAN-specific version of its popular Time Line 3.0 project management software. The LAN version of Time Line allows multiple-user file reading only, but it offers the advantage of saving disk space on individual workstations and significantly reducing the per-user cost of the product.

Many other low-end packages are already certified to run on LANs and offer advantages comparable to those of Time Line even though they are not marketed as LAN-specific products (Zarley 1989). No low-end product had yet been designed to allow multiple users to update multiple files at the same time. Multiple-users/multiple-files operation will permit the project management system to function as an interactive database.

The primary advantage of running low-end project management software on a LAN is to take advantage of the capabilities available on the LAN and not necessarily increase the functionality of the software. With a LAN version of a project management package, you can access the program and centralized files from the individual terminals. Ordinarily, a single user can only support about two hundred activities relating to a project. On a network, you can easily schedule over 1,000 activities. A LAN facilitates the sharing of data. In a network, users do not need to hand-deliver disks to other analysts or upload them to a minicomputer or mainframe.

Most project management operations in the business and industry communities involve more than one person working at various locations. When you want to review the status of a project, you might have to wait for several printouts from different individuals. Your decision might be delayed if the required printouts don't all arrive in a coordinated fashion. Sometimes, the printout is ''in the mail'' somewhere in the organization and might never get to its destination despite the level of urgency associated with it. This scenario can be improved under a LAN operation because the review of the printouts can be taken out of the batch mode into a real-time process.

There has to be close cooperation between the project management software developer and the vendors of LAN products. The functions offered by the software must be in line with the capabilities available on the LAN on which it is expected to run. Thus, coordination of functionality is very important. The Triple C principle of communication, cooperation, and coordination can be effectively implemented in the relationship between software developers and vendors. If care is taken during the software development stage, a low-end project management package that incorporates too many features of LAN can turn out to be a source of disparity. Multiple-user reading and writing capabilities might stifle the original functionality of the project management software. Fierce competition is driving many project management software developers to join the LAN craze without proper planning and sound product design. The consumer must, therefore, be careful in evaluating and selecting products that are advertised as being LAN-compatible.

Some low-end project management packages that can run on LAN are: Harvard Project Manager 3.0, Superproject Expert 1.1, Time Line 3.0, Insta-Plan, Project Scheduler 4, Microsoft Project 4.0, Qwiknet Professional, and Micro Planner for Windows. Many of these products support the popular LAN configurations such as Novell Inc.'s Netwave, 3Com Corp.'s LAN, IBM Token-Ring LAN, TOPS Network, AST Research Inc.'s AST Network, Orchid Technology Inc.'s PCnet, IBM's PC Network, 3Com Corp.'s Ether series, and Ungermann-Bass Inc.'s Net/One. Due to the variety of product offerings, prospective buyers of LAN-compatible project management software must carefully evaluate all the options.

6.3 DATABASE FILE SERVERS

The growing need to share information among personal computers has given rise to a technology that centralizes data-storage and data-management operations on a network server. This database-server approach consists of two parts: a shared database and a Structured Query Language (SQL) engine (or back-end server) that performs the house-keeping and database operations for all PC's on the network. Each PC is equipped with tools and applications known as front-ends. The front-ends are used to query and retrieve information from the database server, which facilitates better performance and a high degree of database integrity when multiple users are trying to access the same pool of information.

The file server configuration also lends itself to the multiuser, multitasking capabilities of OS/2. It moderates the flow of information while protecting data integrity. As database file servers become widely available, a growing number of mini and mainframe level applications should begin to make their way down to the PC level. A database server facilitates data communication better than current database alternatives because the server sends only the data that matches a user's request instead of transmitting entire files.

The following is a project management scenario where a database server could be very helpful. A project analyst sits at his desk and uses an SQL query tool to request the next task on a project operation from a centralized database. At the same time, you, as project manager, update the task list and reshuffle task assignments in the database by using a form-based database entry tool. The file server recognizes your transaction as the priority function. The project analyst's request is withheld while your transaction is processed. The file server informs the query tool that another transaction is being processed and requests the analyst to wait. Once your transaction is complete, the server responds to the analyst's request by sending him an ''up-to-the-minute'' list of tasks. Under the traditional paper record updating, the analyst will find that keeping abreast of changes will be very difficult, particularly if those changes are frequent.

6.4 SYSTEMS CONNECTIVITY

An increasing number of project management vendors are providing direct links to mainframe and minicomputer applications. In some cases, the PC-based packages are hooked up to project management software on the larger systems. In other cases, the connections are to other types of applications, such as databases and financial accounting systems. Such connections are taking on an increasing importance now that organizations are realizing the need to share limited resources. As PCs function less in the independent mode and more as components of information networks, information about managing projects will be spread out throughout the organization by necessity and will not necessarily be restricted to just one computer.

By sending data about managing projects between PCs and larger systems, information about the projects can be consolidatated on the larger systems, thereby permitting a comprehensive information repository. By giving PC project management packages access to data normally found in mainframe environments (e.g., financial data), the local planning, scheduling, and management of small projects can be enhanced. With PC-to-mainframe linkage, someone at an organization's headquarters will be able to conduct company-wide evaluation of all projects. Each project can be managed on a PC-based project management system while the information is periodically uploaded to a mainframe for overall analysis. Information and reports about all projects could be consolidated when you use a mainframe resident software package.

An essential aspect of linking PC software to mainframe software is the question of compatibililty. Both software sources must cooperate to ensure a smooth transition and a proper link. Primavera Systems Inc. makes several project management packages. One of their products, Primavera Project Planner runs on both the PC and DEC VAX minicomputers. In this case, the link is simple. Data can easily be transferred from one end to the other. Like Primavera, the network and VAX versions of Qwiknet Professional project management software can share data. PCs manage individual projects while the VAX systems coordinate the multiple project scheduling. When a complex report needs to be compiled, it can be done on the VAX because of its higher computing power than the PC. But when an analysis needs to be done, the PC might be desirable because it is more flexible and has quicker response time because its processor is typically not shared by multiple users.

M*PM project management software (Micro-Frame Technologies, Inc.), originally designed for aerospace and defense contractors, is now available to run on local area networks. The multiuser version of M*PM can support up to 100 simultaneous users on IBM PC and compatible workstations. The software differs from the traditional PC-based project management software because it is designed in a work-breakdown structure (WBS) format to facilitate government-required reporting. M*PM addresses the problem of performance reporting very well.

This software was truly designed for large-scale businesses when you consider the cost. The networked version costs from $30,000 to $60,000 depending on the number of users. The single-user version costs $7,500 per copy.

If full connectivity is effected between systems in a project management environment, the exchange of data will be possible. Data-affecting projects can be automatically imported into the project management system. Likewise, data generated by the project management system can be automatically sent to the application it affects. FIGURE 6-1 presents a graphical representation of file transfer between project management software and several other application programs.

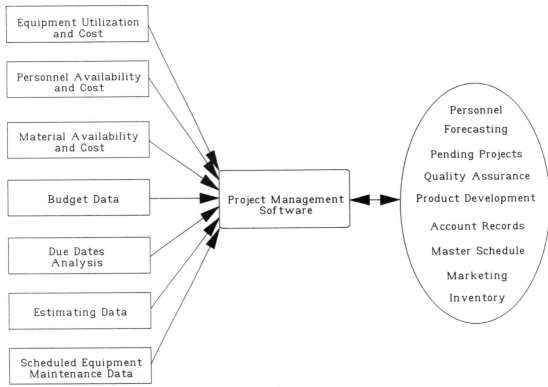

Fig. 6-1. Applications systems connectivity.

6.5 FAX MACHINES

Telephone facsimile machines are changing the way business people communicate. They are quickly becoming the telecommunications tool of choice. Almost one million fax machines were sold in 1988. That number is double the number sold in 1987. The fastest growing segment of the market is for desktop fax machines priced under $2,000. With that relatively low price, fax machines are now within reach of most businesses.

Fax machines are electronic devices that instantaneously transfer documents from one place to another over ordinary telephone lines. The machines work by converting the dark and light pixels (picture elements) in a document into an electrical signal that represents various shades of gray in the original material. These shades of gray are reproduced into a printed document at the receiving end by another fax machine. A fax machine electronically scans a document, converts the scanned information into a digital format, and then transfers the data to a modem for telephone transmission. Fax machines were once bulky contraptions that used spinning drum devices. The original versions have now been replaced by small machines that fit nicely on a desk.

A fax machine capable of transmitting as many as 64 shades of gray will reproduce better copies of photographs and other graphic material than a machine capable of transmitting only 8 shades of gray. The machines are classified into four groups according to how fast they transmit data. The best of the new technology is in Group III. The machines in this group transmit at a maximum rate of 9,600 bits per second (bps). A transmission rate of 9,600 bps (or 9,600 baud) implies that a typical page of data can be transmitted in about 12 seconds under ideal transmitting conditions.

Group III machines can communicate with slower Group II machines that transmit at rates from 2,400 bps to 7,200 bps. Group I machines date back to the 1970s and are essentially obsolete. Group IV machines transmit as fast as 3 seconds per page and are used by high-volume institutions with private digital telephone networks.

Fax machines can be extremely instrumental in transmitting project data. Items such as cost reports, graphical schedules, and job assignments can be sent quickly to remote locations (e.g., project headquarters) for prompt review and decisions. Important information that typically would be sent by mail and be subject to abuse or loss can be safely transmitted by fax machines. Not only is the transmission safe, but the original document is not exposed to any accidental damage while in transit. So, in addition to expediting communication, fax machines help protect documents so their original integrity can be preserved.

Document Conference

Like telephone conferences, document conferences should be gaining grounds fast in the near future. Many times, overnight mail is not fast enough to get an important project document signed on a tight schedule by people located in different geographical areas. If the people must jointly write or revise the document, teleconferencing systems can be utilized. However, they are expensive and not effective when dealing with very fine print.

A satisfactory solution now emerging is the document conferencing system. Databeam Corporation of Lexington, Kentucky, has introduced a document conferencing system called CT 1000. The system enables up to eight standard personal computers located virtually anywhere in the world to display the same electronic document simultaneously. Except for minor communications delay, all eight machines show exactly the same image on their screens, even as the text or picture is modified with a pen-like screen marker by any or all of the participants.

In addition to special hardware and software for each PC, Databeam Corp. supplies a device called a data bridge. The data bridge feeds data from each computer into standard telephone lines. The complete system costs from $25,000 to $40,000. Despite high cost, organizations involved in crucial project management functions are purchasing the system. Fortunately, as with most electronic products the price of the document conference system is expected to drop in the future. A reduction in cost will make the system more affordable to the small-scale project management offices. Document conferencing can be very helpful for multiproject operations where documents containing information such as cost data, schedules, and personnel need to be distributed quickly.

Video Fax

A product similar to the document conferencing system is the Videofax system developed by Interactive Picture Systems, Inc. The system transmits full-color video snapshots from PC to PC over telephone lines. This method can be very useful for transmitting color-coded charts of project schedules and other high-quality project presentation graphics. The complete system costs $15,000. It works by taking a single video frame from any source, such as a video cassette recorder, and converting it into a digital form that the computer can store or send to another computer. Transmitting an image can take as little as 45 seconds.

At the receiving end, a PC equipped with Videofax software and an add-in circuit board can store up to 400 images on magnetic disk. The images can then be viewed selectively on standard video monitor or paper copies can be generated on video printer. For Videofax billing purposes, the receiving machine keeps track of which images are viewed and how often. The company expects that future enhancements to the system will enable the video frames to be sent to standard facsimile machines as well. In the future, there will probably be a network of fax machines, document-conferencing equipment, and Videofax systems that work together to facilitate better management of projects.

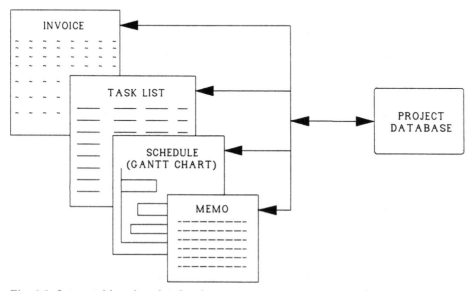

Fig. 6-2. Integrated imaging of project documents.

Integrated Imaging

A network of FAX machines, document-conferencing equipment, Videofax system, Scanners, and PCs will provide capabilities that make it possible to obtain *integrated imaging*. Integrated imaging refers to an on-line display of a combination of text and graphics screens. This will facilitate remote review of project documents. FIGURE 6-2 shows an example of a potential layout of an integrated imaging screen. With integrated imaging, real-time project monitoring and control can be implemented.

6.6 LAN CONFIGURATIONS

What is a local area network? LAN is a private communications facility extending over a limited geographical area. The size of the communications area can range from a single building to a large manufacturing facility comprising of several closely related buildings. LAN offers the opportunity to customize the communications facility to suit the needs of an organization. In a project management environment, the transmission of project documents (e.g., graphs, memos, and tables) can be significantly improved by using local area networks. LAN communications typically operate at very high speeds. The motivations for LAN include the following:

1. To connect computing and communication devices
   - Achieve full logical connectivity
   - Achieve simplified wiring
   - Facilitate relocation and reconnection of devices
   - Enhance dissemination of information
2. To provide shared services
   - Share disk, printer, modem, plotter, etc.
   - Provide means for electronic mail
   - Provide access to licensed software
   - Provide alternate communication routes
   - Facilitate the development of a central database
3. To achieve higher system performance
   - Reduce operating errors
   - Improve response times
   - Protect data integrity
   - Coordinate operations
   - Provide on-line information

There are three basic types of LAN: Institutional Broadband (multimode operation similar to cable TV system), Institutional Baseband (for computer only), and PC LAN (for connecting small computers over limited areas such as laboratories). *Baseband* uses a single channel and pulse transmission. *Broadband* uses multiple channels and modulated carriage and caters to multiple traffic types. TABLE 6-1 shows the components and requirements of the basic LAN types.

The LAN technology is described in terms of five characteristics: *topology, media, signaling, access,* and *protocols.*

Topology refers to the physical arrangement of the components in the LAN configuration. The most popular configurations are *star, bus, ring,* and *mesh.*

Media refers to the specific communication mechanasim used in connecting devices in the network. The basic media types are *wire pairs, coax cables,* and *fiber optics.*

Signaling refers to the type of signals sent over the network. The two conventional signals are broadband and baseband.

Access refers to the logistics for gaining access to transmissions on the network. Two of the popular access procedures are *token passing* and *contention.*

Protocol refers to the communication standard used by the network. The most prevalent standard is the ISO reference model.

In a tokensharing network, a special bit pattern, called a token, is sent to each computer sequentially around the network. Only the computer that has the token at a given instance can transmit. Once a transmission is made by a computer in the network, the token is passed to the next computer. In conten-

Table 6-1. Characteristics of LAN Types.

	Institutional Broadband	Institutional Baseband	PC LAN
Types of Devices	Hosts, PCs, Video	Hosts, PCs	PCs
Number of Devices	Thousands	Hundreds	Dozens
Channels Needed	Many	One or Two	One
Bandwidth Needed	Over 100M BPS	Less than 10M BPS	Less than 1M BPS
Distance Served	About 10 km	About 1 km	About 1 km

tion transmission, also called *multiple access network*, all computers can transmit at any time. Collisions of signals might occur during contention but collision detecting software is used to control the transmissions. Signals on a collision course are retransmitted after a random delay.

Star Configuration

The *star LAN configuration* (FIG. 6-3) uses a single root node to which other communication nodes are connected. In other words, one "host" computer has several "slave" computers connected to it. There is a unique path from each node to the root node. The distance of a particular node from the root node can indicate the node's echelon in the network communication hierarchy. The star configuration provides a good model for timesharing systems for front-end computers, concentrators, multiplexors, and terminals. Communications between any two computers must be routed through the host computer, which controls all data communications, Thus, if the host computer fails, the whole network will go down.

Bus Configuration

Bus network configuration (FIG. 6-4) has computers that tie into a main cable, or *bus,* without a central computer. This configuration is a single multipoint channel similar to an unrooted tree. The failure of any one computer does not affect the overall performance of the network. A bus network can be interconnected with other bus networks or extended with repeaters. However, no

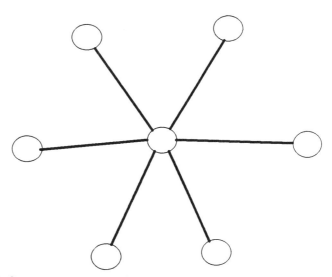

Fig. 6-3. Star network configuration.

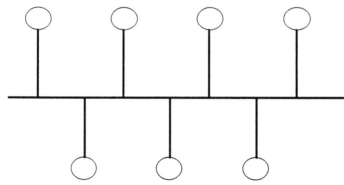

Fig. 6-4. Bus network configuration.

loops back to the original bus are permitted. A single unique path exists between any pair of nodes.

Mesh Configuration

A *mesh* network (FIG. 6-5) constitutes a collection of arbitrarily distributed communication nodes. The arbitrary nature of the configuration implies that there is much flexibility in locating nodes within the network. There are multiple links between nodes. Consequently, routing decisions are necessary to determine which routes a transmission can take to reach its destination. A quantita-

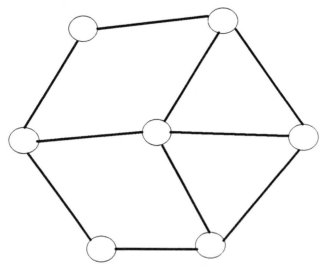

Fig. 6-5. Mesh network configuration.

tive measure of the connectivity of a mesh network is given by the average number of links per node.

Ring Configuration

A *ring network* (FIG. 6-6) is a distributed network with minimal connectivity. In the ring, all computers are on the same level and any communications between two computers are on the same level and any communications between two computers must be processed by any intermediate computer. Consequently, if any one computer goes down, the whole system will also go down. Each communication node is connected to exactly two other nodes. Network connectivity is preserved if one link is cut, but is lost if two or more links are cut. Data flow in the ring network can be unidirectional or bidirectional.

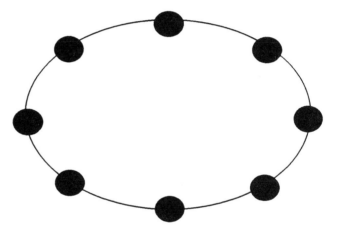

Fig. 6-6. Ring network configuration.

Star-shaped Ring

A variation of the ring configuration is the *star-shaped ring* (FIG. 6-7). This variation retains the simplicity of the ring network coupled with the advantages of the star configuration. It provides a central point of control. Malfunctioning links or nodes can be bypassed at the control center, thus, the major disadvantage of the regular ring configuration is avoided.

Bus-shaped Ring

A *bus-shaped ring* (FIG. 6-8) is a variation of the ring configuration introduced by 3Com for IBM Token-Ring compatible products. A special Y-connector permits nodes to be extended in a daisy-chain fashion, thus, the ring is extended each time a node is added to the network. A loop back plug at the end of the chain preserves the ring.

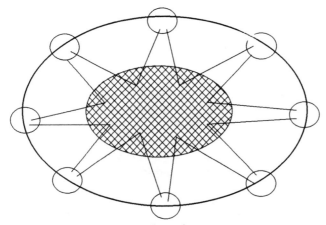

Fig. 6-7. Star-shaped ring network configuration.

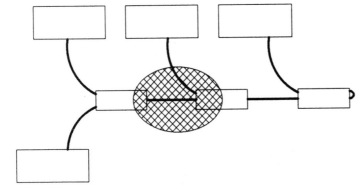

Fig. 6-8. Bus-shaped network configuration.

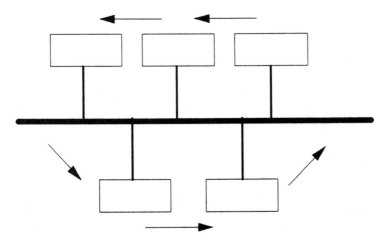

Fig. 6-9. Logical ring network configuration.

Logical Ring

A *logical ring* (FIG. 6-9) is a network configuration implemented on a physical bus configuration. The ring is implemented with appropriate protocols only when it is necessary. The logical ring is used to provide deterministic timing on a bus medium.

6.7 LAN PLANNING AND MANAGEMENT

Local area networking can significantly enhance project management communication needs. However, careful planning must be done for the installation of the network. The planning for LAN covers the following six evaluations:

1. Why LAN Is Needed
   - Determine communication scope
   - Evaluate type and number of connections needed
   - Evaluate geographic coverage
2. Technology Evaluation
   - Determine currently available technology
   - Evaluate available commercial products
   - Establish maintenance procedures
3. Site Planning
   - Determine hardware needs
   - Determine cabling requirements
   - Specify whether network is integrated with phone system or not
4. Software Planning
   - Determine which network software to use
   - Establish network applications
   - Evaluate user interface
5. Operations Planning
   - Arrange how the network will be managed
   - Establish network responsibilities
6. Vendor Selection
   - Establish vendor selection criteria
   - Determine service support needs

The vendor selection criteria should cover such things as *functionality* (interfaces supported and capabilities provided), *performance* (speed, error rate, and delay), *maintainability* (network control), *extensibility* (upper limits on growth and granularity of growth), *vendor stability* (reputation, length of service, and support structure), and *price* (network capability versus cost).

A project communication network should be managed by going through several iterative steps which may be summarized as follows:

- Evaluate the overall network in view of desired performance and personnel productivity.

- Evaluate each component of the network based on level of management and control.
- Compute the maintenance cost of each network element.
- Identify and minimize idle times at critical communication links.
- Review the configuration of the network for efficient node proximity.
- Review the capability of current equipment based on project communication needs.
- Review the capability and cost of new equipment available in the market.
- Estimate the benefit-cost ratio for any proposed addition to the communication network.
- Develop a forecast of future project communication requirements.
- Integrate the network hardware and software with the human functions in the project environment.

6.8 ELECTRONIC MAIL AND PROJECT REPORTS

Sending documents, graphs, reports, and messages to one or more people via the computer has potential benefits in project management, including:

- Facilitating real-time monitoring and controlling of project functions
- Creating an avenue to quickly track the progress of projects
- Avoiding the hassles associated with conventional typing and reporting procedures
- Reducing paperwork and the cost of making photocopies for distribution to project analysts or managers
- Ensuring prompt responses to messages and reports thereby increasing the probability of getting a response to a message

In the conventional ''paper-pushing'' approach, you must first find time to prepare a draft of the document, find a secretary to type the document, send the document through the mail, and then wait for a reply from the recipient. The recipient will need to find time to read the document, find time to prepare a response, find a secretary to type the response, and then send the response back to you. In addition to the delays at each end of the communication channel, there are potential delays or risk of loss within the conventional mail system.

In contrast, with an electronic mail system, you simply turn on your computer, enter the appropriate commands, type in the document, specify the name and location of the recipient, and send the document on its electronic journey with a simple push of a button. Instantly, a ''mail waiting'' message appears at the terminal when the mail arrives, he can read and respond to the mail immediately. If not, the message is received the next time he turns on his computer.

In a project management office, electronic mail can significantly reduce the amount of time spent waiting for a reply to interoffice memos or telephone calls and the time spent waiting to see someone. Combined with word processing, electronic mail can make the preparation and distribution of documents more efficient. With electronic filing, project reports can be saved in a central location where it can be copied or read by the appropriate personnel. With an expert system, mail-routing rules can be developed to automatically determine which mail in the central electronic "mail box" can be accessed by different categories of personnel.

As an example, managing tax collection is not an easy task. The US Internal Revenue Service (IRS), in an effort to improve its operations, has given credence to electronic filing. The IRS now has a mechanism for tax payers to electronically file their income tax returns. Authorized tax preparers can transmit returns electronically to two of the IRS's ten service centers: Ogden, Utah and Cincinnati, Ohio. The day after receiving a return, IRS computers send out a report verifying each return's receipt and specify whether the return has been accepted or rejected.

The present electronic filing system includes the most popular tax forms and covers about 20 metropolitan areas across the nation. By 1990, the IRS expects that electronic filing will reach all tax districts. The IRS also expects that "after-filing" tax refunds and payments will be handled by electronic transmission. After full implementation, electronic filing will help eliminate mounds of paperwork currently handled by the IRS. This filing will save the agency considerable time and money and significantly improve its operations.

6.9 TELECOMMUTING AND TELECOMPUTING

The introduction of the personal computer has made telecommunications easier. Under a telecommuting arrangement, you can work at home on a personal computer, store the results on disk, and then transfer the results to a mainframe computer at the office. There are three types of telecommuting:

1. Accessing a mainframe computer using your personal computer at home to avoid a trip to the office
2. Using your home computer to continue or finish work that was started at the office
3. Working at home most of the time and only reporting to the office occasionally to consult with coworkers

For the first two types of telecommuting, a home computer is a convenience that allows you to complete your work quickly and easily. For the third type, working at home or in a remote location is a professional routine. This last type can be very instrumental in organizations that handle multiple projects. If some of the projects are located in rural settings with no major computing facilities, telecommuting can offer a way to have you close to the project site while maintaining a close link with the project headquarters. This role can significantly reduce the cost of managing multiple projects.

In telecomputing, while located in a remote project site, you can log on to the computer facilities in the main project office to perform any analysis just as if you were located at the office. Thus, telecomputing is a wide-area distribution of terminals linked to a central computing facility. Depending on the distance, the telecomputing workstation can be connected to the host system via a modem or hardwired on a local area network. Unlike telecommuting, telecomputing is more susceptible to computer breakdowns at the main office. FIGURE 6-10 shows a conceptual layout of a telecommuting facility.

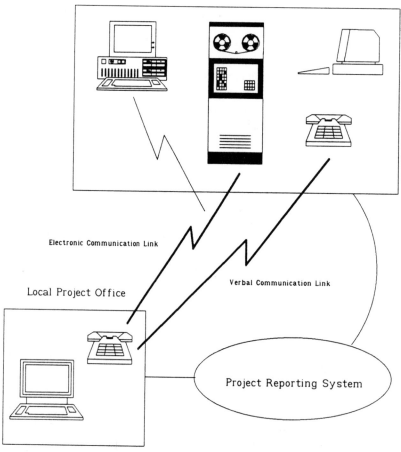

Fig. 6-10. Telecommuting/telecomputing layout.

6.10 ROLE OF TECHNICAL WORD PROCESSORS

The incorporation of technical material into text documents has become a popular practice among technical writers Technical writers have needs well above those of ordinary word processor users. They often write long, highly structured documents which require complex formatting and processing. Tables and graphics are now used extensively to enhance the quality of printed technical documents. Project management is one area where the presentation of technical information is very important. Technical word processors can play very significant roles in the preparation of project management reports.

In the past, technical word processing capabilities were limited to expensive software packages on mainframe computers. The proliferation of personal computers has created a big demand for PC based packages that can provide the technical capabilities comparable to those of mainframe packages.

Lotus Manuscript 2.0 is one of the few PC based word processors that offers the full functionality for technical writing in one convenient package. Until Manuscript came along, such capabilities were only available on a piecemeal basis. For example, one capability (e.g., equations) might be from one package while another capability (e.g., table formatting) might be from another package. The provision of all the common mathematical symbols and the greek alphabet makes Manuscript a unique tool compared to packages that only offer the rudiments of technical word processing.

Manuscript 2.0 is a marvelous tool for all functional environments including engineering, R and D, data processing, financial management, information management, and science. Manuscript integrates very nicely with many of the popular software packages on the market. From record keeping with Lotus 1-2-3, statistical analysis with STATGRAPHICS, graphics enhancement with Lotus Freelance Plus, to report generation with Manuscript 2.0, you will find the functionality of Manuscript to be a good reporting asset.

This section presents graphics and file merge capabilities of Lotus Manuscript 2.0. This section should serve as a guide in case you need to evaluate the capabilities of a technical word processor for project management document processing needs. You can import graphics images from any graphics program that can create metafiles. You can import ASCII files and spreadsheet documents from Lotus 1-2-3 or Symphony into Manuscript documents. You can capture and save screen images into special files, which are imported into Manuscript documents during final printing. You also can capture the graphics image of a keyboard element and insert the image at any desired place in your document.

Screen Capture

Manuscript comes with a Screen Capture utility that enables you to capture the graphic image of your computer display screen. The utility can be used with other programs apart from Manuscript. Screen Capture is a memory resident program that is loaded from the DOS prompt. You must, therefore, have enough system memory on your computer to successfully run Screen Capture while you are running your regular programs. If you already have other memory resident programs, Screen Capture might be deprived of enough space to run. With the Screen Capture utility, you have a quick way of capturing an image shown on your computer screen. For example, Gantt charts drawn on the screen can be captured and inserted into documents directly, instead of getting it printed conventionally and then cutting and pasting it into a printed document.

Loading Screen Capture. You must first load Screen Capture before you load the program whose screens you want to capture. If you are already in your regular program and you want to load Screen Capture, you must exit completely from the regular program, load Screen Capture, and then restart your regular program. Do not load Screen Capture from a temporary exit to DOS. Here are the three steps to load Screen Capture:

1. Make sure that the screen capture program, scr.exe, is in your default directory (Manuscript's directory).
2. Type scr at the DOS prompt and press Enter.
3. Start your regular program.

Removing Screen Capture. If you no longer need the services of Screen Capture and you want the memory space occupied by it to be freed up for other purposes, you need to remove it from the computer memory. Here are the steps to remove Screen Capture:

1. Return to the DOS level. This can be a temporary exit to DOS.
2. Type scr quit and press Enter. A message will be displayed to confirm the removal of Screen Capture from memory.

Capturing a Screen Image. The following steps to capture the graphic image of a screen from within any application program.

1. Make sure that Screen Capture has been loaded.
2. Display the screen to be captured.
3. Press Shift Prtsc to start the Screen Capture process. A prompt will be displayed requesting you to enter a filename in which to store the captured image.
4. Type a filename (include drive designation if necessary). Do not specify an extension for the file name. Screen Capture automatically appends the extension .SCT (for text screen) or .SCG (for graphics screen).
5. Press Enter. The screen will now be displayed in reverse video.
6. Use the Up, Down, Right, and Left arrows to highlight the screen area to be captured. The cursor is initially located at the upper-left corner of

the screen. Press the Space bar to switch the cursor between the upper-left corner and the lower-right corner of the screen. To speed up the cursor movement, hold down the Shift key while you press the Up, Down, Right, and Left arrows.

7. Press Ins to save the image of the highlighted region.

Inserting the Captured Screen in Documents. The screen image that you capture using the Screen Capture utility can be inserted in your documents with the following procedure:

1. Make sure that the file containing the captured screen is saved in the appropriate directory.
2. Move the cursor to the intended location of the captured image.
3. Press Ctrl ∖ and type sc.

The screen insert panel will appear. To complete the screen insert panel, follow these steps:

1. *File Name*   Specify the file that contains the screen image to be inserted in the document.
2. *Position*   Press the Space bar to display the position options. Select the desired position.
   - Fixed   Fixed sets the screen image in the relative position where you place the Screen Marker in the document. If the entire screen image does not fit on the page, white space will remain at the bottom of the original page and the screen image will move to the top of the succeeding page.
   - Floating   Floating allows the screen image to have a floating location among the surrounding text in the the document. If the entire screen image does not fit on a page, succeeding text moves up ahead of the screen image to fill the space left at the bottom of the original page and the screen image moves to the top of the succeeding page.
3. *Show Cursor*   Select Yes to include the cursor in the printed screen image.
4. *Width*   Type a number to specify the width of the screen image in the measurement units (e.g., inches). To extend the image width to the right margin, type RM. You can specify a unit of measurement different from that specified on the Global Options panel by including the appropriate unit abbreviation. For example, 24pt for a 24-point height or 1cm for a one-centimeter height. If a different unit of measurement is specified, Manuscript automatically converts the request to the appropriate magnitude in the Global units. For example, a request of a ten-centi-

meter height is automatically converted to a 3.937-inch height, if the Global unit is in inches.

5. *Height* Specify the desired height of the screen image in the prevailing units of measurement. Refer to the previous explanation for width specification. You do not need to specify both width and height for an image. If you specify only width, the height is automatically adjusted to fit the requested width. If you specify only height, the width is automatically adjusted to fit the requested height. If you specify both width and height magnitudes that are not compatible with the default shape and size of the image, the image will be distorted.

6. *Scale* Type a scaling factor from 0 to 10 to adjust the size of the screen image in multiples of its default size. A scale of 3, for example, prints an image at three times its original size. A scale of 0.5, on the other hand, would print the image at half of its original size. You cannot specify Scale if you already have a specification for Width or Height.

7. *Normal Video Foreground* Type a number (0 to 100: 0 = Black; 100 = White) to specify the shading of gray to use for the standard foreground of the screen.

8. *Normal Video Background* Type a number (0 to 100: 0 = Black; 100 = White) to specify the shading of gray to use for the standard background of the screen.

9. *Reverse Video Foreground* Type a number (0 to 100: 0 = Black; 100 = White) to specify the shading of gray to use for the reverse video foreground of the screen (e.g., a highlighted bar). The reverse video shading specification does not work for nonPostScript printers.

10. *Reverse Video Background* Type a number (0 to 100: 0 = Black; 100 = White) to specify the shading of gray to use for the reverse foreground of the screen (e.g., a highlighted bar). The reverse video shading specification does not work for nonPostScript printers.

11. *Name (for Table of Figures)* Type a name if you want the name of the screen image to be included in the table of figures.

12. *Print/Preview* Select Print to print the screen image immediately. Select Preview to preview the screen image immediately. Select No if you don't want to print or preview the screen immediately.

Merging Graphics with Text

You can merge graphics elements with text in your documents with the PICTURE command. PICTURE merges graphics images imported from the following programs:

- Graphic files with the extension .PIC from Lotus 1-2-3 or Symphony
- Metafiles with the extension .GMF imported from Lotus Freelance Plus or Lotus Graphwriter II

- PostScript image files with the extension .PS or encapsulated PostScript image files with the extension .EPS
- AutoCAD or AutoSketch image files with the extension .DXF
- Scanned image files with the extension .IMG (must first be converted to .BIT or .RLE files using File Conversion Utilities)
- HP ScanJet or DEST image files with the extension .TIF (must first be converted to .BIT or .RLE files using File Conversion Utilities)
- PC Paintbrush image files with the extension .PCX (must first be converted to .BIT files using File Conversion Utilities)
- MacPaint image files with the extension .MPT (must first be converted to .BIT files using File Conversion Utilities)

Here is the procedure for merging graphics images with document text:

1. Create the graphics image using your graphics program.
2. Save the image in the appropriate format for export to Manuscript.
3. While in the Manuscript document, move the cursor to the desired location for the graphics image.
4. Press Ctrl \ and type pi.
5. Complete the PICTURE panel as previously explained for screen capture.

Importing ASCII Files. You can import document files to be processed by Manuscript. To import a file into Manuscript from another program, you must save the file in the ASCII format using that program. Here is how to import an ASCII file:

1. Press F10 for the main menu.
2. Select File.
3. Select Import.
4. Specify the file to be imported.

ASCII File Import Options. There are several import options available on the ASCII file import panel:

- *Ignore Line Endings*—Ignore line endings converts two consecutive end-of-line characters into block dividers and ignores all single end-of-line characters. ASCII documents having blank lines separating paragraphs will have the paragraphs divided into blocks where the words wrap from line to line. This option does not preserve the layout of columns and tables.
- *Preserve Line Endings*—Preserve line endings converts two consecutive end-of-line characters into block dividers and keeps all end-of-line characters in the imported file. This options maintains the layout of columns

and tables. Once in Manuscript, you must delete the appropriate end-of-line characters to achieve proper word wrap where needed.

- *Code Page Options*—The next five options denote the code page that was used in creating the file to be imported. If you don't know the code that was used, accept the default option (*IBM Extended ASCII (CP 437)*). If that does not provide a suitable import, try each of the other options.

Weird looking characters might appear in the imported document because certain codes (e.g., subscripts) are not amenable to standard import formats. You can globally replace such characters by using the Replace command.

Importing Spreadsheet Files. You can import Lotus 1-2-3 and Symphony worksheet data into Manuscript as document files. Details of spreadsheet import and export can be found in your spreadsheet manual and the Manuscript reference guide. The import procedure is briefly outlined:

1. Select Import 1-2-3/Symphony File from the Manuscript Document Manager Menu.
2. Complete the panel that appears.

The prompts on the panel are briefly explained:

- *Working Directory*—Specify the working directory if different from the default specified on the panel.
- *Worksheet File Name*—Type the name and extension of the worksheet file to be imported.
- *Window Name*—If you are importing from Symphony, type the name of the window (SHEET, DOC, or FORM) to use for the import. If the window is not specified, the last active window will be assumed by Manuscript. The window name is not relevant for importing from Lotus 1-2-3.
- *Range Name*—Enter the range of the data to convert either directly (e.g., F2..G25) or by name (e.g., INFO). If no range is specified, the whole worksheet will be imported.
- *Format*—Press the Space bar to display the format options. Select the format to be used for the import (Table, Column, Tab, Document, or Document Image). Table and column will preserve the layout of the worksheet with blocks and columns. Tab will preserve the layout with blocks and tabs. Document and Document Image will convert the data to blocks of text. Refer to the Manuscript reference guide for more details.
- *Document Name*—Type the name of the document to create for the imported worksheet.

Lotus 1-2-3 Example. The budget statement shown in TABLE 6-2 was imported as a spreadsheet from Lotus 1-2-3. The steps involved in the spread-

Table 6-2. Spreadsheet Imported From Lotus 1-2-3.

1987 QUARTERLY BUDGET PROJECTION

	QTR1	QTR2	QTR3	QTR4	TOTAL
	***************	***************	***************	***************	***************
Sales	20000.00	20000.00	20000.00	20000.00	80000.00
Cst/Gds	5000.00	5000.00	5000.00	5000.00	20000.00
Gross Margin	$15,000.00	$15,000.00	$15,000.00	$15,000.00	$60,000.00
Expenses:					
Overhead	3000.00	3000.00	3000.00	3000.00	12000.00
Marketing	1000.00	1000.00	1000.00	1000.00	4000.00
Salaries	6000.00	6000.00	6000.00	6000.00	24000.00
Lgl Fees	1500.00	1500.00	1500.00	1500.00	6000.00
TTL EXPENSES	$11,500.00	$11,500.00	$11,500.00	$11,500.00	$46,000.00
PROFIT	$3,500.00	$3,500.00	$3,500.00	$3,500.00	$14,000.00

sheet importation process are:

1. The budget statement is developed as a regular spreadsheet in Lotus 1-2-3.
2. The spreadsheet is saved as a Lotus 1-2-3 file named TBL6_2.WK1.
3. At the Manuscript Document Manager menu, Import from 1-2-3/Symphony File is selected as the desired option.
4. The Worksheet Import Panel is completed as explained below:
   - *Worksheet File Name*   c:\123\files\TBL6_2.WK1
   - *Format*   Table
   - *Document Name*   c:\ms\msfiles\TBL6_2.DOC
   - The other fields are left at their default settings
5. After pressing Ins at the Worksheet Import Panel, the 1-2-3 worksheet is automatically imported and saved in the Manuscript files directory as TBL6_2.DOC.
6. The Manuscript file, TBL6_2.DOC, is retrieved and edited as desired just like any other Manuscript document file. Lines and borders could be added to the imported worksheet to enhance its appearance.

7. The edited worksheet document file is then retrieved and inserted in a regular document file to be printed. The spreadsheet is shown in TABLE 6-2.

Importing DCA (Revisable) Files. A DCA file uses the IBM Document Content Architecture (DCA) revisable text format as an alternative to ASCII format for data exchange. To import a DCA file from another program into Manuscript, you must save the file in the DCA (Revisable) text format using the other program. This procedure will convert the DCA file to a Manuscript document:

1. Select FILE CONVERSION UTILITIES on the Document Manager.
2. Select DCA (Revisable) File Import.
3. Type the name of the file to be imported.
4. Specify a document name under which to save the imported file.
5. Press Ins.

If you do not specify a document name, Manuscript uses the DCA file name with extension .DOC as a default.

Manuscript returns to the Document Manager menu after the conversion. You can now retrieve and edit the imported file.

Import from Freelance Plus. Graphics files created by Lotus Freelance Plus can easily be imported into a Manuscript document file. Here are the required steps:

1. Create your graphics drawing as usual with Freelance Plus.
2. Select FILE EXPORT METAFILE options from the Freelance Plus menus. This will save the graphics file as a GMF file (i.e., the file will be saved as *filename*.GMF in a specified directory).
3. Use the PICTURE command marker discussed earlier to import the GMF file into any desired location in your word processing document.

Import from Harvard Graphics. Graphics files created by Harvard Graphics also can be imported into a Manuscript document file. Here are the required steps:

1. Create your graphics drawing as usual with Harvard Graphics.
2. Select EXPORT METAFILE options from the file menus. This selection will save the graphics file as a CGM file (i.e., the file will be saved as *filename*.CGM in a specified directory).
3. Use the PICTURE command marker discussed earlier to import the CGM file into any desired location in your word processing document.

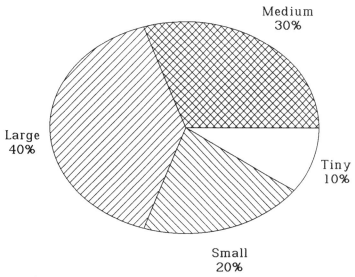

Fig. 6-11. Pie chart import from Harvard Graphics.

The charts shown in FIG. 6-11 and FIG. 6-12 were imported from Harvard Graphics.

Importing Lotus 1-2-3 Graphs. Graphs created by Lotus 1-2-3 also can be imported into Manuscript documents. Here are the steps:

1. Create your Lotus graphs as usual.
2. Select FILE SAVE options from the Lotus Graph menus. This option will save the graph file as a PIC file (i.e., the file will be saved as *file-name*.PIC in a specified directory.
3. Use the PICTURE command marker discussed earlier to import the PIC file into any desired location in your word processing document.

The chart shown in FIG. 6-13 was imported from Lotus 1-2-3.

Import from STATGRAPHICS. Plots created by STATGRAPHICS can be imported into Manuscript document files using the CGM format. Here are the required steps:

1. Create your graphics drawing as usual with STATGRAPHICS.
2. Save the plot in a metafile following the procedures outlined in the STATGRAPHICS manual. STATGRAPHICS does not automatically append a file extension to the metafile. However, it saves the file in the

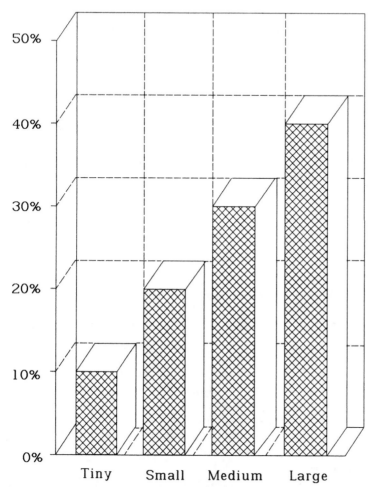

Fig. 6-12. Bar chart import from Harvard Graphics.

CGM format. You might want to explicitly specify a file extension (e.g., .CGM) when you specify the metafile name.

3. Use the PICTURE command marker discussed earlier to import the CGM file into any desired location in your word processing document.

The plot shown in FIG. 6-14 was imported from STATGRAPHICS. You might want to first import the STATGRAPHICS plots into Lotus Freelance so that you can easily edit the plots.

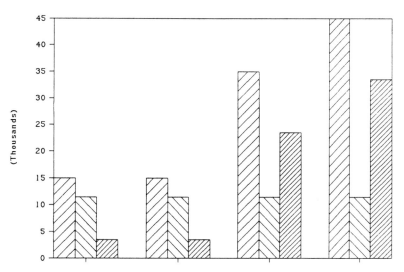

Fig. 6-13. Bar chart graph import from Lotus 1-2-3.

Three-D Histogram

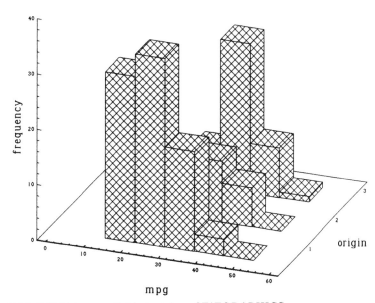

Fig. 6-14. 3-D histogram plot import from STATGRAPHICS.

7

xpert Systems
oject Management

ert system is a software package designed to mimic the
 expert to solve complex problems in a specific domain.
xpert system is:

s a computerized consultant that uses both facts and heu-
fficult decision problems that are beyond the capability of a
. It is akin to a consultant resident in computer RAM.

EMS CHARACTERISTICS

are an emerging technology with many areas for applica-
ns range from the expert system MYCIN, that detects
ases, to XCON, that is used to configure large computer
rt systems have proven to be quite successful. Other suit-
xpert systems will fall into one of the following categories:

d identifying

d testing
d training

Domain Specificity

Expert systems are usually very domain specific. They most likely will cover a specific area of expertise. For example, you might have a diagnostic expert system for trouble shooting computers. The expert system must actually perform all the necessary data manipulation as a human expert would. The knowledge engineer must limit his or her scope of expert system only to what is needed to solve the target problem.

Special Programming Languages

Expert systems are usually written in a special programming language. The use of languages like LISP, PROLOG, and OPS5 in the development of an expert system simplifies the coding process. The major advantage of these languages, as compared to conventional programming languages, is the simplicity of the addition, elimination, or substitution of new rules.

7.2 EXPERT SYSTEMS STRUCTURE

Expert systems are organized in three distinct levels:

1. *Knowledge Base*—Problem solving rules, procedures, and data relevant to the problem domain
2. *Working Memory*—Task specific data for the problem under consideration
3. *Inference Engine*—Generic control mechanism that applies the axiomatic knowledge in the knowledge base to the task-specific data to arrive at some solution or conclusion

These three distinct levels are unique in that the three pieces might very well come from different sources. The inference engine, like EXSYS or VP-Expert, might come from a vendor. The knowledge base might be a specific knowledge base on diagnosing heart problems that comes from a medical consulting firm. Finally, the session data might be supplied by the end user. The dynamism of the application environment for expert systems is based on the individual dynamism of the components. Dynamism can be classified as follows:

- *Most Dynamic*—The working memory changes with each problem situation. Consequently, it is the most dynamic component of an expert system, assuming, of course, that it is utilized and updated when necessary.
- *Moderately Dynamic*—The knowledge base does not change unless there is a new piece of information that indicates a change in the problem solution procedure. Changes in the knowledge base should be carefully evaluated before being implemented. In effect, changes should not be based on just one consultation experience. For example, a rule that is found to

be irrelevant under one problem situation might turn out to be indispensible in other problem scenarios.

- *Least Dynamic*—Because of the strict control and coding structure of an inference engine, changes are made only if absolutely necessary to correct a bug or to enhance the inferential process. Commercial inference engines, in particular, change only at the discretion of the developer. Because frequent updates can be disrupting and costly to clients, most commercial software developers try to minimize the frequency of update.

The modularity of an expert system is what distinguishes it from a conventional computer program. Modularity is effected in an expert system by organizing it in three distinct components of knowledge base, working memory, and inference engine. A functional integration of expert system components is shown in FIG. 7-1.

The knowledge base constitutes the problem-solving rules, facts, or intuition that a human expert might use in solving problems in a given problem

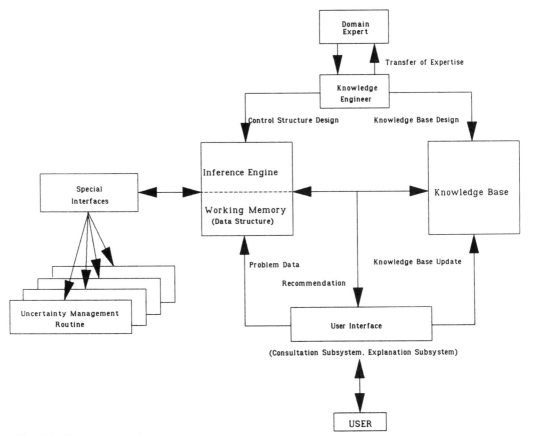

Fig. 7-1. Expert system structure.

domain. The knowledge base is usually stored in terms of *If-Then* rules. The working memory represents relevant data for the current problem being solved. The inference engine is the control mechanism that organizes the problem data and searches through the knowledge base for applicable rules. With the increasing popularity of expert systems, many commercial inference engines are coming onto the market. Thus, the development of a functional expert system usually centers around the compilation of the knowledge base.

The Benefits of Expert Systems

Some of the most obvious benefits typically associated with expert systems are:

- Increase the probability, frequency, and consistency of making good decisions
- Help distribute human expertise
- Facilitate real-time, low-cost expert-level decisions by the nonexpert
- Enhance the utilization of all available data
- Permit objectivity by weighing evidence without bias and without regard for the user's personal and emotional feelings
- Permit dynamism through modularity of structure
- Free up the mind and time of the human expert to enable him or her to concentrate on more creative activities

No matter what area of business you are engaged in, expert systems can fulfill the need for higher productivity and reliability of decisions. You can capitalize on the benefits of expert systems by participating in one or more of the following areas of interest:

- Expert system basic research
- Expert system applied research
- Knowledge engineering
- Expert system programming and software analysis
- Management of expert systems professionals
- Expert systems training
- Expert systems sales and marketing
- Expert systems end user (passive or active role)

The Need for Expert Systems

Expert systems are needed for various reasons. However, the most pressing need for expert systems is created by the shortcomings associated in the decision making process of humans. Some of the human shortcomings are:

- Scarcity of expertise
- Fatigue
- Forgetfulness
- Inconsistency
- Limited working memory
- Inability to comprehend, retain, or recall large amounts of data quickly
- Capability to lie, die, and hide at any time

7.3 HEURISTIC REASONING

Human experts use a type of problem-solving technique called *heuristic reasoning*, also called "rules of thumb." Heuristic reasoning allows the expert to quickly and efficiently arrive at a good solution. Expert systems base their reasoning process on symbolic manipulation and heuristic inference procedures that closely match the human-like thinking process. Conventional programs can only recognize numeric or alphabetic strings and manipulate them in a programmed, predefined manner. The heuristic approach of expert systems makes heuristic reasoning attractive for project management applications. Project management has been one of the very futile areas for applying decision-making heuristics.

Search Control Methods

All expert systems are search intensive. Many techniques have been employed to try to make these intensive searches more efficient. *Branch and bound, pruning, depth first search,* and *breadth first search* are just some of the search techniques used to search a knowledge base. Because of the intensity of the search process, it is important that search control strategies be used to handle the accounting aspects of a good search.

Forward Chaining

Forward chaining involves the checking of a rule's premise for truth and taking action on the rule's conclusion if the premise proves to be true. This procedure will continue until a solution is found or a dead end is reached. Forward chaining is commonly referred to as data-driven reasoning.

Backward Chaining

Backward chaining is used to backtrack from a goal to the paths that lead to the goal. It is the reverse of forward-chaining. Backward chaining is very good when all outcomes are known and the number of possible outcomes is not large.

7.4 USER INTERFACE

Initial Development and Maintenance

The initial development of an expert system is performed by the expert and the knowledge engineer. Unlike most conventional programs in which only programmers can make changes, changes in expert systems are discussed and implemented by a group of people. These changes usually are time consuming and costly. Even with the easily changed expert system, strict rules and guidelines need to be established to authorize new or modified rules. A careless user might accidentally introduce some unacceptable rules. Any changes to an expert system should be carefully monitored. Only individuals who are not completely familiar with the expert system should evaluate and authorize permanent or temporary changes in the system.

Natural Language

The programming languages used for expert systems operate more like talk and answer questions than a cryptic language. The premise is usually stated in the form of a question and actions are stated like answers to the question. In the future, some expert systems might even be capable of modifying themselves. If the expert system determines that a piece of its data or knowledge base is incorrect during or after a program is run, or is no longer applicable because the problem environment has changed, the system should be able to update its information accordingly.

Summaries and Explanations

One of the key characteristics of an expert system is the ability to explain how it arrived at its recommendation. With this ability, you can always question the expert system about a specific recommendation and the reasoning path used to arrive at the recommendation. In addition, a printed summary of a consultation can be generated by an expert system.

Quantitative and Qualitative Factors

Expert systems not only arrive at solutions or recommendations, but can give you a level of confidence about the solution. In this manner, the expert system can handle both quantitative and qualitative factors when analyzing problems. This aspect is very important when you consider how inexact most input data are for day-to-day decision-making problems.

Dynamic Decisions

The problems addressed by expert systems can have more than one solution path or, in some cases, no solution path. This characteristic is quite different from the conventional programs that follow a rigid program path and always arrive at one solution. Expert systems can be designed to solve one or more problems within a given problem domain simultaneously while considering all of the information available in the knowledge base. Sometimes, an expert system is required to solve other problems not necessarily directly related to the specific problem at hand, but whose solution will have an impact on the total problem-solving process.

Multiple Solutions

Because of the dynamic decision process that an expert system is capable of, multiple solutions can be recommended by the system. In other words, the system could be intelligent enough to realize that there might not be one over-all best solution. By recommending more than one solution, the system attempts to mimic the human expert as he would have offered alternative paths to the solution of a problem.

Data Characteristics

One of the most unique characteristics of expert systems is the capability of working with inexact data. The expert system allows the user to assign probabilities, certainty factors, or confidence levels to any or all input data. This feature more closely represents how most questions are handled in the real world. The computer can take into account all of these factors and make a recommendation based on the best possible solution rather than the only solution.

What data has been to the previous generations of computing, knowledge is to the present generation of computing. Conventional data can now be manipulated to form durable knowledge, which can be processed to generate timely information, which is used to enhance human decisions.

7.5 FUTURE DIRECTIONS FOR EXPERT SYSTEMS

The intensity of the ongoing efforts in the area of expert systems has created unique opportunities in many spheres of human endeavor. Following is a list of what can be expected in this burgeoning field in the coming years.

- Large-scale research into natural language systems
- Further research in knowledge base organization
- Insatiable demand for expert system related consulting services
- Commercial knowledge bases
- Drive for advanced hardware and software capabilities
- Continuing growth in the market for expert systems products and services

These opportunities should be practically utilized to solve many of the business and industry problems that are now impeding productivity in many organizations. Project management offers one avenue through which the practical utilization can be effected.

7.6 KNOWLEDGE REPRESENTATION MODELS

The purpose of knowledge representation is to organize the required knowledge into a form so the expert system can readily access it for decision-making purposes. Knowledge does not always come compiled and ready for use. The term *knowledge* is used to describe a variety of bits of understanding that enable people and machines to perform their intended functions.

Types of Knowledge

Knowledge can be broadly classified into two types: *Surface Knowledge* and *Deep Knowledge*. The classification is based on the prevailing information circumstances and the intended (conscious or subconscious) uses of knowledge. Some of the characteristics of the two types of knowledge are:

1. Surface Knowledge
   - Composed of situation and action pairs
   - Capable of solving simple domain problems
   - Often used in a cursory situation
   - Faster to implement
2. Deep Knowledge
   - Composed of cause and effect relationships
   - Based on hierarchical cognition of events
   - Involves goals and plans to achieve the goals
   - Capable of solving difficult problems

Knowledge, whether surface or deep, must be extracted and encoded into usable forms for solving problems. Sometimes, the source of knowledge can be so dormant that a great effort must be made to extract it. Once extracted, an element of knowledge must undergo other transformations before it acquires an operative value. Extraction involves eliciting the basic concepts of the problem domain from a reliable knowledge source. The two major sources of knowledge are:

1. Active human expertise
2. Latent literature expertise

The major representational models for achieving the transformation of knowledge into a form that can be used by a computer are:

- Semantic networks
- Frames
- Production rules
- Predicate logic
- O-A-V (Object-Attribute-Value) triplets
- Hybrids
- Scripts

Semantic Networks

A semantic network is the most general and perhaps the oldest representational structure for an expert system knowledge base. It serves as the basis for other knowledge representations and is a scheme for representing abstract relations among objects in a problem domain, such as membership in a class. The network consists of a collection of nodes that are linked to form object relationships. Arcs linking nodes carry notations that indicate the type of relationships.

Semantic networks have been a useful way to represent knowledge in domains that use well-established taxonomies to simplify problem solving. Some of the advantages of semantic networks are:

- Flexibility in adding, modifying, or deleting nodes and arcs
- Ability to inherit relationships from other nodes
- Ease of drawing inferences about inheritance hierarchy

The disadvantage of a semantic network is the lack of a formal definitive structure which makes it difficult to implement in an operational setting. An example of a semantic network for manufacturing and inspecting a gear is presented in FIG. 7-2.

Frames

A frame consists of a collection of slots that contain attributes to describe an object, a class of objects, a situation, an action, or an event. Frames differ slightly from semantic networks. In a semantic network, information about an object can be randomly placed throughout the knowledge base, whereas a frame is information grouped together into a single unit. Frames provide a description of an object by using a tabulation of information associated with it. This organization of useful relationships helps to mimic the way an expert typically organizes the information about an object into chunks of data. Frame-

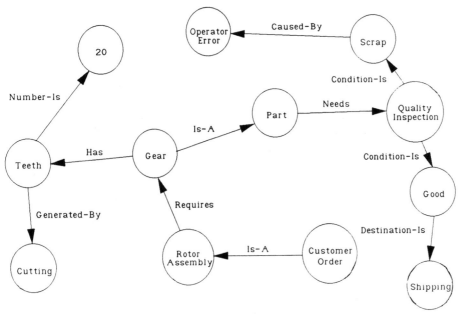

Fig. 7-2. Semantic network example.

based reasoning is based on seeking confirmation of expectations or "filling in the slots." If a frame is not relevant to a given situation, control will move to another frame. Two advantages of frames are:

1. Frames are arranged in a hierarchical manner to inherit relationships from other frames.
2. Through the concise and compact representation of information, frames facilitate faster searches of the knowledge base.

Using the earlier gear example, a frame representation might be constructed as shown in FIG. 7-3. The knowledge base presented in TABLE 7-1 is a sample knowledge base in the PC PLUS expert systems development package from Texas Instruments, Inc. The knowledge base analyzes the problem of buying or leasing an asset. Once a buy or lease conclusion has been reached, the knowledge base determines the best financing method for the acquisition of the asset. The consultation process involves three goal parameters ordered as follows:

HOW-TO-ACQUIRE = = > > PAYMENT = = > > FINANCE-IT

HOW-TO-ACQUIRE represents the "buy or lease" decision option, PAYMENT represents the installment payment needed to acquire the asset, and

Gear	
Teeth Number	20
Assembly	Rotor
Production Method	Cutting
Delivery Date	9/2/88

Fig. 7-3. Frame representation.

Table 7-1. Root Frame and Subframe Organization.

ROOT FRAME	SUB FRAME
Frame Name: ASSET	Frame Name: FINANCE
PARMS:	PARMS:
LESSEE-CASH	FINANCE-INTEREST
CASH-RESERVE-NEEDED	FINANCE-PERIOD
PRESERVES-CASH	DOWN-PAYMENT
CANNOT-BORROW	ASSET-COST
ACQUIRE-BY	
RULES:	RULES:
1. IF LESSEE-CREDIT = POOR	1. IF ACQUIRE-BY = PURCHASE
THEN CANNOT-BORROW AND ACQUIRE = LEASE	THEN FINANCE-IT (calculation)
2. IF CANNOT-BORROW OR PRESERVES-CASH	2. IF ACQUIRE-BY = LEASE
THEN HOW-TO-ACQUIRE = LEASE	THEN FINANCE-IT = (calculation)
AND ACQUIRE-BY = LEASE	3. IF FINANCE-IT IS KNOWN
3. IF LESSEE-CREDIT = FAIR AND LESSEE-CASH = FAIR	THEN PAYMENT = (calculation)
AND CASH-RESERVE-NEEDED	
THEN PRESERVES-CASH	
4. IF HOW-TO-ACQUIRE IS NOTKNOWN	
THEN HOW-TO-ACQUIRE = BUY-THE-ASSET	
AND ACQUIRE-BY = PURCHASE	
	GOAL:
GOALS:	FINANCE-IT
HOW-TO-ACQUIRE, PAYMENT	

FINANCE-IT represents the finance method appropriate for the particular scenario of the client. Organizing the knowledge base rules into frames according to their relationships with the goal parameters is a logical idea. As shown in TABLE 7-1, rules relevant to HOW-TO-ACQUIRE and PAYMENT are located in the root frame. Rules relevant to FINANCE-IT are in the subframe. When dealing with large knowledge bases (large sets of knowledge elements), you will find it helpful to have an analytical tool for investigating the relationships and logical groupings of the knowledge elements. Frames facilitate such an efficient organization.

Production Rules

Production rules are the most popular of all the representation schemes. Rules provide a formal way of representing recommendations, directives, or strategies. *If-Then* rules link antecedents to their associated consequents. They are appropriate when the knowledge domain results from empirical associations developed through years of experience solving problems in a given area.

The rule antecedent typically contains several clauses linked by the logical connectives AND and OR. The rule consequent consists of one or more verb phrases that specify the action to be taken. Advantages of production rules are:

- Flexible in that individual rules can be easily added, removed, or updated independently of their relationship to other rules
- Provide a homogeneous representation of knowledge which provides ease of interpretation
- Structured similarly to the way people think about solving problems
- Useful as a mechanism for controlling the interaction between statements of declarative and procedural knowledge

Disadvantages of production rules include the following:

- Inability to maintain modularity between rules in large systems
- Inefficiencies due to constraining interactions between rules
- Prevailing inefficiency of search techniques
- Separation of knowledge and control is poor when dealing with sequential information in large knowledge bases

An example of a rule that might be used in the gear production example is:

ANTECEDENT
IF thickness for any tooth is large
    and circular pitch is small
    and face width is medium

CONSEQUENT
THEN production method is cutting

Rules can be classified into two categories: *first-order* rules and *meta* rules (higher-order). A first-order rule is a simple rule consisting of antecedents and consequents. A meta rule is a rule whose antecedents and consequents contain information about other rules.

An example of a first-order rule with a rule certainty factor of 75 percent:

IF   node j is inactive and arc i has a reliability <0.9,
THEN   set (1,n) connectedness = 0 [cf = 0.75].

A meta rule example with a rule certainty factor of 82 percent:

IF   arc k has a failure rate similar to arc m
AND   arc k uses rule $R1$,
THEN   activate rule $R1$ [cf = 0.82].

A familiar example of a meta rule is the popular office sign which says:

Rule Number One:

The Boss is always right.

Rule Number Two:

IF the boss is wrong,
THEN see rule Number One.

Predicate Logic

Logical expressions use predicate calculus to generate inferences by asserting the truthfulness or otherwise of propositional statements. For example:

Gear is-a machined part

This statement is either true or not-true in the context of the problem being addressed. Many forms of logic have been developed for use within AI. Propositional calculus, predicate calculus, first-order logic, modal logic, temporal logic, and fuzzy logic are just a few of the prevailing logic forms. First-order logic, an extension of predicate logic, is perhaps the most commonly used form. A predicate symbol expresses a statement about individual elements, either singly or in relation to other elements. A function symbol expresses a mapping from one element or a group of elements to another element. For example, in the following formula, the predicate product denotes a relationship between three arguments: a particular class of item, material, and shape.

Product (Shaft, Metal, Cylindrical)

The predicate will return a value of "true" if a given item matches the description of a cylindrical metal shaft. Similarly, the function symbol "Use" in the next formula maps metal shafts to a particular usage category.

Product (Shaft, Metal, Use (Crank-Shaft))

If "crank-shaft" is used as the argument in the function "use," the function will probably return the value "cylindrical" because most crank-shafts are cylindrical in shape. The value "cylindrical" is then used by the predicate "Product" to identify a specific type of product. Subsets of product types can be formed, for example, by further classifying cylindrical metal shafts into diameter size categories. Thus, product inheritance relationships can be represented by considering the predicate "part-of" as shown in the formula:

$$\{\text{PART-OF}(x,y)\} \cap \{\text{PART-OF}(y,z)\} = \text{PART-OF}(x,z)$$

Predicate logic relies on the truth and rules of inferences to represent symbols and their relationships to each other. It can be used to determine the truthfulness or falsity of a statement and also be used to represent statements about specific objects or individuals. The advantages of predicate logic include:

- Simplicity of notation allows descriptions to be readily understandable.
- Modularity allows statements to be added, deleted, or modified without affecting other statements in the knowledge base.
- Conciseness because each fact has to be represented only once.
- Derivation of new facts from old ones can be automated by using versions of theorem-proving techniques.

Predicate logic is best used in domains of concise unified theories such as physics, chemistry, and other mathematical or theoretical fields. The disadvantages of predicate logic are:

- Difficulty in representing procedural and heuristic knowledge.
- Difficulty in managing large knowledge bases due to poor organizational structure.
- Weak data manipulation procedures.

O-A-V Triplets

An O-A-B Triplet is a common type of semantic network commonly used within the framework of other representation models. The network is divided into three parts: *Object, Attribute,* and *Value.* The representation presents a serial list of an Object and an Attribute of interest. Objects are viewed as physical or conceptual species, similar to the noun in a structured sentence. Attributes are general properties defining the Object, while the Values indicate the specific descriptions of the Attribute. Within the O-A-V, Object and Value are graphically represented by nodes, while Attribute is designated by an arc or link. Using a segment of the semantic network presented earlier in FIG. 7-2, an O-A-B triplet could be given as:

	OBJECT	ATTRIBUTE	VALUE	
Gear	= = = = >	Number of teeth	= = = = >	20

Because of the formalized structure required by an O-A-V model, the use of triplets allows semantic networks to be organized in a tree structure (or similar) format, which allows a starting point for reasoning and gathering information.

Hybrids

Each knowledge representation technique has its advantages. For example, production rules are especially useful for representing procedural knowledge (methods for accomplishing goals). Semantic networks are good for representing relations among objects. Frame-based semantic networks can concisely store an immense amount of knowledge about object properties and relations. Predicate logic supplies a means for explicitly expressing different types of knowledge. Early expert systems tended to use one technique or another exclusively.

The tendency recently has been to combine different representation techniques to take advantage of the best capability of each within the context of the prevailing problem. A system might use production rules to define procedures for discovering attributes of objects, semantic networks to define the relationships among the objects referenced in the rules, and frames to describe the objects' typical attributes. The frame in TABLE 7-1 is a good example of combining rule and frame representations.

Scripts

Scripts form an extension of frames that present the expected sequence of events and their associated information in a linked time-based series of frames.

For example, the frame discussed previously for gear production might be linked to other frames which contain detailed information on the cutting operation in the time sequence of events in the production schedule.

7.7 REASONING MODELS

Once problem solving knowledge has been identified, the way the knowledge is encoded for drawing inferences depends on the reasoning approach desired for the chosen problem domain. The structure of the problems in some domains dictates which reasoning approach is applicable or effective. An *inference* is the logical conclusion or implication based on available information. *Reasoning* is the process of drawing inferences from known or assumed facts. Sometimes, you can draw an inference based on *intuition*. In such a case, you can reach a conclusion without a conscious use of reasoning.

- Deductive Reasoning—The process of reasoning from general information about a class of objects or events to specific information about a given member of the class.
- Inductive Reasoning—Drawing a general conclusion based on specific facts. For example, the specific information about individual members of a class of objects or events might lead to a general conjecture about the whole class.
- Monotonic Reasoning—A one-way path for data. In monotonic reasoning, parameter instantiation (the assignment of a value to a parameter) is irrevocable regardless of whatever new information might become available.
- Nonmonotonic Reasoning—Reinstantiating parameters if new information warrants the assignment of a new value to the parameter.

Forward Chaining

Forward chaining is the process of reasoning forward from a given set of data to some possibly remote goal state or conclusion. It is also commonly known as *forward reasoning* or *data-driven search*. Forward chaining is generally of the heuristic form:

IF (data condition)
THEN (conclusion)

An example of a forward rule might be:

IF *person x* trusts *person y*
THEN *person x* likes *person y*

The assumption must be made that people normally like those that they trust. The conclusion or goal state of a given rule can become the condition or data state of subsequent rules.

Backward Chaining

In backward chaining, the reasoning process starts from a goal state and backtracks to the paths that might have led to the goal. It is also called *backward reasoning* or *goal-driven*. Backward chaining is generally of the form:

Goal State
IF (data condition)

An example of backward rule is:

person x likes *person y*
IF *person x* trusts *person y*

This example asserts that liking someone implies a precondition of trust. As you shall see later, such an assertion might not be precise. For example, if only 80 percent of the population falls in the category of the rule assertion, then you could assign some level of certainty to the rule. Then the rule might be stated as:

person x likes *person y*
IF *person x* trusts *person y*
Certainty Factor = 0.80

Backward chaining is often implemented in expert systems in the coding format of a forward rule. In that case, the goal is specified in the antecedent of the rule and the condition leading to the goal is specified in the conclusion of the rule. For the example of interpersonal relationship, the backward rule can be written as:

IF *person x* likes *person y*
THEN *person x* trusts *person y*

Breadth-first Search

The process of drawing inferences using an expert system knowledge base involves searching for parameters and values that match certain conditions. In breadth-first search, all the available premises at a decision node are evaluated before going into the deeper details of each premise.

Depth-first Search

Depth-first search involves the evaluation of all the ramifications of each premise before going to the next one. The comparison of depth-first search to breadth-first search can be drawn from the screening of job applicants. Under breadth-first search, all the applicants are broadly reviewed before deciding whom to invite for an interview. Whereas, under depth-first search, the first applicant is reviewed, interviewed, and evaluated before considering other applicants.

7.8 REASONING UNDER UNCERTAINTY

The difference between human reasoning and machine reasoning has been a subject of great debate for many years. Humans have very definite differences from computers in the way they reason. Humans have intuitive insight that has, thus far, been difficult to implement in AI.

Amount of Information Used in Human Decision Making

Most people are not very disturbed by making some decisions under uncertain conditions, especially when a high level of accuracy is not crucial. People make many decisions every day under uncertain conditions and don't even realize it.

One method humans have of working under uncertain conditions is the use of nonmonotonic reasoning. This reasoning is an inductive process in which a person can assume a statement to be true and then follow where that assumption leads. If the assumption leads to a contradiction to what the person believes to be true, then it is withdrawn. People can fairly easily make and retract assumptions, which is also a valuable asset in expert systems.

Bayesian Approach to Handling Uncertainty

By using probability, you can generalize observations about events to arrive at statements about a population of objects or conversely from the population to specific events. The Bayesian approach uses Bayes' Theorem for handling uncertainty in the process of drawing inference about objects or events. Bayes' Theorem states:

Let $\{B_1, B_2..., B_n\}$ be a set of events forming a partition of the sample space S, where $P(B_i) \neq 0$, for $i = 1, 2, ..., n$. Let A be any event of S such that $P(A) \neq 0$. Then, for $k = 1, 2, ... n$, there is:

$$P(B_k \mid A) = \frac{P(B_k \cap A)}{\sum_{i=1}^{n} P(B_i \cap A)}$$

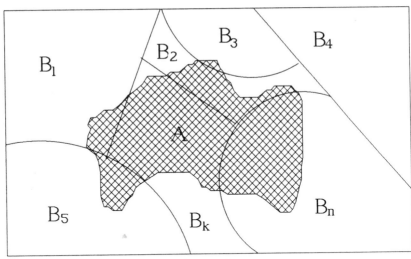

Fig. 7-4. Partitioning of the knowledge sample space.

$$= \frac{P(B_k)P(A \mid B_k)}{\sum\limits_{i=1}^{n} P(B_i)\, P(A \mid B_i)}$$

Referring to FIG. 7-4, the shaded area is the event A that is given and the events labeled B_i are the events about which the inferences are drawn. Bayes' Rule shows how to calculate the probability of having an event B_i, given that the event A has occurred.

For example, if 2 percent of a population has tuberculosis (T), then the following probabilities and rule of inference can be defined:

$P(T)$	= .02
IF	
$P(X\mid T)$	= probability that an X-ray of a tubercular person is positive
	= .90, and
$P(X\mid\text{Not-}T)$	= probability that an X-ray of a healthy person is positive
	= .01
THEN	
$P(T\mid X)$	= probability that a person with a positive X-ray has tuberculosis

Using Bayes' Rule, the calculation $P(T\mid X)$ is as follows:

$$P(T \mid X) = \frac{P(T)\,P(X\mid T)}{P(T)\,P(X\mid T) + P(\text{Not}-T)\,P(X\mid \text{Not}-T)}$$

187

$$= \frac{(.02)\,(.90)}{(.02)\,(.90)\ +\ (.98)\,(.01)}$$

$$= .648$$

Although the techniques for applying the probability approach are well developed, there are many reasons why pure probabilistic analyses have not been very popular in expert systems. Some of these reasons are:

- The events that partition the sample space (knowledge base) must be disjoint. Of course, this disjointedness is not necessarily the case in the reasoning approach that humans use in solving problems.
- The prior probabilities, $P(A|B_i)$, must be known. Because most heuristic problem solving methods rely on expert judgment rather than mathematical facts, these prior probabilities are usually not available. Even when they are available, they are often unreliable.
- Bayesian reasoning could lead to combinatorial explosion of the analysis. Because the boundaries of the events leading to a problem solution are usually indeterminate or ambiguous, there is the tendency to over-partition the sample space. Over-partitioning leads to large data requirements and analysis.
- Users not familiar with probabilistic statements are likely to misinterpret the results of a probability analysis.

7.9 CONFIDENCE FACTORS

Most heuristic methods use some sort of quasi-probabilistic techniques to handle uncertainty. Two of these techniques are *certainty factors* and *fuzzy logic*.

Fuzzy Logic

Fuzzy logic uses a multivalued membership function to denote membership of an object in a class rather than the classical binary true or false values used to denote membership. In fuzzy logic, the source of imprecision is the absence of sharply defined criteria for class membership rather than the presence of random variables. Each class contains a continuum of grades of membership. Thus, a person will not be considered to be either old or young. Depending on his or her actual age, the person will have a certain degree of being old (or being young). This degree of membership will depend on the membership functions that people define for the concepts of being old or young.

Certainty Factors

The most common representation of heuristic weights is the use of *certainty factors* (or confidence factors). In this approach, numbers greater than 0 are used for positive evidence and numbers less than 0 are used for negative evidence (e.g., -1 to 1, -100 to 100). These numbers are used merely as heuristics, and no criterion of optimality is associated with them. However, a common belief is that the distinction between positive and negative certainty factors helps in the extraction of information from human experts.

1. The CF of a conjunction of several facts is taken to be the minimum of the CFs of the individual facts.
2. The CF of a disjunction of several facts is taken to be the maximum of the CFs of the individual facts.
3. The CF for the conclusion produced by a rule is the CF of its premise multiplied by the CF of the rule.
4. The CF for a fact produced as the conclusion of one or more rules is the maximum of the CFs produced by the rules yielding that conclusion.

For example, suppose you are trying to establish fact D, and the only rules concluding anything about D are the following:

Rule 1: IF A and B and C, THEN CONCLUDE D (CF = .8)
Rule 2: IF H and I and J, THEN CONCLUDE D (CF = .7)

If facts A, B, C, H, I, and J are known with the respective CFs of 0.7, 0.3, 0.5, 0.8, 0.7, and 0.9, then the following computations would produce a CF of 0.49 for D.

From Rule 1:

Min {CF(A), CF(B), CF(C)}	= Min {0.7, 0.3, 0.5}
	= 0.3
CF(D) based on Rule 1	= 0.3(0.8)
	= 0.24

From Rule 2:

Min {CF(H), CF(I), CF(J)}	= Min {0.8, 0.7, 0.9}
	= 0.7
CF(D) based on Rule 2	= 0.7(0.7)
	= 0.49

Rule Combination:

CF(D)	= Max {CF(D)$_1$, CF(D)$_2$}
	= MAX {0.24, 0.49}
	= 0.49

This method of handling uncertainty has been used quite extensively in many expert systems. However, it does have some flaws. For example, the method is not suitable for situations involving high levels of interactions between goals. Several variations of the mathematical approach to combining certainty factors have been proposed and used in many systems.

7.10 EXPERT SYSTEMS AND PROJECT DECISION MAKING

The concept of integrating cost into project network analysis provides management the tools for effective control of project resources. In today's complex organizational cost structures, there are several factors that influence project implementations. Such factors include variable interest rates, inflation, technology changes, resource allocation, project incentives, penalties, cash flow changes, budget restrictions, reporting regulations, work breakdown structure (WBS), forecasting, cost estimating, shortage of technical personnel, and competitions.

Many computer-based cost systems are now in operation in many project environments. Unfortunately, these cost systems are often implemented for only a limited number of the factors that affect the overall cost performance of projects. Fortunately, this problem can be overcome by taking advantage of new computer technologies.

Expert systems can facilitate effective and prompt managerial cost control without the need for extensive run-time data collection. An expert system can increase the probability and frequency of making good project decisions.

The Network Plan

The increased complexity, size, and amount of development required by today's project systems have made the traditional cost management methods obsolete. While seeking more effective means for managing these projects, network cost techniques have evolved. A network is a representation of a project plan such that the relationships between jobs or activities are clarified and can easily be examined. Network analysis reduces the project evaluation to four stages:

1. Breaking down the project into a set of individual jobs and events and arranging them into a logical network
2. Estimating the duration and resource requirements of each job
3. Developing a schedule, and finding which job controls the completion of the project
4. Reallocating funds or other resources to improve the schedule

If done properly, network cost analysis offers the following ten advantages:

1. Forces a thorough preplanning of project tasks
2. Increases coordination
3. Identifies trouble spots in advance and pinpoints responsibility

4. Focuses management's attention on the activities that are cost-critical
5. Indicates cost effective start and finish times for project activities
6. Enables revisions of project plans without extensive cost changes
7. Suggests where alternative project methods should be sought
8. Makes costs tractable
9. Facilitates fair allocation of resources
10. Minimizes cost overruns

An expert system can serve as the effective mechanism that aids management in answering questions such as:

1. What are the actual project costs to date?
   - Single cost estimate
   - Activity direct costs
   - Project indirect costs
   - Three cost estimates
   - Normal and crash activity costs
2. How do the actual costs to date compare with planned costs to date?
3. By how much might the project be expected to overrun the total planned cost?
4. How can resources be best allocated?

The first step in the network cost planning is constructing a network and performing the basic scheduling that gives the earliest and latest start and finish times for each activity. Then the estimated cost data for each activity can be added to the network and the first cost computation can be made.

As the project progresses, actual expenditures are recorded by activity at specified reporting dates. Any revised estimate of duration or costs of activities are also accounted for at the reporting times. The following five computations can be made:

1. Summation of all actual costs
2. Summation of budgeted costs at this point in time
3. Summation of budgeted costs for all activities completed and partial costs of activities partially completed
4. Computation of differences in actual costs and planned costs for completed portions of the project
5. Computation of a projection on the expected cost of the total project based on the progress made so far

Based on the above cost computations and other prevailing cost circumstances, rules can be developed to serve as guides for courses of managerial actions in diverse cost and project scenarios. These rules can then be incorporated into an expert system to facilitate quick real-time managerial decisions.

Rule-based Cost Analysis

Cost rules compiled as discussed in the previous section can be organized into an expert system knowledge base. For example, the following cost rules might apply to a given project.

Rule 1—If the total budget exceeds $100,000 and the expected project duration exceeds 1 year, then allocate 10 percent of the budget to each 10 percent of the expected duration.

Rule 1 establishes the procedure for spreading the project budget evenly over the duration of the project. This rule can be particularly useful for fixed-budget projects that extend over several years. The rule provides a safeguard against expending a larger portion of the budget early in the project at the expense of later project needs. The rule, of course, assumes that any initial fixed-cost (lump sum) requirements of the project have been accounted for. If not, a subrule such as the following may be utilized:

> If the fixed-cost exceeds 10 percent of total budget and 10 percent of the expected duration is less than 1 day, then compute the new budget as the total budget minus the fixed cost and allocate 10 percent of the new budget to each 10 percent of the expected duration.

Rule 2—If the project activities are numerous (>20), then record half of the budget for each activity at the activity's scheduled start time and record the other half of the budget at the activity's scheduled completion time.

Rule 2 is the common 50/50 rule (Kerzner, 1984) used in reducing cost variance in projects with a large number of elements. One advantage of the 50/50 rule is that it reduces the necessity to continuously determine the percent complete for each activity in the process of allocating cost.

Rule 3—If current costs are more than 5 percent above the initial budget, then review the cost of higher-salaried personnel.

Rule 3 might not be a popular rule, especially in a union environment. However, it can give management an indication of where to start troubleshooting.

Rule 4—If the cost of any given project element exceeds 10 percent of the total cost, then reexamine the work breakdown structure.

Inadequate work breakdown structure often leads to intractable cost control problems. Elemental definition of project activities and their associated costs can greatly alleviate the problems of chasing cost "ghosts."

Rules similar to the ones presented can be developed to fit specific organizational needs. Many practical expert systems have been developed using as few as 20 rules. Some systems designed for more robust applications have been known to contain as many as 1000 rules. Specific organizational needs and available expertise generally should determine the contents and size of a knowledge base.

Project Knowledge Base Structure

The exact structure of a rule in an expert system is determined by the particular shell (inference engine or development tool) being used. This section illustrates how rules can be developed using facts from a decision tree. Then, directions to show how the rules can be organized into a knowledge base using a generic structure will be given. For the examples, use the partial cost structure shown in FIG. 7-5.

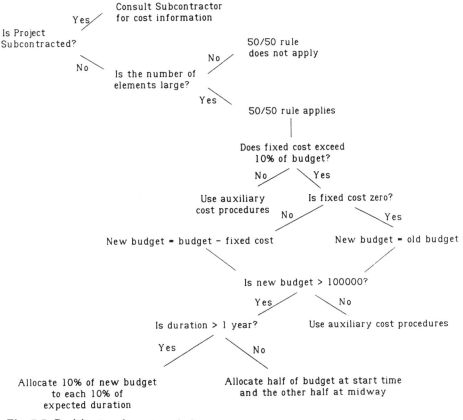

Fig. 7-5. Decision tree for cost analysis.

The decision tree can be as complex and detailed as there are relevant cost relationships. In the representation technique used by most expert systems, a rule is composed of an antecedent (premise) and a consequent (conclusion). The antecedent forms the IF part of the rule and the consequent forms the THEN part. Each antecedent and consequent consists of one or more statements of facts linked by "and." Each statement of fact consists of three parts:

1. Attribute—An attribute is a keyword or phrase chosen to represent the subject of the fact to be determined (e.g., budget).
2. Value—A value is a qualitative or numeric measure assigned to the attribute (e.g., large).
3. Predicate—A predicate is a link used to relate the value to the attribute (e.g., is).

Referring to FIG. 7-5 again, the following generic rules can be generated:

- If the project is subcontracted, then cost information is from a subcontractor.
- If the project elements are large, then the 50/50 rule is applicable.
- If the fixed cost is not zero, then the new budget is procedure new budget.
- If the 50/50 rule is applicable, the new budget is greater than $100,000, and the expected duration is greater than one year, then use the 10 percent allocation procedure.

A procedure is a computational subroutine used to calculate variable values. The computation procedure for new budget might be:

$$\text{New Budget} = \text{Current Budget} - \text{Fixed Cost}$$

The computation procedure for cost allocation might be:

$$\text{Allocation for 10 percent of duration} = 0.10(\text{New Budget})$$

7.11 PROJECT STATE SPACE REPRESENTATION

A state is a set of conditions or values that describe a system at a specified point during processing. The *state space* is the set of all possible states the system could be in during the problem-solving process. State space representation solves problems by moving from an initial state in the space to another state, and eventually to a goal state. The movement from state to state is achieved by the means of operators, typically rules or procedures. A *goal* is a description of an intended state that has not yet been achieved. The process of solving a problem involves finding a sequence of operators that represent a solution path from the initial state to the goal state.

State space techniques have been used extensively to model many management decision problems. By using an expert system and state space modeling, the project management decision process can be greatly enhanced.

A state space model consists of definition state variables that describe the internal state or prevailing configuration of the system being represented. The state variables are related to the system inputs by an equation. An equation also relates both the state variables and system inputs to the outputs of the system. Examples of potential state variables in a project system include product quality level, budget, due date, resource, skill, and productivity level.

In the case of a model described by a system of differential equations, the state-space representation is of the form:

$$\dot{z} = f(z(t), x(t))$$
$$y(t) = g(z(t), x(t))$$

where f and g are vector-valued functions. In the case of linear systems, the representation is of the form:

$$z = Az(t) + Bx(t)$$
$$y(t) = Cz(t) + Dx(t)$$

where $z(t)$, $x(t)$, and $y(t)$ are vectors and A, B, C, and D are matrices. The variable y is the output vector, the variable x denotes the inputs. The state vector $z(t)$ is an intermediate vector relating $x(t)$ to $y(t)$.

The state space representation of a discrete-time linear dynamic system, with respect to a suitable time index, is given by:

$$\dot{z}(t+1) = Az(t) + Bx(t)$$
$$y(t) = Cz(t) + Dx(t)$$

In generic terms, a project system is transformed from one state to another by a driving function that produces a transitional equation given by:

$$\psi = f(x|\Theta) + \epsilon$$

where ψ is the subsequent state, x is the state variable, Θ is the initial state, and ϵ is the error component. The function f is composed of a given action (or a set of actions) applied to the project structure. Each intermediate state can represent a significant milestone in the project system. Thus, a descriptive state space model facilitates an analysis of what actions to apply in order to achieve the next desired state or milestone.

The Project Model

Any human endeavor can be defined as a project. Potential application domains include automated process planning for manufacturing systems, patient monitoring systems in medical applications, military logistics, production scheduling, business movements, economic planning, R & D planning and control, and conventional construction jobs.

A project can be considered as a process of producing a product. The product can be a measurable physical quantity or an intangible conceptual entity. You can consider the product as a single object constructed from a set of subobjects, which are themselves constructed from sub-subobjects. A simple project model is the application of an action to an object that is in a given state or condition.

The application of action constitutes a project activity. The production process involves the planning, coordination, and control of a collection of activities. Project objectives are achieved by state-to-state transformation of successive task phases. FIGURE 7-6 shows the transformation of an object from one state to another through the application of action. The simple representation can be expanded to include other components within the project framework. The hierarchical linking of objects provides a detailed description of the project profile, as shown in FIG. 7-7.

Model Enhancement

The project model can be expanded further in accordance with implicit project requirements. These considerations might include grouping of object classes, precedence linking (both technical and procedural), required communication links, and reporting requirements.

The actions to be taken at each state depend on the prevailing conditions. The natures of the subsequent alternate states depend on what actions are actually implemented. Sometimes there are multiple paths that can lead to the desired end result. At other times, there exists only one unique path to the desired objective. In conventional practice, the characteristics of the future states can only be recognized after the fact, making the development of adaptive plans impossible. In terms of control, deviations are often recognized too

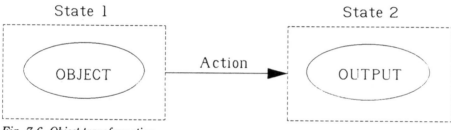

Fig. 7-6. Object transformation.

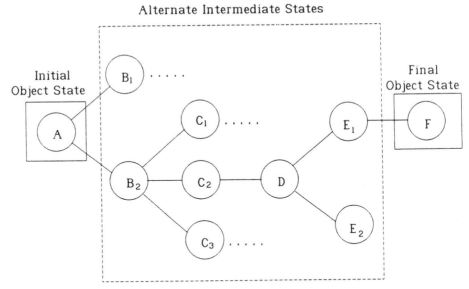

Fig. 7-7. Object state paths.

late to take effective corrective actions. Events occurring inside and outside the project state boundaries can be taken into account in the planning function. These environmental influences are shown in FIG. 7-8.

Project State Representation

A project system can be described by M state variables s_i. The composite state of the system at any given time can then be represented by an M-component vector S.

$$S = \{s_1, s_2 ..., s_M\}$$

The components of the state vector could represent either quantatative or qualitative variables (voltage, investments, energy, color, etc.). You can visualize every state vector as a point in the M-dimensional state space. The representation is unique because every state vector corresponds to one and only one point in the state space.

Project State Transformation

Suppose you have a set of actions (transformation agents) that can be applied to a project to change it from one state to another within the state space. The transformation will change a state vector into another state vector. A transformation, in practical terms, might be heat treatment, firing of a rocket, or a change in management policy. Let T_k be the kth type of transformation. If

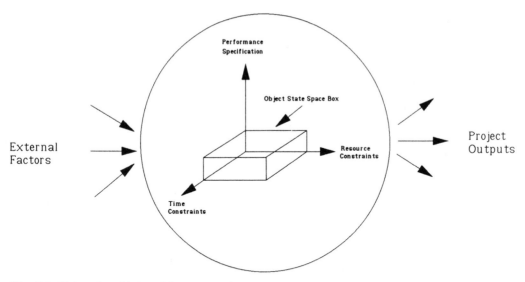

Fig. 7-8. External and internal forces on projects.

T_k is applied to the project when it is in state S, the new state vector will be $T_k(S)$, which is another point in the state space. The number of transformations (or actions) available for a project can be finite or countably infinite. You can construct trajectories that describe the potential states of a project as successive transformations are applied. Each transformation can be repeated as many times as needed. For convenience, you can use the notation T_i to indicate the ith transformation in the sequence of transformations applied to the project. Given an initial state S, the sequence of state vectors is then given by:

$$S_1 = T_1(S)$$
$$S_2 = T_2(S_1)$$
$$S_3 = T_3(S_2)$$
$$\cdot$$
$$\cdot$$
$$\cdot$$
$$S_n = T_n(S_{n-1})$$

The final state S_n depends on the initial state S and the effects of the transformations applied.

State Performance Measurement

A measure of project performance can be obtained at each state of the transformation trajectories. Thus, you can develop a reward function $r^k(S)$ associated with the kth type transformation. The reward specifies the magnitude of gain (time, quality, money, revenue, equipment utilization, etc.) to be achieved by applying a given transformation. The difference between a reward and a performance specification might be used as a criterion for determining project control actions. The performance deviation can be defined as:

$$\delta = r^k(S) - p$$

where p is the performance specification.

Project Policy Development

Given the number of transformations still available and the current state vector, you can develop a policy, P, to be the rule for determining the next transformation to be applied. The total project reward can then be denoted as:

$$r(S|n,P) = r_1(S) + r_2(S_1) + \ldots + r_n(S_{n-1})$$

where n is the number of transformations applied and $r_i(.)$ is the ith reward in the sequence of transformations. You can now visualize a project environment where the starting state vector and the possible actions (transformations) are specified. You must decide what transformations to use in what order to maximize the total reward, i.e., develop the best project plan.

If you let v represent a quantatative measure of the worth of a project plan based on the reward system previously described, then the maximum reward is given by:

$$v(S|n) = \text{Max}\{r(S|n,P)\}$$

The maximization of the reward function is carried out over all possible project policies that can be obtained with n given transformations.

Probabilistic States

In many project situations, the results of applying transformations to the system might not be deterministic. Rather, the new state vector, the reward generated, or both might have to be described by random variables. You can define an expected total reward, $Q(S|n)$, as the sum of the individual expected rewards from all possible states. Let S^p be a possible new state vector generated by the probabilistic process and let $P(S^p|S,T^k)$ be the probability that the new state vector will be S^p if the initial state vector is S and the transformation T^k is applied. Now write a recursive relation for the expected total reward as:

$$Q(S|n) = \underset{k}{\text{Max}} \{r^k(S) + \underset{S^p}{\Sigma} Q(S^p|n-1)P(S^p|S,T^k)\},$$

for n = 1,2,3,...

The notation $r^{-k}(S)$ is used to designate the expected reward received by applying the kth type transformation to the system when it is described by state vector S. The above procedure allows the possibility that the terminal reward itself might be a random variable. Thus, the state space model permits a complete analysis of all the ramifications and uncertainties of the project management system.

7.12 STATE SPACE AND EXPERT SYSTEMS IMPLEMENTATION

The IF-THEN structure of knowledge representation for expert systems provides a mechanism for evaluating the multiplicity of project states under diversified actions. Expert systems have the advantages of consistency, comprehensive evaluation of all available data, accessibility, infinite retention of information, and lack of bias. An integrated project planning and control system using state space and expert systems is shown in FIG. 7-9.

As project manager, you might interact with the state space model and the expert system by doing the following:

- Perform the real-time monitoring of the project and then supply inputs to the state space model
- Get feedback from the state model
- Consult the expert system based on the state space information
- Get recommendations from the expert system

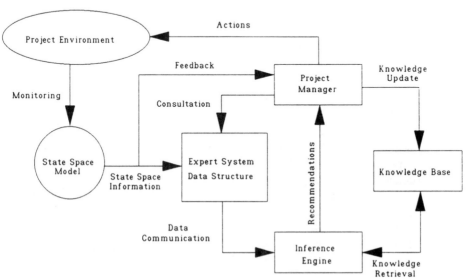

Fig. 7-9. State space and expert system model.

- Take project actions that eventually generate further inputs to the state model
- Update the expert system knowledge base as new project management knowledge is acquired

The supply of state space information to both you and the expert system in FIG. 7-9 will serve as a control measure. In case you do not utilize all available information, the expert system can query you for justification.

Consultation with an expert system is effected by logging on the computer, loading the inference engine, identifying the knowledge base, and entering relevant project data. Valuable cost control recommendations can be obtained in a matter of minutes. You will no longer need to read voluminous cost guides or waste productive time trying to locate an expert to handle routine cost functions. Expert systems can significantly enhance the functions of project analysts. The systems can handle routine cost analysis and rule-based decision analysis, thus, freeing you, the expert, to concentrate your efforts on crucial project problems.

8

Computer-aided
Project Control

The number of project management software packages has been growing steadily for the past several years. Gido (1985) presents a comprehensive directory of project management software available as of 1985. The directory listing for project management packages has grown substantially since then, however, Assad (1986) suggests that the market for microcomputer-based project management software was around $10 million in 1984. That appears to be an underestimation based on the strength of the current trend in the market. Day-Copeland (1988) also presents a trend analysis that indicates a strong growth in the project management software market.

This chapter presents a brief evaluation of some selected project management systems. The use of computer software in project management and control is also discussed. The significance of computer information flow for project monitoring and control is emphasized. A few selected case studies are presented to illustrate the use of computer software in managing projects. Appendix B presents the names and addresses of some vendors of project management software vendors.

8.1 COMMERCIAL PROJECT MANAGEMENT PACKAGES

Project management software packages available on mainframe computers are essentially directed toward large, complex projects. The microcomputer-based packages are geared toward small projects. The major advantage of microcomputer packages lies in their user friendliness, ease of use, accessibility, and interactive features. A few selected project management software packages are discussed in this section.

The features discussed are representative of what is available in the market. Due to the frequency of changes in the products and the available features, the best way to get an up-to-date evaluation (price, characteristics, size, etc.) of the available commercial packages is to refer to frequently published trade magazines. Magazines such as PC Week carry regular buyers' guides and comparative evaluations of project management software. Due to the limited space available, many deserving project management packages have been omitted from our discussions. Hence, the fact that a product is mentioned or not mentioned here is neither an indication of its superiority nor its mediocrity. The discussions are presented only to suggest a basis for evaluating project management software packages. By observing the list of capabilities presented, you can put together a shopping list containing items to look for when buying project management software. Appendix A provides a directory of some of the available software packages.

Microsoft Project

Microsoft Project, developed by Microsoft Corporation, requires 256K RAM and DOS 2.0 or later to run. This package is noted for its simplicity and straightforward approach to project management. The software is based on the Gantt chart. The network is created by entering the activity parameters such as predecessors, duration, start date, percent completed, resource requirements, and so on in the Gantt chart itself. The duration parameter can be minutes, hours, days, weeks, months, or years. Thus, a suitable time scale can be developed for any given project. The number of predecessors per activity is restricted to 16, and the number of resources per activity is limited to 8. This is adequate for most of the small projects that you are likely to encounter.

For large projects, Microsoft Project has a provision for linking different subprojects together. Each subproject appears as an activity in the main project. The program also allows you to replace one linked file in a master project with another, allowing you to customize your master project by substituting small pieces of projects in a modular fashion. The Gantt chart associated with the project being managed is shown on the screen and permits viewing of up to 18 activities at a time. This feature facilitates better tracking of a project. Symbols denoting crucial activities, milestones, predecessors, and so on are easy to understand. Microsoft Project can sort activities by criticality as well as by any other secondary parameters such as duration, early start, and so on. Like most other packages, the PERT chart is very poorly portrayed on the computer screen and presents hardly any significant information.

A noteworthy feature of Microsoft Project is the effective use of split screens. The program permits you to view both the forecasted and the actual project Gantt chart at the same time. You can make a quick performance appraisal of the project progress with displays of both charts.

By using another split screen feature, you can view the list of activities that a particular resource is assigned to and the resource histogram at the same time. The resource histogram shows the pattern of resource utilization over a period of time.

The report writing feature of the software is very flexible. It is designed in a way that you can customize your reports to emphasize specific parameters of interest. The cost tracking capability by the software appears to be poor. However, an analyst can export the project data to a spreadsheet program for a better cost analysis. An on-line tutorial is provided with the program. The tutorial helps you quickly get up to speed in use of the software.

In summary, Microsoft Project is a low-cost project management package devoid of fancy features. As a low-end product, this package is easy to use and can be effectively used to manage most small projects.

Advanced Project Workbench

Advanced Project Workbench was developed by Applied Business Technology Corporation. It requires 512K RAM and DOS 2.0 or higher. The package is oriented toward people as project resources. It offers the choice of hierarchical level in a project schedule. You can enter data into a phase level, activity level, or task level. Data is entered into a Gantt chart model of the project being managed. Task bars of appropriate length are generated automatically.

For managing resources, Advanced Project workbench calculates the total work effort instead of effort by each resource. This method leads to a problem: you must count the little boxes in a bar to see how long a task will take in real time. Also, the only resources that the program is designed to handle are human resources. Data relating to the personnel's name, ID initials, working days per week, pay per week, and so on are required to be entered to get reports on resource scheduling. Even though the program specifically deals with human resources, you can use it for other resource types by simply describing those resources as if they were people. For example, a machine might be described as a person whose name is Machine A, with initials M. A., working five days per week, and making $1,500 per week. In that case, the weekly pay of the machine can be prorated based on the operating cost of the machine.

The Gantt chart displays the resource, the resource ID, and a spreadsheet of the resource's associated work effort. The time scale divisions are either in weeks or months. The average work effort of each resource is reported, and automatic resource leveling can be performed by the program. Because the program is based on people as resources, cost reports are somewhat limited. The only cost reports that are generated are the total project plan reports concerning different costs, and the status report. The status report compares the actual costs against planned costs for each activity. The report-generation capabilities of the packages are flexible, and the project data can be sorted in a variety of ways.

The graphics capabilities in the program are used to develop the Gantt chart, the PERT chart, and the dependency definition diagram. The program appears to be an excellent tool for people-oriented project management environments.

Qwiknet Professional

Qwiknet Professional, developed by Project Software and Development Inc., is designed for professional project management analysts. It requires 512K RAM and DOS 2.0 and up. A lot of time and effort is required to learn the program in order to make full use of its capabilities. You can customize project views and report layouts, but will need to spend a lot of time organizing and entering data to take advantage of the unique features of the program. You can create a project by filling out the numerous forms and adding constraints and resource usage levels.

The package has a well-developed automatic resource-leveling feature. The first type of leveling is resource-limited leveling: the project is delayed to enable the availability of 100% of the resources for all the activities in the project. The other type of leveling considers both time and resource availability when smoothing out a resource use. An auto scheduling feature in the program is also provided in the program. This feature automatically generates CPM analysis. It can be turned off to enable editing a project without slowing down the computation process.

The report generation capability of Qwiknet Professional is good and allows for sorting and selecting to create flexible reports. A project can be sorted in many ways to be used in combination with the 25 report forms. The package does not have a good graphics capability, and the printed version of charts is not very easy to understand. The time scale is confusing because the initials for days are all squeezed together; the bar chart symbols are also unclear.

The user interface of the package makes Qwiknet Professional easy to use. It uses a mouse for invoking commands, picking menu options, and even filling forms. Qwiknet also allows the opening of multiple windows to work on more than one part of the project simultaneously, and allows the importing and exporting of files. Because the program is oriented toward textual reporting, the software might not appeal much to you if you like information presented graphically.

Artemis Project

Metier Management Systems has introduced a PC version of its Artemis mainframe project management software. The PC version, named Artemis Project, provides full-featured mainframe and minicomputer project management capability. It runs on IBM XTs, ATs, and compatibles equipped with 512K

RAM and 3.5M bytes of hard disk space. The program lets you enter information about each activity involved in completing a project, including a description, duration, and cost. You also can specify the order (precedence relationships) in which activities must be performed.

Artemis Project can track up to 60,000 activities at a time, giving you the capability to handle multiple projects. The software package comes with its own built-in relational database. Files can be converted to and from Artemis mainframe and minicomputer formats, as well as dBASE III and Lotus 1-2-3 formats. Pull-down menus and an on-line help feature guide you through the program.

Super Project Plus

Super Project Plus is a product of Computer Associates International, Inc. It requires 320K RAM and DOS 2.0 or later. You can customize the program to fit your level of expertise. No matter what skill level you might be, you can benefit from Super features. In the beginner's mode, the program allows only basic project planning and scheduling. In the expert mode, you can take advantage of the full potential of the software.

Super Project Plus is oriented toward the PERT chart. You can create a project by entering the data such as task number, task name, resource, duration, start and end dates in a task box. One limitation with task data entry is that duration in minutes cannot be entered in the unit. The program allows task windows, but a window can only display six tasks at a time. This limitation makes it difficult to comprehend the precedence relationships.

The Gantt chart layout is one of the better features of this software. The differentiation of symbols in the charts is clear. Crucial activities are color-coded making the chart easy to review. Activity additions are done in the PERT chart. The program is very flexible with respect to calendars. Every resource has a calendar, and you can set work hours in the project calendar for any time of day. You can specify, both long and short work days.

There is no limitation to the number of tasks and resources the software can handle. One drawback of the package is its report writing feature. A few canned report formats are provided in the program, and you cannot customize reports. No resource histograms are provided by the program. The program has file export facilities to Lotus 1-2-3 and dBASE, but not file-import capability. On-screen help is available in the program. The user interface uses both pull-down menus and keyboard commands.

Time Line

Time Line was developed by Breakthrough Software Company. It requires 256K RAM and DOS 2.0 or higher. A graphics add-on module is available for the package. Time Line is one of the most popular PC-level project management software packages. It is powerful and versatile, and an effective tool for both professionals and beginners. One of the first things to do before constructing a project is set up a calendar. The program allows you to set any day and all hours of the day and night as work time. After the calendar is set, data is required to be entered into the Gantt chart.

Crucial activities can be made to appear as highlighted bars in Gantt charts. As many as 19 activities can be viewed on the Gantt chart at one time. The Gantt chart in Time Line provides more information than is available in most other project management packages. Partial dependencies and resource conflicts, as well as both negative and positive slacks are displayed on the chart.

The PERT chart is represented on the screen along one horizontal line that obscures the visual clues to activity relationships and makes the chart difficult to read. Also, there are not directional arrows on the PERT chart.

The program does not have the facility to zoom in on the overall project. The filter feature available in the program allows you to highlight tasks by criticality, resources, data ranges, and so on. Tasks that do not fit a specified set of criteria can be hidden from view. This feature is very useful for analyzing a project to identify potential problems. It helps in giving special attention to certain aspects of the project.

In order to simplify its operations and keep tasks up to date, Time Line has a tickler feature called the "alarm clock." The system will give an audio as well as visual signal with tasks that need to be updated. It also provides an automatic resource-leveling features to resolve resource conflicts.

The reporting features of Time Line are fairly standard with about 12 basic reports that can be customized. Filtering helps to attain a fair degree of flexibility. Unfortunately, despite having excellent Gantt chart features, you cannot compare planned versus actual progress graphically. An on-line tutorial provides an excellent user interface for learning the program.

Version 3.0 of Time Line was released in 1988. It offers expanded capabilities that in no way compromise its utility and simplicity. The new capabilities of this versatile project management program include outlining, long note fields, customizable screen layouts, and reports. The ability to undo or redo up to 999 steps in a project allows you to explore alternate project plans.

Project Scheduler Network

This software was developed by Scitor Corporation and requires 320K RAM. Project Scheduler has some of the best graphics available in low-end project management packages. The PERT chart is the core of the program, and it is there that the task relationships are established. To create a PERT chart, you must list all the activities in the data entry screen. You must then use a mouse to place each activity on the screen. The PERT chart displays a lot of information including work breakdown structure code, activity name, activity number, start and finish dates, and the current status as a percentage of the duration.

Project Scheduler is equipped with seven levels of magnification to choose from. You can view either an overall picture or a detailed picture of the project.

Color coding is effectively used in the Gantt chart. Solid green bars denote completed activities and incomplete tasks are shown as outlines. Red is used for critical tasks and white for noncritical tasks. Slacks are represented by hatched bars. Time scale on the Gantt chart can be adjusted to display in days, weeks, or months. By using the split screen feature, you can view a Gantt chart as well as a resource histogram at the same time. The Gantt chart reflects only those tasks to which the particular resource is assigned.

Several cost curves can be developed in Project Scheduler. One of the possible curves is the three-line comparative cost curve depicting current planned costs, baseline planned costs, and actual costs. However, sorting of tasks is somewhat limited and tasks cannot be sorted by critical activities, resource, and so on. Project Scheduler makes use of pull-down menus, mouse pointing, and function keys.

Primavera

Primavera is a product offered by Primavera Systems. It requires 640K RAM and a hard disk. Price discounts are available for the purchase of multiple copies. A graphics option for Primavera is available.

The package can handle up to 10,000 tasks per project and the number of resources per project is unlimited. Facilities are provided for linking multiple projects. The package also has an interface to mini or mainframe packages such as the Primavera Project Planner package. Different levels of user access and authority can be assigned in the program. Some of the data integrity capabilities of Primavera include file locking and user passwords.

The package caters to both Gantt and PERT charts and provides resource loading reports. Resource leveling is performed in a simplified format. Activities can be entered in precedence or I-J format. It allows up to 130 successors per activity in precedence networks. The package also supports 64-character activity coding and allows work breakdown structuring and the assignment of organizational responsibilities. Project schedule parameters and criteria can be used to generate reports, sort files, and provide "task select" capabilities.

On the economic side, Primavera adjusts cost estimates for inflation and computes an earned value measure for projects. It provides on-line viewing of bar charts, resource/cost histograms, and resource/cost cumulative curves. Primavera is a complete tool for planning and scheduling all types of projects and can handle very large and complex projects efficiently. With its extensive capabilities, Primavera can handle what-if analysis to enhance project management functions.

ViewPoint

ViewPoint was developed by Computer Aided Management company. This package is an excellent program with no limitations on the size of projects or the amount of resources one can assign to a task. It is one of the best low-priced packages available. ViewPoint combines power and user friendliness very well.

You can create a project on a time scaled network screen. The time scale gives a temporal dimension to the network along with the structural dimension. Resources are entered into a separate form where they are allocated to tasks. In addition to specifying the general resource information, you can specify that a resource rate be variable with respect to a given time period.

ViewPoint's multiple project capability is one of its most powerful features. In addition to grouping projects together, ViewPoint allows each project to maintain its file integrity. The standard report formats provided by the program can be expanded by using the sorting and selecting facilities available. The program is equipped with an ASCII word processor. With the processor, you can design a customized form and save it as a standard report format.

In addition to the time scaled PERT chart, you can display a Gantt chart. You also can display the baseline bars for comparison of planned versus actual progress. The on-screen graphics includes a network tree which shows a structural diagram of the main task divisions in a project. Resource histograms can also be generated. Simplified user interfaces are used extensively in the program that include: pull-down menus, pop-up forms, mouse, and function key commands. The package is also equipped with a rudimentary programming language for creating macros and customized reports. Version 3.1 of ViewPoint has eight capabilities:

1. Adjusts a previously saved project model by a specified percentage (e.g., 10 percent) to handle additional amounts of work
2. Reports progress from a dBASE III application
3. Generates outputs of project data in dBASE III, Lotus, or ASCII formats
4. Estimates labor and materials for a project
5. Has an interface to other project management packages
6. Creates an audit trail by importing time card data on human resources as they relate to project work and automatically exports it directly into an accounting system
7. Uses pick-up and copy-down keys in form and table formats to facilitate ease of data entry
8. Has file-locking capability for the management or multiuser access on project files

Promis

Strategic Software Planning Corp. has released version 3.0 of Promis, one of the mid-range project management packages. This software significantly increases the number of activities you can schedule on a network. Promis version 3.0 runs on the IBM PC XT, AT, PS/2, and compatibles and requires 512K RAM and a hard disk.

Promis is used to manage the schedules, resources, and costs of a task. It is typically used by managers of large, complex projects. The software has found extensive uses in the aerospace, defense, and electronic telecommunications industries. It provides managers with the ability to break down a project network into subnetworks. Subnetworking divides activities into more detailed levels. As many as 2,000 activities can be scheduled at any network level.

Promis version 3.0 supports *hammocking,* which links different levels of a project so that changes in one level are made throughout the entire network. Promis also lets managers separate the project levels for individual needs. Hammocking facilitates the generation of reports that are meaningful to everyone from the supervisor on a job site, who only wants the list of tasks to be performed on a given day, to top management executives, who only want to know whether or not a contracted deadline can be met.

Topdown Project Planner

Topdown Project Planner is a product of Ajida Technology, Inc. It is an intuitive project management system that emphasizes planning. Projects that are properly planned identify potential management problems before they occur. Topdown uses an hierarchical model of a PERT chart. Tasks are divided into groups of smaller tasks, which are further divided into groups of smaller and smaller tasks. This dividing permits you to enter project data with as much detail you want.

An unlimited number of resources (e.g., personnel, equipment, etc.) and expenses (e.g., overhead costs) can be assigned to any task. The program monitors resource usage and costs automatically. It will level resources to prevent overloading. Costs are automatically calculated as task dates are calculated. Costs can be displayed for any task, or group of tasks, by period or as cumulative over time. Because the hierarchical project definition implicitly defines the work breakdown structure, summary reports can be easily generated.

Topdown generates presentation quality reports that are suitable for distribution. Reports can be filtered and sorted by more than 20 different attributes. Thus, you can get desired information in a desired format.

Harvard Project Manager

Software Publishing Corporation has struck a balance with its latest project management software product, Harvard Project Manager 3.0 The product provides proficient users with advanced reporting and scheduling features and novice users with a simple "get-started" module. It offers expanded import/export capabilities to popular PC programs such as Lotus 1-2-3 and dBASE III, more flexible reporting options, and new project planning tools. This software package requires 512K RAM.

If you are new to project management software, you can invoke Fast Track, a new module designed to get you scheduling tasks in 15 minutes. Fast Track employs a time scale, allowing you to manage an entire project easily. You can plug in task names and durations along the scale, and then add, delete, or move tasks to modify the project. If a PERT chart, Gantt chart or work breakdown outline is required, Harvard Project Manager 3.0 automatically builds the charts from the Fast Track data. For more complex projects, the program includes a work breakdown feature that lets a project be broken down into scheduling tasks, either graphically or in outline form. After the project is broken down, summary reports and charts can be generated.

An enhanced resource calendar in the program monitors resources over the life of a project. Individual calendars can be created for each resource that takes into account vacation time or nonstandard work weeks. The program automatically tracks resource allocations across all projects and has a feature that will resolve resource conflicts automatically. Up to 200 resources can be leveled simultaneously and resource histograms can be generated.

The new reporting features of Harvard Project Manager include the ability to output 26 graphs or reports, a batch capability for unattended printing, and a template option that lets you save predefined formatting criteria for quick generation of custom reports.

PAC III

PAC III, developed by AGS Management Systems, is a totally integrated project management system. The package is a mainframe product that combines sophisticated networking, resource scheduling, estimating, and cost accounting functions into a single project management system. It operates on IBM mainframes and DEC VAX minicomputers.

PAC III offers a fast, easy, simple, and reliable way to plan and manage complex multitask projects. It can be used to plan single or multiple projects and has the capability for sharing multiple resources across functional project lines. Some of the specific functions provided by PAC III include budgeting, planning, networking, time analysis, simulation, resource leveling, critical path analysis, progress reporting, status accounting, statistical analysis, project monitoring, cost accounting, automatic audit trail, custom reporting, and graphics.

The interactive capabilities of PAC III permit you to do the following quickly: define new projects, generate cost estimates and budgets, review network resources, report project status, evaluate "what-if" scenarios, and monitor project progress. An on-line editing function checks inputs and immediately reports any problems or inconsistencies.

The system generates more than 40 standard report formats for planning, simulation, and management of projects. Reports can be individually selected for management-by-exception (MBO) reporting needs. PAC III uses color-coded network graphics that make it easy to visualize the relationships between events in a project. The program's automated visual display provides clear, informative network diagrams that show the project tasks, critical activities with float, and project progress compared to schedule.

In addition to project network graphics, PAC III also has a management graphics module that displays schedules and budgets in Gantt or Pie chart format by project, phase, activity, or resource. The outputs of the management graphics module are very useful for quick status reports of projects. The earned value capability in PAC III compares scheduled work and budgets with actual performance and provides an automated facility for detailed performance analysis.

Even though PAC III is a mainframe product, it offers an interface to PC-based packages such as PAC Micro and Estiplan. PAC Micro and Estiplan are also products of AGS Management Systems. With PAC Micro, you can plan, budget, and analyze alternatives on a personal computer before invoking the full power of PAC III on a mainframe. Estiplan builds custom work breakdown structures, creates time and cost estimates for evaluation, and then automatically creates input for PAC III.

VISION

VISION is a minicomputer based project management system from Systonetics, Inc. VISION is an advanced user-oriented management information system that transforms data into information for managing projects. It is developed to run on DEC VAX and Prime minicomputers. Its "cousins," Acu-VISION, and VISIONmicro run on IBM mainframe and IBM PC/XT/AT respectively. VISION automates the creation and maintenance of a database that models all aspects of a project. Cost and resource-related data are totally integrated with activity and schedule data. Some of the specific capabilities of the package are:

- Network scheduling of critical path and precedence models
- Multiple resource allocation, tracking, and projection
- Resource-constrained scheduling and leveling
- Cost tracking projection and reporting
- What-if analysis
- Sophisticated graphical representation in the form of Networks, Bar charts, and management graphs
- Standard, flexible reporting formats for cost, resource, and scheduling information
- User-oriented, free-format report writer for customized reporting
- Performance measurement reporting and graphics

A user interacts with VISION through a friendly user interface. New or updated project information is entered directly into the database. A change in project data and its impact can be reviewed quickly and you can make any additions and corrections immediately. The program enables you to cope with masses of details and be able to respond quickly to project crises.

VISION has the ability to satisfy reporting requirements at any level of management. You can stratify the database of a project into arbitrarily defined levels based on managerial needs. Selected activities can be combined from the databases of many projects based on some common attribute. With this capability, you can get a top-down perspective on what is crucial in managing multiple projects. VISION provides the ability to conditionally select, summarize, and sort information to narrow the focus and precision of desired reporting and graphical representations.

8.2 COMPUTER INFORMATION FLOW

The flow of information in project management is a crucial aspect of the function of project analysts. Information is the basis for making all project decisions. Information must be available in the right quantity, in the right format, in the right place, and at the right time. Computers can play a significant role in ensuring the proper flow of information for project management. The capabilities of conventional project management software packages can be coupled with the capabilities of other software tools to facilitate efficient computer information flow (CIF).

Information must be tracked from its origination all the way to its destination. The information tracking system will encompass the following elements:

- Data acquisition
- Data processing
- Data storage
- Data retrieval
- Data transmission
- Data reception
- Data usage

Within a given environment, one or more of these elements will be given particular emphasis. There are specific software tools designed for managing each of the elements. Thus, the ability to integrate the various software capabilities in achieving the desired management and control of project information becomes necessary. Data entry systems and real-time monitoring systems will emphasize the efficiency of the data collection procedures. Query systems will emphasize data communication by using appropriate user interfaces. Modeling systems will emphasize the processing of data to generate information, and data communication systems will emphasize the transmission of project data from one location to another. Tracking of computer information flow will enable you to:

- Identify value-added points in a project
- Identify potential failure points in a project

One mechanism for enhancing the control of information flow is to establish a centralized project database library whenever possible. With this library, any project analyst will have access to the needed information by going through formal retrieve channels, as shown in FIG. 8-1.

To resolve the problems caused by separate project databases within an organization, the concept of an integrated database could be implemented. In an integrated database, all information used by separate departments is stored in a single database that can be accessed by all users. Each user might not need all of the information, but any information that is needed can be found in the integrated database.

A good example of managing computer information flow is provided by American Airlines, Inc. The airline is revolutionizing the way it handles information. American has created an electronic platform that will eliminate much of the paperwork in its operations. The platform will be one universal system of interconnected PCs, minicomputers, and mainframe computers. The system, named InterAct, will provide almost all of American's employees around the world with a consistent set of tools to automate functions now performed by personnel on a wide array of equipment types. Users will work from Hewlett-Packard's NewWave graphical user interface to access a centralized collection of general and customized applications.

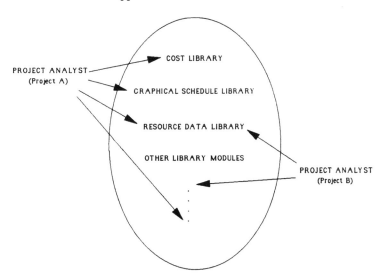

Fig. 8-1. Centralized flow of project information.

The aim of InterAct is to put information at the fingertips of employees at all operational levels. People seeking information would not have to go through the traditional intermediate points, such as middle managers. Employees access information directly so that they can make appropriate decisions in a timely manner. People in different geographical locations can interrelate and pull information together quickly. The initial phase of the InterAct system will make about 14,000 networked PCs available to clerical workers and middle managers. Personal computers on Token-Ring networks, which are internetworked with Hewlett-Packard minicomputers, will provide workers with a central foundation for electronic mail, document filing, and word processing.

Another technology that can enhance computer information flow for project management is ISDN (Integrated Services Digital Network). ISDN permits the transmission of voice, text, or data over a single communication device. With ISDN, specific information about a project can be dictated over a telephone line, merged with data from a centralized database, and manipulated to generate printed reports. It then can be transmitted through an ISDN to associated project offices.

The use of reporting capabilities in project management software packages has facilitated better communication among project members. Through the use of computer-generated reports, project analysts who typically relied on verbal reports of project updates now can be made fully aware of crucial project information, such as the costs associated with each task, the location of a project in relation to the original plan, and the resources necessary to get a project back on schedule. Upper-level managers can obtain summary reports that provide them with general project status information, which can be used for project control purposes.

Through the use of an itemized chart showing costs according to task, the project accounting department is better informed about project expenditures. If a project management software package lacks the flexibility of customized reports, project data can be downloaded from the program to tools like dBASE III PLUS, where the desired report formats can be generated. The major focus of computer information flow is to provide a reporting mechanism that can be used for project monitoring and control.

8.3 PROJECT MONITORING AND CONTROL

Time, cost, and performance form the basis for the operating characteristics of a project. These same factors help determine the basis for project control. *Project control* is the process of reducing the deviation between actual performance and planned performance. To be able to control a project, you must be able to measure performance. Measurements are taken on each of the three components of project constraints: time, performance, and cost. FIGURE 8-2 presents a conceptual model of the interaction among these three control elements in a project management environment. The traditional procedures for measur-

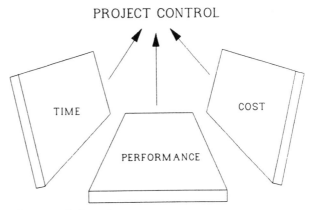

Fig. 8-2. Project control elements.

ing project progress, evaluating performance, and taking control actions are not adequate for modern project management environments where technology-induced events occur at a rapid rate and at different locations.

Computers are needed to provide the capabilities for acquiring large amounts of data, measuring the data, and presenting a formal analysis in a consistent and timely manner. The use of expert systems and real-time data entry and analysis techniques will enable project managers to keep track of small and large projects. Appropriate control actions also can be instituted in real time before project problems get out of hand. Some of the things that can cause a project to require control are:

1. Time
   - Missed milestones
   - Delay of key tasks
   - Increased need for expediting
   - Unreliable time estimates
   - Time-consuming technical problems
   - Lack of explicit precedence relationships
   - Change of due dates
   - New industry regulations that need time to implement
   - Supply delays
2. Performance
   - Poor quality
   - Low reliability
   - Fragile components
   - Poor functionality
   - Maintenance problems
   - High risk implementation
   - Restricted access

- Poor mobility
- Technical difficulties
- Resources not available when needed
- Change order from client
- Conflict of functional objectives
- New technology adaptation

3. Cost
- Cost overruns
- Budget revisions
- Inadequate resources
- Price changes
- Poor cost reporting
- Increase in scope of work
- Incorrect bids
- Insufficient Project Cash Flows
- High overhead rates
- High labor cost
- Increased delay penalties

When a deviation from expectation occurs, the project analyst should conduct variance analysis. The five key questions to be asked in the analysis include:

1. What is the cause of the variance?
2. How does the variance affect the project?
3. How does the variance affect other ongoing operations?
4. What corrective action should be taken to reduce the variance?
5. What is the expected result of the corrective action?

Schedule Control

The Gantt Charts developed in the scheduling phase of a project can serve as the yardstick for measuring project progress. Project status should be monitored frequently. Symbols can be used to mark actual activity positions on the Gantt chart. A record should be maintained of the difference between where the activity should be and where it actually is. This information is then conveyed to the appropriate personnel. The more milestones or control points in the project, the better. A larger number allows for more frequent and distinct avenues for monitoring the schedule. With more milestones, problems can be identified and controlled before they accumulate into an unmanageable magnitude.

Scheduled variance magnitudes can be plotted on a time scale (e.g., on a daily basis). If the variance continues to get worse, drastic actions might be needed. Temporary deviations without a lasting effect on the project might not be a cause for concern. Some corrective actions that can be taken for project schedule delays are:

- Crashing of activities (expediting)
- Minor redesign
- Elimination of unnecessary activities
- Productive improvement
- Reevaluation of milestones or due dates
- Revision of project master plan
- Revision of time estimates for pending activities
- Recomputation of activity network data

Performance Control

Most project performance problems will not surface until after the project is completed, making performance control very difficult. However, every effort should be made to measure all the interim factors of the project. After-the-fact measurements generally don't serve the purpose of control very well.

Some of the performance problems might be indicated by time and cost deviations. So, when project time and cost have problems, an analysis of how the problems affect performance should be made. Because project performance requirements usually relate to the performance of the end products, controlling performance problems might necessitate altering the product specifications. Performance analysis will involve checking key elements of the product such as:

1. Scope
   - Is the scope reasonably based on the project environment (too wide versus too narrow)?
   - Can the required reliability (grade, level, etc.) be achieved with the available resources?
2. Documentation
   - Is the requirement specification accurate?
   - Are statements clearly understood?
3. Requirement
   - Is the technical basis for the specification sound?
   - Are requirements properly organized?
   - What are the interations between specific requirements?
   - How does the prototype or sample perform?
   - Is the material appropriate?
   - What is a reasonable level of reliability?
   - What is the durability of the product?
   - What are the maintainability characteristics?
   - Is the product transportable as needed?
   - What are the chemical and physical properties, if any?

- Are the dimensions satisfactory (weight, color, size, finish, etc.)?
- Is the workmanship acceptable?
4. Quality Assurance
   - Who is responsible for inspection?
   - What are the inspection policies and methods?
   - What actions are needed for a nonconforming item?
5. Function
   - Is the product usable as designed?
   - Can the expected use be achieved by other means?
   - What are the potentials for misuse?

Careful evaluation of the performance basis throughout a project's life cycle should help identify problems early so that managerial actions can be taken to forestall greater problems later.

Cost Control

Cost control is a very expansive topic. Numerous accounting and reporting systems have been developed over the years for project cost monitoring and control. The level of interest in this topic is probably an indication of the sensitivity of the subject matter. The complete cost management involves a good control of each of the following:

- Cost estimating
- Cost accounting
- Project cash flow
- Company cash flow
- Direct labor costing
- Overhead rate costing
- Incentives, penalties, and bonuses
- Overtime pays

Each of the first four items in the previous list could be a whole subject by itself. Costs can become so intractable that we rarely find manual cost tracking in today's complex projects. Most project cost analyses are now done by computerized accounting systems. The process of controlling cost covers ten key issues that management must address:

1. Proper planning of the project to justify the basis for cost elements
2. Reliable estimation of time, resources, and cost
3. Clear communication of project requirements, constraints, and available resources
4. Sustained cooperation of project personnel
5. Good coordination of project functions
6. Strict policy of expenditure authorization

7. Timely recording and reporting of project consumptions: time, materials, labor, and budget
8. Frequent review of project progress
9. Periodic revision of schedule to account for prevailing project scenario
10. Periodic evaluation of the reasonableness of budget depletion versus actual progress

These ten items must be evaluated as an integrated control effort, rather than as individual functions. The interactions among the various actions needed might be so unpredictable that the success achieved on one side can be masked by failure on another side, making cost performance tracking even more elusive. Management must, therefore, be alert and persistent in the cost monitoring function.

Some government agencies, such as DOE, have implemented cost control techniques aimed at managing large projects that are typical in government contracts. The cost and schedule control system (C/SCS) of DOE is based on work breakdown structure (WBS) and can quantitatively measure project performance at a particular point in the project life cycle.

Another useful cost control technique is the Accomplishment Cost Procedure (ACP). This technique is a simple approach for relating resources allocated to actual work accomplished. It presents costs based on scheduled accomplishments, rather than as a function of time. In order to determine the progress of an individual effort with respect to cost, the cost/progress relationship in the project plan is compared to the cost/progress relationship actually achieved. The major aspect of the ACP technique is that it is not biased against high costs. It gives proper credit to high costs as long as comparable project progress is maintained.

FIGURE 8-3 presents a model of how a computer-based project monitoring and control system might be implemented. In the model, a computer tool is

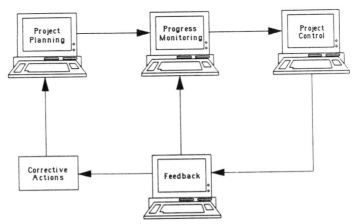

Fig. 8-3. Project feedback control system.

used during the project planning stage. In the monitoring stage, a computer tool monitors the progress of the project by comparing actual performance to expected performance. A feedback of the observed deviation between plan and accomplishment is then sent back to the planning stages, along with potential corrective actions. With the feedback information, appropriate replanning is done to bring the project back in line with the time-phased objectives of the project.

Control charts similar to that shown in FIG. 8-4 also can be developed for monitoring and controlling projects. Control limits can be incorporated into the chart trigger when control actions should be taken. Multiple control limits can be used to determine various levels of control points. The incorporation of fuzzy logic and expert systems (Kangari and Boyer 1989) can indicate shades of control areas and levels of risk management required. Control charts can be developed for cost, schedule, resource utilization, performance, and other measures of project evaluation.

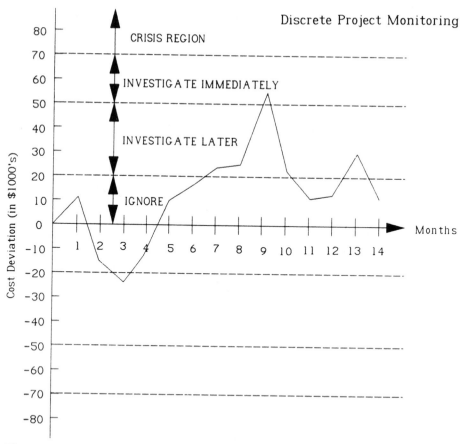

Fig. 8-4. Project control chart limits (discrete monitoring).

FIGURE 8-4 represents a case of discrete monitoring of project progress. Cost is monitored and recorded on a monthly basis. If the cost is monitored on a more frequent basis, days for example, then we might be able to draw a more curvelinear cost plot as shown in the control chart in FIG. 8-5. Of course, you will need to decide whether the additional time needed for continuous monitoring is justified by the extra level of control provided. The control limits can be calculated with the same procedures used for X-bar and R charts in quality control or they can be based on management stipulations. In addition to drawing control charts for cost, you can draw them for other measures of performance, such as task duration, quality, or resource utilization.

FIGURE 8-6 shows a control chart for cumulative cost. The control limits on the chart are indexed to the project percent complete. At each percent complete point, there is a control limit that the cumulative project cost is not expected to exceed. A review of FIG. 8-6 shows that the cumulative cost is out of control at the 10%, 30%, 40%, 50%, 60%, and 80% completion points. Thus,

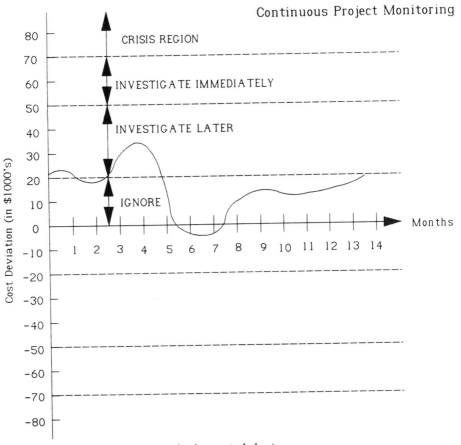

Fig. 8-5. Continuous project monitoring control chart.

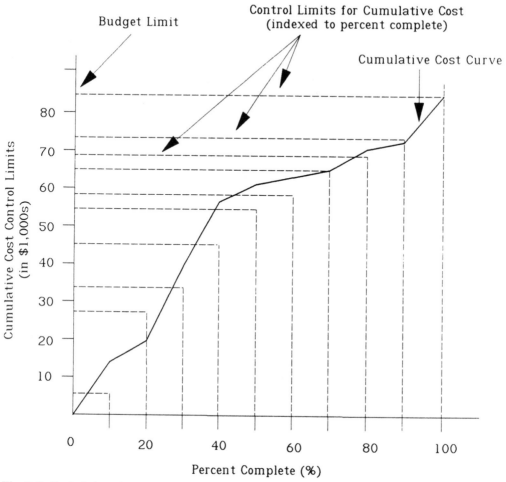

Fig. 8-6. Control chart for cumulative cost.

the indication is that managerial control should be instituted right from the 10% completion point. If no control action is taken, the cumulative cost might continue to be out of control and eventually exceed the budget limit by the time the project is finished.

The information obtained from the project monitoring capabilities of project management software can be transformed into meaningful charts that quickly identify when control actions are needed. For example, FIG. 8-7 shows the resource loading plots for three different resource types. The percent of the project complete is shown on the same chart to provide information about resource expenditure relative to work accomplished. The chart can provide information about resource overallocation, as well as sluggish progress of the project.

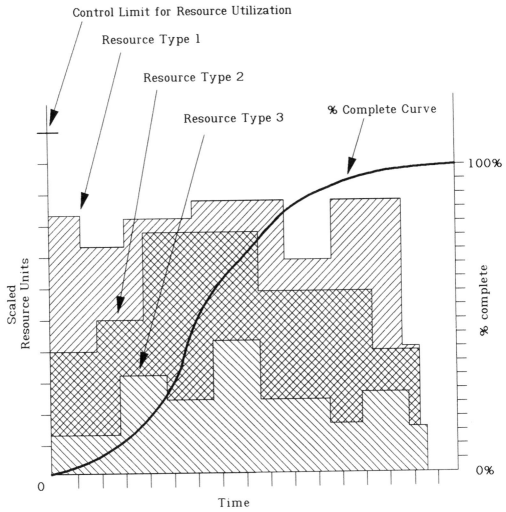

Fig. 8-7. Resource loading versus project progress.

8.4 CASE STUDIES

There are numerous successful case studies of the application of project management software. Presented in this section are a few selected case studies to point out the benefits that can be derived from the proper implementation of computer-aided project management.

City Planning

In 1986, the city of Greensboro, North Carolina, used a PC-based project management software package to manage the timely completion of Bryan Park, the Civic Cultural Center, Southeast Park, a fire station, street beautification works, and many other projects totaling about $40 million in value. The Greensboro Public Works Engineering Design Department used Primavera Project Planner to stay within the city's budget for projects funded by a 1985 bond issue.

Time constraint was the major factor in using the project management software. The city government had a limited time period to spend a large portion of the bond money in order for the people purchasing the bonds to get a good price. In conjunction with the Primavera Project Planner, the department used Primavision, a reporting and plotting tool. The use of Primavision helped clarify project proposals and status throughout the massive undertaking. Verbal reporting typically does not generate the type of attention that the use of project charts can command. City planners subscribed to the concept of "a picture is worth a thousand words" and made extensive use of the graphics capabilities of the Primavera/Primavision alliance.

The project committee at the Public Works Department presented the deputy city manager with big, colorful charts each month. The charts portrayed the status of all projects in progress. The deputy city manager then used the reports and charts to make presentations to the city council and the city manager. For example, with different colors, bar charts were used to show how far each project was toward completion. With the appropriate levels of detail, the charts gave the city council an indication of what percentage of a project had been finished compared to target dates. If problems were spotted, corrective decisions were made quickly during the council meeting. There was no need for council members to take voluminous reports home to read and study before deciding what to do.

Before computerization, the city knew there were problems associated with city projects, but was not able to trace all the problems. After computerization, the locations of the problems became clear, and the city had the opportunity to do something about these problems.

Under conventional reporting, people could not believe that it was taking so long to complete a project. When graphical schedules and time tables were presented, the durations and resource requirements became obvious to everyone. The ability to track projects, foresee problems, and take control actions saved the city a significant amount of time and money. Better investment planning of available funds was possible because the city knew exactly when funds would be needed or not needed for project allocations. If, at a particular point in the project, some of the available funds were not needed for a period of time, the city's project managers were able to make a quick decision to invest the money in another part of the project. Thus, public funds were not just sitting idle while waiting for allocation to projects that would not start for several months. Based on the success of the project management software, the city has decided to also use Primavera on future public projects.

Public Facilities Management

A success story similar to that of the city of Greensboro is found in the case of the Water Resources Department in the Environmental Services Division of Brevard County, Florida (Kintner, 1986). The department has a wide array of responsibilities ranging from developing groundwater-monitoring plans to administrating a $24 million wastewater treatment plant. The department also oversees and coordinates the activities of a number of outside consultants, contractors, and other county departments.

The department might work on 15 to 20 different projects at a time. The scope of each project extends from fewer than half a dozen tasks covering two to three months to projects containing more than 100 tasks in a multilevel project extending two or more years. All projects are tracked as a part of a big project that shows the start and end of each project and the percentage completed. In 1984, after extensive consultations with other users of project management software and a search through printed literature, the department decided to start using Harvard Total Project Manager software to manage the varied projects.

The department staff now uses the software on a routine basis. The two HTPM reports used most often are the task detail and the projects to-do list. The task list allows a listing of each task that is due to start during a specified period. The list also is helpful in evaluating the overall progress of the department at any given time. Reports on tasks are listed in a variety of ways: by starting dates, by persons responsible, or by task names.

The construction of the Merritt Island Regional Wastewater Treatment Plant is an example of how the Water Resources Department keeps track of a project that involved coordination with three other departments, at least two consultants, and up to six general contractors. The responsibility of the department was to track all of the paperwork, reports, payment requests, inspections, and other functions involved in the $24 million construction project. The project was broken down into 40 major subprojects. Some of the subprojects were further broken down into sub-subprojects, each of which sometimes contained more than 20 tasks. Thus, the project was a complex, multileveled project that spanned a period of three years. Harvard Total Project Manager software was used to successfully manage and track the progress of the project. Future projects handled by the department now have the benefit of being managed by this popular software package.

Managing Olympic Events

The 1988 Winter Olympic Games in Calgary, Alberta, Canada, offered an opportunity for project management software to make a good showing, not on the race tracks, but in the planning board rooms. The Olympic organizers used PROJECT/2 and QWIKNET in an interactive fashion to plan and schedule the games (Lucas 1986).

An integrated use of QWIKNET and PROJECT/2 helped the Olympic committee get the most effective assistance from volunteers and other individuals. The software combination offered comprehensive management and control of the Olympic project. Professional project managers, volunteers, and other organizers were able to access the PROJECT/2 database through the QWIKNET personal computer program.

The scope of staging the Olympic Winter Games involved a myriad of tasks, all of which had to be carried out in a logical sequence and on a precise schedule. The organizers broke the games down into several areas that could be planned, scheduled, and managed with the help of a computerized project management system. The duration of the entire project lasted two to three years. Some of the components of the project included building sports facilities and accommodations, designing security systems, arranging television coverage, arranging transportation and food services, and organizing special cultural events for visitors. Planning for some functions required progress reporting to start two years before the planned occurrence of those functions. The larger project management functions were handled by PROJECT/2 on a mainframe computer and the smaller functions of one- to six-month durations were handled by QWIKNET on personal computers. All applications at the PC level were uploaded and integrated with other applications on the mainframe computer.

Approximately $450 million in Canadian dollars were spent on the Olympic project. All of the standard project management functions regarding baseline planning, scheduling, and resource estimation were performed in each application area. The project was controlled by periodically comparing progress to target schedules and making the appropriate updates. The ease of use of QWIKNET allowed many more of the participants and contributors to the games to work effectively towards the overall goal of the project. Timing was of the utmost importance and was very crucial in avoiding delays in planning and implementating the Olympic events. Project management software made that realization possible.

Conference Management

Organizing a national conference is like any typical project. There is a series of activities that must be performed in an orderly and timely fashion. There is an extensive coordination of the efforts of several people. Many of those involved in organizing national conferences are normally located in different geographical locations across the nation, making the communication and coordination functions even more difficult. Resource allocation problems are also a major concern when organizing conferences. All these factors make conference management a prime candidate for the application of project management techniques.

Conferences now managed by conventional pencil and paper approaches can be managed more effectively by a direct application of project management concepts with the support of computer tools. Dr. Sid G. Gilbreath, professor of Industrial Engineering at Tennessee Technological University, used the support of computer tools to improve conference management. Gilbreath was the conference chairman for the 1987 Fall conference of the Institute of Industrial Engineers held in Nashville, Tennessee. Faced with very little time and limited resources, he sought the help of computer tools.

In addition to employing the traditional project management principles throughout the planning, organizing, directing, and scheduling phases of the conference, Gilbreath used Lotus 1-2-3 and dBASE III PLUS to develop custom application programs to suit the needs of the conference. With innovative uses of the spreadsheet and database programs, he was able to implement computer routines that are normally found in commercial project management packages.

First, he developed a straightforward data base file (IE87_COM.DBF) containing information about members of the Nashville host committee and members of the ''Tennessee network.'' He used the file as a directory for communication purposes and as a file folder to accumulate needed information about each person whose record was included in the database file. He developed another database file (IE87_COM.LBL), which contained label formats for the information in the file IE87_COM.BDF. The mailing label formats were used for printing address mailing labels when distributing or requesting information concerning conference planning. He developed another database file (IE87_SCD.DBF) containing the following four items:

1. The list of items to be accomplished in planning and delivering the conference. This list is furnished by IIE staff at the national headquarters in Atlanta. By automating the list, Gillbreath was able to make sure that the conference plans were in line with the objectives of the national headquarters.
2. Responsibility assignments.
3. Due dates.
4. Completion dates.

The other database files that Gilbreath developed and their contents and functions are presented below:

- SCH_R_DD.NDX—This file was an index file that enabled the reporting of the data in IE87_SCD.DBF in a format that grouped tasks by persons responsible and in due date order.
- SCH_R_DD.FRM—This file was a report file that prints the data from SCH_R_DD.DBF in a tabulated format that made it simple to analyze tasks.
- SEMINARS.DBF—This file was a database file that collected information concerning seminar host volunteers for reporting to IIE staff personnel.

- SEMINARS.LBL—This file was for printing the information from SEMINARS.DBF in a convenient format.
- WORKSHOP.DBF—This file was a database file to collect information that concerned evening workshop-host volunteers for reporting to IIE staff personnel.
- WORKSHOP.LBL—This file was for printing the information from WORKSHOP.DBF in a convenient format.

Several Lotus 1-2-3 spreadsheet files were also created. One spreadsheet file, named ESMATRIX.WK1, contained the conference educational sessions matrix. Traditionally, the sessions matrix was prepared on poster boards, which made updating very difficult. Session cancellations and room changes were often difficult to track. In addition to being difficult to update, the poster boards were cumbersome to use for operational purposes at the conference.

Under the direction of Gilbreath, one of the conference staff members transposed the poster board information into an electronic spreadsheet. The large poster board matrix furnished by the IIE headquarters was used as a model in developing the electronic spreadsheet. The spreadsheet was updated as conference arrangements progressed on site and information became available. Periodically, hard copies of the sessions matrix were printed to reflect the current status of events at the conference, which made it possible for the conference organizers to quickly monitor the progress of the conference and provide timely and accurate information to conference participants and volunteers.

The other spreadsheet files contained the daily conference functional schedule. The printout of these files provided all persons with the official conference management responsibilities. The automated schedule format was easier to handle in the conference control center, where it was used for informational purposes, such as ongoing events.

This case example shows how conventional computer software tools could be used in managing projects. Despite the absence of a commercial project management software package, the conference organizers were still able to take advantage of the power of computers as management and decision support tools.

Construction Management

In 1986, McSha Properties of Norman, Oklahoma, was in dire trouble. The firm won a competitive award of over $5 million to build 184 two-bedroom apartment units in 9 months. Unless completed on time, the project would cost McSha severe monetary penalties. To satisfactorily complete the contract, McSha overcame significant financial problems and construction delays by creatively using microcomputers and several software packages to solve the financial and project management challenges (Carlson 1987).

Financial Approach. In developing the winning proposal, McSha never considered financing a problem. Later, after the contract to build was awarded, obtaining the funds required for construction became a major problem. Financial institutions were in the midst of their own crises. Defaults on buildings, farm, and energy loans contributed to the closing of many banks in the state of Oklahoma. Some unscrupulous builders obtained large portions of their loans by intentionally overestimating the percentage of construction complete. A bank representative normally inspected the site to confirm that percentage. Because of the difficulty in estimating the percent completion on a multiple-unit project, the bank representative often agreed with the builder's estimate.

Based on the contractor's claim and the bank's validation, funds for the next phase of the construction were advanced. The bank did not know that many subcontractors and material suppliers never received payment; the unscrupulous builder left town with the money. The bank, the subcontractors, and the materials suppliers were left with nothing. In too many cases, the Federal Deposit Insurance Corporation ended up with the bank, passing the loss to the taxpayer.

McSha proposed a novel approach to accounting to reduce the lender's level of risk. They proposed to provide a completed bank draft to the bank for signature and a copy of each invoice at defined contractual milestones. Each milestones tied to a point in the financial system which represented completion of an activity in the management system. The bank compared the invoice with the draft, analyzed detailed management reports, checked construction, and countersigned the draft.

Management eliminated percentage-completion guesswork. This elimination permitted the bank to base decisions of factual information. Management used an integrated, general ledger, accounts payable, and job cost package to eliminate the guesswork. This package also used a standard AIA-type progressive draw form program. McSha used the Open Systems software by Uccel Company to control the turn-around of invoices and payments. This satisfied lenders and subcontractors. Use of the microcomputer-based financial package made it possible to apply the "Continuous Draw" concept.

McSha enhanced the Open Systems package with a Funds Committed report and a Financial Draw package. With these enhanced functions, they produced an automated check register. They also produced cost reports by job and phase. *Job* would represent the major tasks shown on the draw report. *Phase* would be a subdivision of these major tasks, used for additional control.

A software subcontractor developed a history file for producing additional reports. This history file also helped integrate a draw package into the financial system. It worked by entering a purchase order in the accounts payable package to represent committed funds. The history file reports indicated total purchase orders, total cost, and a budget by job and phase. These reports were useful in preventing surprises that might have occurred during the final phases of construction.

As in many software development or modification projects, there were delays. While the software subcontractor completed the new program, McSha created a database using Symphony. With this database, McSha developed semiautomated Draw Schedule and Funds Committed reports. With the integrated financial package delivered, McSha officers established a rigid cost-control process. Estimated material costs were entered into the system for each activity. The estimates became budget. Then a purchase order was entered for the job or material. When an invoice arrived, estimated and actual costs were compared. When actual cost exceeded the estimate, supervisors contacted the subcontractor to resolve the situation. The financial system permitted McSha to closely track all invoices, eliminating duplicate billing. Management then knew their financial position at all times and made rational decisions based on timely and accurate information.

Program Management. A drastic reduction of construction time became the next challenge to face McSha. It took five months to obtain financing. Now, less than four months remained to complete the project. However, superior planning and adherence to plan enabled the firm to avoid financial disaster.

McSha responded to the critical construction challenge with yet another innovative approach. They developed a detailed plan using Harvard Total Project Manager software. This plan described all of the major construction tasks and the interrelationship between tasks. The plan prevented electrical, plumbing, and other services subcontractors from working in the same areas at the same time. HTPM generated plans for the apartment units in the first phase. Using the same system, plans for the second and third phases were generated, varying the start dates. A major Construction innovation occurred when McSha realized the need to motivate the subcontractors to follow the plan. Each subcontractor had to meet the scheduled dates.

To convince subcontractors that the project could be highly successful, McSha contracted the University of Oklahoma. Dr. Harold Connor of the Construction Sciences Department discussed the requirements with management. Dr. Connor then set up a seminar on Critical Path Method (CPM) management. All potential bidders were invited to attend the two-evening seminar (with homework) as a prerequisite for bidding. Dr. Connor described the CPM process, emphasizing the teamwork required to complete a project on time. The subcontractors left the seminar eager to participate in the project, but concerned. When they were confronted with the first computerized schedules and activity networks, their panic was clear. McSha quickly reverted to hand-drawn activity flow diagrams to develop their proposals.

When the subcontractors' proposals were received, McSha could see that the subcontractors' reputations were being put on the line. Each proposal showed how the subcontractor would manage resources to guarantee quality work within the specified time frames. A few firms indicated they would not subscribe to the mandatory completion dates and were not given the contract. Other firms were not selected because they did not have the flexibility or staff to meet the schedule. McSha selected subcontractors who were financially strong and had an adequate staff with a reputation for professional performance.

After the subcontractors were selected, their individual plans were entered into the McSha HTPM network. The initial plan rapidly changed to reflect the information contained in the winning proposals. As the revised plan took shape, HTPM guaranteed that each subcontractor's resources were effectively deployed across each phase. The HTPM Resource Leveling function calculated the manpower loading on each activity for each trade skill. Thus, the program indicated how an electrician could work on a task on phase one. From there, he would move to phase two, and then possibly back to phase one. Although subcontractors were responsible for assignment of their personnel, McSha provided invaluable information for sound assignment decisions.

The automated project management package provided a flexible and disciplined tool for managing the project. The package permitted rapid change of activities, start dates, completion dates, relationships, and progress. Often, changes were made in a few minutes and plotted in an hour. In the past, those changes might have taken days to analyze and redraw. The automated package provided a discipline because it identified problems immediately. This forced managers to make decisions that alleviated deficiencies. Slow progress of a crucial task often required that management assign additional resources to the task or change the completion date.

Although a financial institution had agreed to lend the required funds, the bank wanted a second look before the company broke ground. A negative second look would enable the lender to pull out with a minimal loss. McSha provided financial and management information, along with the subcontractor proposal plans. Most important in gaining approval to proceed was the automation of the financial and project management system. These systems produced cost statements associated with milestones.

Word Processing. Once again, McSha was ready to use an ordinary product in an unusual way. McSha wanted a printed checksheet to check completion of each milestone. The concept start with self-appraisal by the subcontractor. After that came an evaluation by the McSha phase supervisor, followed by approval from the country building inspectors. The concept was that each subcontractor would complete a task and then administer a self-appraisal by using a checksheet tailored to that specific task. Entering the checksheet into a word processing package permitted McSha to modify the form rapidly for use in different localities. Once again, McSha ran into some problems. Contact with the local building inspectors determined that they did not use checksheets. Inspectors felt each job was unique and that building regulations required changes in each situation. The inspectors thought that an all-inclusive checksheet was impractical. The only way McSha could acquire the checksheets would be to make them.

Officers at McSha researched state, county, and local building codes and developed a series of draft checksheets for each trade. They circulated the drafts among local inspectors and requested their professional evaluation. After the comments were received, the checksheets were updated in the word processing system. Completed checksheets were distributed to McSha phase supervisors, subcontractors, and building inspectors. Although such a requirement was not in their contracts, subcontractors knew that the checksheets must be completed before payment would be authorized.

Many benefits resulted from the implementation of the checksheet process. First, the subcontractors knew exactly what to expect. Each one could conduct a self appraisal before notifying McSha that the task was complete. Second, the phase supervisor would evaluate the task to make certain it was ready for the building inspectors.

Use of the checksheet placed a powerful management tool in the hands of McSha's supervisors. McSha's excellent reputation with the building inspectors quickly rose even higher. When McSha informed them that the site was ready, the inspectors knew there would be no waiting. When McSha said it was ready, it was ready. The result of the checksheet effort was that subcontractors and McSha worked closely to eliminate project failures. Even the inspectors were convinced of the use of checksheets. They became part of the team effort to deliver a quality product in a tight time frame.

The word processing package selected for the effort was Writing Assistant 2 from IBM. This program provided a powerful set of word processing functions at the managerial and professional level. A good spelling check feature is in the package, along with the capability of identifying synonyms. McSha also used Rightwriter by Decisionware Inc., to perform grammar analysis and produce readability and strength indices. This additional capability enabled McSha to tailor its writing to the comprehension level of target audiences. These audiences included banks, investors, future clients, press, and subcontractors.

The success of McSha was tied directly to the success of this project. Had management or financial control deteriorated, the project and company would have suffered serious financial consequences. The use of the computer provided the discipline and control needed to sell, manage, and complete the project successfully. HTPM software greatly enhanced the planning and detail that went into the project before the request for proposals. The level of detail enabled McSha to develop extremely tight contract specifications. These specifications resulted in a minimum of change orders. The low number of change orders led to fewer construction delays and cost increases. In the past, subcontractors relied on increasing profit through change orders. Now change orders turn a profit on better use of resources. Most subcontractors indicated they made more money on this job than on any other job that was bid as competitively.

McSha delivered 184 two-bedroom apartments with a clubhouse. The clubhouse contains a commercial laundry, delicatessen, TV room, and game room. The entire project contained 180,000 square feet. McSha completed the complex in 73 days, not including 17 weather days. Although this might not be a construction record, the work represents expedient use of time without sacrificing quality.

The successful and profitable conclusion of this project demonstrates that even little companies must employ automated management systems to be competitive. Construction giants aren't the only companies that effectively use automation. Automation is necessary for the little company that must squeeze out every penny of profit. The example of McSha Properties further attests to the benefits of computer tools in managing projects to improve productivity and increase profit. That is the bottom line!

Appendix A

Guide to Software

DATABASE MANAGEMENT SOFTWARE

PRODUCT	COMPANY	OPERATING REQUIREMENTS	SPECIFICATIONS
ACCELL/SQL for Unify 2,000 first version	Unify Corp.	2M bytes of RAM; Unix and Xenix environments	2.3 billion fields per record, 2.3 billion-character field size, 2.3 billion records per file, 2.3 billion-character record size, automatic indexing, 2.3 billion active indexes, 2.3 billion indexes per file
Team-Up version 2.1	Unlimited Processing, Inc.	155K bytes of RAM; DOS 3.1 and higher environments	1,000 fields per record, 1,900-character field size, 4 billion records per file, 8,187-character record size, automatic indexing, 100 active indexes, 100 indexes per file
dbMAN V = Microport386 version 5.1	VeraSoft Corp.	512K bytes of RAM; Microport 386 environments	128 fields per record, 254-character filed size, 2 billion records per file, record size limited by disk space, automatic indexing, active indexes and indexes per file limited by disk space
dbMAN V = Novell version 5.1		512K bytes of RAM; Novell environments	128 field per record, 254-character field size, 2 billion records per file, record size limited by disk space, automatic indexing, active indexes and indexes per file limited by disk space
dbMAN V = PC DOS version 5.1		480K bytes of RAM; PC-DOS and MS-DOS	128 fields per record, 254-character field size, 2 billion records field size, 2 billion

PRODUCT	COMPANY	OPERATING REQUIREMENTS	SPECIFICATIONS
		environments	records per file, record size limited by disk space, automatic indexing, active indexes and indexes per file limited by disk space
dbMAN V = PC NET version 5.1		512K bytes of RAM; PC-DOS, PC-MOS and Concurrent DOS environments	128 fields per record, 254-character field size, 2 billion records per file, record size limited by disk space, automatic indexing, active indexes and indexes per file limited by disk space
dbMAN V = Xenix 286 version 5.1		512K bytes of RAM; Xenix 286 environment	128 fields per record, 254-character field size, 2 billion records per file-character record size, automatic indexing, active indexes and indexes per file limited by disk space
Quick silver version 1.2C	Word Tech Systems Inc.	360K bytes of RAM; DOS 2.0 and higher environments	128 fields per record, 254-character field size, 1 billion records per file 4,000-character record size, automatic indexing, 1 per file active indexes, 7 indexes per file
dBXL version 1.2C		430K bytes of RAM; DOS 2.0 and higher environments	128 fields per records, 2254-character field size, 1 billion records per file 4,000-character record size, automatic indexing, 1 per file, 10 total active indexes, 7 indexes per file
dBXL/LAN version 1.2		440K bytes of RAM; DOS 3.1 and higher environments	128 fields per record, 254-character field size, 1 billion records per file 4,000-character record size, automatic indexing, 1 per file active indexes, 7 indexes per file
XDB-SQL version 2.20	XDB Systems Inc.	270 bytes of RAM; DOS Xenix and Unix environments	400 fields per record, 1,500-character field size, records per file limited by disk space, 32,767-character record size, automatic indexing, over 400 active indexes, up to 400 indexes per file
ZIM version 3.02	Zanthe Information Inc.	640K bytes of RAM; VAX/VMS, VM/CM, Unix, Xenix, QNX, LANs, DOS, AOS/VS environments	16,383 fields per record, 32,000-character field size, records per file limited by disk space, 32,000-character record size, automatic indexing, active indexes limited by disk space, 200 indexes per file
Zfour version 3.5.0	Zfour, Inc.	512K bytes of RAM; MS-DOS, Unix, Xenix, AIX, Wang OS, VMS and OS/2 environments	65,535 fields per record, 65,535-character field size, 4,294,967,296 records per file 65,535-character record size, automatic indexing, 65,535 active indexes, 65,535 indexes per file

PRODUCT	COMPANY	OPERATING REQUIREMENTS	SPECIFICATIONS
B.O.S.S	American Planning Corp.	512K bytes of RAM; DOS, PC LAN and Xenix environments	255 fields per record, 255-character field size, 2 billion records per file, 64,000-character record size, automatic indexing, 15 active indexes
VersaForm XL version 5.0	Applied Software Technology	500K bytes of RAM; MS-DOS 2.1 and higher environments	250 fields per record, 78-character field size, 2 billion records per file, 16-character record size, automatic indexing, 1 active index, 1 index per file
dBASE III Plus version 1.1	Ashton-Tate Corp.	256K bytes of RAM; MS-DOS 2.1 and higher environments	128 fields per record, 256-character field size, 1 billion records per file, 4,000-character record size
dBASE IV version 1.0		530K bytes of RAM; PC-DOS, MS-DOS and Windows 386 environments	255 fields per record, 254-character field size, 1 billion records per file, 4,000-character record size, automatic indexing, 47 active indexes, 47 indexes per file
Omnis Quartz version 2.00	Blyth Software, Inc.	640K bytes of RAM; Microsoft Windows environment	120 fields per record, 2,400-character field size, records per file limited by disk space, 288,000-character record size, 720 active indexes, 12 indexes per file
Paradox 386 version 2.0	Borland International, Inc.	512K bytes of RAM; DOS 2.0 and higher environments	255 fields per record, 255-character field size, 2 billion records per file, 4,000-character record size, automatic indexing, 255 active indexes, 255 indexes per file
Paradox OS/2 version 2.0		512K bytes of RAM; DOS 2.0 and higher environments	255 fields per record, 255-character field size, 2 billion records per file, 4,000-character record size, automatic indexing, 255 active indexes, 255 indexes per file
Paradox version 2.0		512K bytes of of RAM; DOS 2.0 and higher environments	255 fields per record, 255-character field size, 2 billion records per file, 4,000-character record size, automatic indexing, 255 active indexes, 255 indexes per file
Paradox version 3.0		512K bytes of RAM; DOS 2.0 and higher environments	255 fields per record, 255-character field size, 2 billion records per file, 4,000-character record size, automatic indexing, 255 active indexes, 255 indexes per file
D the Data Language version 2.7	Caltex Software, Inc.	440K bytes of RAM; DOS, Xenix and Novell environments	4,088 fields per record, 4,088-character field size, records per file limited by disk space, 4,088-character record size,

PRODUCT	COMPANY	OPERATING REQUIREMENTS	SPECIFICATIONS
			automatic indexing, active indexes and indexes per file limited by disk space
CA-1deal Escort version 1.2	Computer Associates International, Inc.	300K bytes of RAM; PC-DOS and OS/2 environments	500 fields per record, 2,000-character field size, records per file limited by disk space, 2,000-character record size, automatic indexing, active indexes limited by memory, 40 indexes per file
DABL versions 3	Computer Control Systems Inc.	50K bytes of RAM; MS-DOS 3.1 and higher environments	128 fields per record, 255-character field size, records per file limited by disk space, 32,640-character record size, automatic indexing, 1 active index, 129 indexes per file
DB-FABS version 3		135K bytes of RAM; MS-DOS 3.1 and higher environments	128 fields per record, 255-character field size, record per file limited by disk space, 32,640-character record size, automatic indexing, 1 active index
Thoroughbred IDOL-IV version 4.3	Concept Omega Corp.	640K bytes of RAM; Unix, Xenix, DOS, VMS and Thoroughbred/-OS environments	Field per record and field size limited by disk space, records per file and record size limited by disk space, automatic indexing, active indexes and indexes per file limited by disk space
PRODAS version 3.2	Conceptual Software, Inc.	320K bytes of RAM; DOS, Xenix and VAX environments	32,000 fields per record, 200-character field size, records per file limited by disk space, 32,000-character record size, automatic indexing, active indexes and indexes per file limited by disk space
Condor 3 version 2.20	Condor Computer Corp.	256K bytes of RAM; PC-DOS and CP/M environments	127 fields per record, 127-character field size, 65,534 records per file, 1,024-character record size, 1 active index, 8 indexes per file
NPL/R Plus Database Applications System version 3.2	Database Applications, Inc.	335K bytes of RAM; DOS 2.1 and higher environments	256 fields per record, 999-character field size, records per file limited by disk space, 10,000-character record size, automatic indexing, 40 active indexes
DataEase version 4.0	DataEase International, Inc.	640K bytes of RAM; DOS environments	255 fields per record, 255-character field size, 2 billion records per file, 4,000-character record size, automatic indexing, 254 active indexes, 254 indexes per file
Formula IV version 1.19	Dynamic Microprocessor Associates, Inc.	256K bytes of RAM; DOS 2.0 and higher environments	200 fields per record, 127-character field size, 999,999,999 records per file, 10,240-character record size,

PRODUCT	COMPANY	OPERATING REQUIREMENTS	SPECIFICATIONS
			automatic indexing, 4 active indexes, indexes per file limited by disk space
Enable/OA version 3.0	Enable Software, Inc.	512K bytes of RAM; DOS OS/2, Xenix and Intel-based Unix environments	254 fields per record, 254-character field size, over 1 billion records per file, 245 by 254-character record size, automatic indexing, 10 active indexes, 10 indexes per file
SQLBase version 3.6	Gupta Technologies, Inc.	300K bytes of RAM; PC-DOS, MS-DOS and OS/2 environments	250 fields per record, 5,000-character field size, records per file limited by disk space, 5,000-character record size, automatic indexing, active indexes and indexes per file limited by disk space
INFO-DB+ version 3.40	Henco Software Inc.	1MK bytes of RAM; VMS environments	10,000 fields per record, 4,096-character field size, records per file limited by disk space, 32,000-character record size, automatic indexing, 99 active indexes, 99 indexes per file
pcEXPRESS EM version 2.0	Information Resources, Inc.	640K bytes of RAM; DOS 3.0 and higher environments, 80286 or 80386-based PCs	Fields per record limited by disk space, character field size depends on data type, 16 to 32 million records per file, record size limited by disk space, automatic indexing, indexes per file limited by disk space
Informix-ESQL/C version 2.10.00	Informix Software, Inc.	640K bytes of RAM; DOS, Unix, VMS and OS/2 environments	Fields per record and field size limited by disk space, records per file limited by disk space, record size limited by disk space, automatic indexing, 8 fields per composite index
PDBase version 3.09	IOTC, Inc.	32K bytes of RAM; DOS, P-System and Unix environments	2,000 fields per record, 32,762-character field size, 6.2 billion records per file, 32,764-character record size, automatic indexing, 32 active indexes, 32 indexes per file
Mainstay version 2.53	Mainstay Software, Inc.	640K bytes of RAM; MS-DOS 2.0 and higher and PC-DOS environments	Fields per record limited by disk space, 255-character field size, records per file limited by disk space, record size limited by disk space, automatic indexing, active indexes and indexes per file limited by disk space
Knowledge Man/2 version 2.5	mdbs, Inc.	380K bytes of RAM; PC-DOS, MS-DOS and VMS environments	255 fields per record, 65,535-character field size, 2,147,483,647 records per file, 65,535-character record size, automatic indexing, 65,535 active indexes and indexes per file limited by disk space

PRODUCT	COMPANY	OPERATING REQUIREMENTS	SPECIFICATIONS
Metaview version 1.86	Metafile Information System, Inc.	384K bytes of RAM; PC-DOS and MS-DOS environments	500 fields per record, 1,000-character field size, 2 million records per file, 4,000-character record size, automatic indexing, 100 active indexes, 5 indexes per file
R:BASE for DOS version 2.11	Microrim, Inc.	436K bytes of RAM AM; DOS environments	400 fields per record, 1,500-character field size, records per file limited by disk space, 4,026-character record size, automatic indexing, active indexes and indexes per file limited by disk space
R:BASE for OS/2 version 2.11	Microrim, Inc.	436K bytes of RAM; OS/2 environments	400 fields per record, 1,500-character field size, records per file limited by disk space, 4,026-character record size, automatic indexing, active indexes and indexes per file limited by disk space
Mass-II Manager version 9.0	Micro systems Engineering Corp.	384K bytes of RAM; MS-DOS and VAX/MVS environments	256 fields per record, 1,000-character field size, 65,000 records per file, 4,000-character record size, automatic indexing, 50 active indexes, 50 indexes per file
PC Nomad version 2.03	Must Software International	400K bytes of RAM; PC-DOS 3.0 and higher PS/2 with DOS 3.3 or higher environments	Fields per record limited by disk space, 255-character field size, records per file limited by disk space, 64,512-character record size, automatic indexing, active indexes and indexes per file limited by disk space
1 on 1 = 3! version 1.4	1 on 1 Computer Solutions, Inc.	450K bytes of RAM; PC-DOS and MS-DOS 2.0 and higher environments	128 fields per record, 254-character field size, 1 billion records per file 4,000-character record size, automatic indexing, 7 active indexes
PC Album version 1.0	PC Manager, Inc.	512K bytes of RAM; PC-DOS, MS-DOS 2.0 and higher environments	500 fields per record, 254-character field size, records per file limited by disk space, 16,000-character record size, automatic indexing, 9 active indexes, 9 indexes per file
Data Edge version 1.7		384K bytes of RAM; MS-DOS 2.0 and higher, PC-DOS 2.0 Wang DOS environments	500 fields per record, 254-character field size, records per file limited by disk space, 16,000-character record size, automatic indexing, 9 indexes per file, 9 active indexes
Progress version 4.2	Progress Software Corp.	640K bytes of RAM; MS-DOS, Unix, Xenix, Ultrix, AIX, VAX/VMS,	2,000 fields per record, 2,000-character field size, records per file limited by disk space, 2,000-character record size,

PRODUCT	COMPANY	OPERATING REQUIREMENTS	SPECIFICATIONS
		CTOS/BTOS and other network environments	automatic indexing, 1,023 active indexes, indexes per file limited by disk space
Q-PRO4	QNE International	320K bytes of RAM; PC-DOS, MS-DOS, Lans, PC-MOS, Unix, Xenix environments	Fields per record limited by disk space, 255-character field size, records per file limited by disk space automatic indexing, 9 indexes per file, active indexes limited by disk space
Ingres for PCs version 5.0	Relational Technology, Inc.	450K bytes of RAM; MS-DOS, Unix, VMS, AUX, AIX, VM/CMS and MOS environments	128 fields per record, 2,000-character field size, record per file, 2,000-character record size, automatic indexing, 128 active indexes, 128 indexes per file
Advanced Revelation version 1.1	Revelation Technologies, Inc.	512K bytes of RAM; MS-DOS and OS/2 environments	32,000 fields per record, 65,535-character field size, records per file limited by disk space, 65,535-character record size, automatic indexing, active indexes and indexes per file limited by disk space
Souer Computer Systems version 2F	Souer Computer Systems, Inc.	640K bytes of RAM; MS-DOS environments	80 fields per record, 99-character field size, 32,000 records per file, 512-character record size, automatic indexing, 12 active indexes, indexes per file limited by disk space
Drawbase 4,000 version 1.5	Skok Systems, Inc.	499 bytes of RAM; MS-DOS environments	50 fields per record, 80-character field size, 32,767 records per file, 4,000-character record size
Drawbase 5,000 version 1.5		499 bytes of RAM; MS-DOS environments	50 fields per record, 80-character field size, 32,767 records per file, 4,000-character record size
file Pro-Plus version 3.0	The Small Computer Company, Inc.	300 to 400K bytes of RAM; DOS, OS/2, networks, Xenix, Unix, Ultrix, and VMS environments	999 fields per record, 999-character field size, 250 million records per file, 16,384-character record size, automatic indexing, 8 active indexes, 8 indexes per file
MACH 1 version 5.4	Tominy, Inc.	75K bytes of RAM; PC-DOS, MS-DOS, Unix, Novell and mini/mainframe environments	Fields per record limited by disk space, 245-character field size, records per file, limited by disk space, record size limited by disk space, automatic indexing, 11 active indexes, 11 indexes per file

DATA SECURITY SOFTWARE

VENDOR	PRODUCT NAME	TARGET SYSTEMS	MAJOR FEATURES
American Computer Security Industries Nashville, TN	Compsec II	IBM PC	Data Access Restriction Encryption/Decryption Audit Trail/Reporting
Boole & Babbage Sunnyvale, CA	Backup/CMS	IBM VM/CMS, SP	Backup & Recovery
	Secure	IBM MVS, MVS/XA, VS1	Data Access Restriction Encryption/Decryption
California Software Products, CA	Backpak	IBM PC	Backup & Recovery
Chi/Cor Chicago, IL	Total Recovery & Planning System (TRPS)	IBM PC	Disaster Recovery Planning
Comedia/Lite Software San Francisco, CA	Eclipse	IBM PC	Data Access Restriction Audit Trail/Reporting
Computer Associates International Garden City, NY	CA-ACF2	IBM MVS, VM, DOS/VSE, VS1, DEC VAX/VMS	Data Access Restriction Audit Trail/Reporting
	CA-Top Secret	IBM MVS, VM, DOS/VSE, DEC VAX/VMS	Data Access Restriction Audit Trail/Reporting Backup & Recovery
Computer Security Corporation Chicago, IL	Citadel	IBM PC	Data Access Restriction Encryption/Decryption
Davis, Thomas & Associates Minneapolis, MN	DTA Backup	IBM CICS	Backup & Recovery
DB View, Inc. Waltham, IL	DB/Secure	DB2	Data Access Restriction Encryption/Decryption
Design Software, Inc. Chicago, IL	DS Recover	IBM PC	Backup & Recovery
DTI New York, NY	Codename: Password	IBM PC	Data Access Restriction
Enigma Logic Concord, CA	PC-Safe II	IBM PC	Data Access Restriction Encryption/Decryption Audit Trail/Reporting
	Safeword	DEC VAX, Unix, IBM MVS, Tandem	Encryption/Decryption Audit Trail/Reporting
Fast Track Systems New York, NY	Safetrack	IBM PC	Backup & Recovery

VENDOR	PRODUCT NAME	TARGET SYSTEMS	MAJOR FEATURES
Fifth Generation Systems Baton Rouge, LA	Fastback Plus	IBM PC	Backup & Recovery
Fischer International Naples, FL	Watchdog	IBM PC	Data Access Restriction Encryption/Decryption Audit Trail Reporting
FoundationWare Cleveland, OH	Vaccine Corporate	IBM PC	Data Access Restriction Backup & Recovery Virus Vaccine Audit Trail/Reporting
FWM Digitech New York, NY	MenuTech	Wang VS	Data Access Restriction Audit Trail/Reporting
Goal Systems Columbus, OH	Alert	IBM DOS/VSE, VM/CMS, MVS, CICS	Data Access Restriction
Harcom Security Systems Corporation New York, NY	PC-Watchman	IBM PC	Data Access Restriction Encryption/Decryption Virus Vaccine Audit Trail/Reporting
IBM	Data Encoder	IBM PC	Encryption/Decryption
	RACF	IBM MVS, VM, SP	Data Access Restriction Encryption/Decryption
	ACF/VTAM	IBM MVS, DOS/VSE, VS1	Data Access Restriction Encryption/Decryption
	CICS/VSE	IBM DOS/VSE, CICS	Data Access Restriction Audit Trail/Reporting
Innovation Data Processing Little Falls, NJ	ABR	IBM MVS, MVS/XA, VS1, TSO	Backup & Recovery
Integrity Solutions Littleton, CO	Data Recovery Systems (DRS)	IBM VSAM, CICS/VS	Backup & Recovery
International Security Technology, Inc. New York, NY	IST Virus Protection (VPP)	IBM PC	Virus Vaccine
Kolinar Corporation Santa Clara, CA	KDES	IBM PC	Audit Trail Reporting
Lachman Associates Naperville, IL	The Security Audit	Unix	Data Access Restriction Virus Vaccine Audit Trail/Reporting
Micro Interfaces Corporation Miami, FL	Quiksave	IBM PC	Backup & Recovery

Guide to Software

VENDOR	PRODUCT NAME	TARGET SYSTEMS	MAJOR FEATURES
Micronyx, Inc. Richardson, TX	Triad Plus	IBM PC	Data Access Restriction Encryption/Decryption Audit Trail/Reporting
On-Line Software International Fort Lee, NJ	Omni-Guard	IBM MVS	Data Access Restriction Audit Trail/Reporting
Operations Control Systems Palo Alto, CA	OCS/Private	HP 3000	Data Access Restriction Audit Trail/Reporting
Oxford Software Corp. Hasbrouck Heights, NJ	COSS	IBM DOS/VSE, CICS	Data Access Restriction
Peter Norton Computing Santa Monica, CA	Norton Utilities Advanced	IBM PC	Disaster Recovery Planning
Prime Factors, Inc. Oakland, CA	Descrypt/CS	Wang VS, IBM MVS	Encryption/Decryption
RG Software Systems Willow Grove, PA	Disk Watcher	IBM PC	Data Access Restriction Backup & Recovery Encryption/Decryption Virus Vaccine Audit Trail/Reporting
RSA Data Security Redwood City, CA	Mailsafe	IBM PC, Mainframes, DEC VAX/VMS	Encryption, Decryption
Security Dynamics Cambridge, MA	ACM/6100 Software	IBM MVS, MVS/XA, Unix, DEC VAX/VMS	Data Access Restriction
SoftLogic Solutions Manchester, NH	Data Guardian	IBM PC	Backup & Recovery
Software Integration Los Angeles, CA	Bakup	IBM PC	Backup & Recovery
Software Security Stamford, CT	The Block	IBM PC	Data Access Restriction
Spectrum Computer Services, Inc. North Reading, MA	Rescue	IBM PC, Lotus 1-2-3	Backup & Recovery
Sterlin Software Chatsworth, CA	DYL-Security	IBM DOS/VSE, MVS, VM	Data Access Restriction Encryption/Decryption
ThumbScan, Inc. Oakbrook Terrace, IL	ThumbScan	IBM PC, MVS, VM, DOS/VSE, DEC VAX/VMS	Data Access Restriction
Tower Systems International Costa Mesa, CA	Surveillance	IBM DOS/VSE, MVS, VM	Backup & Recovery

VENDOR	PRODUCT NAME	TARGET SYSTEMS	MAJOR FEATURES
TSI International Wilton, CT	Conductor	IBM MVS	Data Access Restriction
TurningPoint Systems Beverly, MA	Securit	IBM S/38	Backup & Recovery
Unitech Software Reston, VA	USecure	Unix	Data Access Resctriction Backup & Recovery Virus Vaccine Disaster Recovery Planning
United Software Security Vienna, VA	OnGuard	IBM PC	Data Access Restriction
	Take Two	IBM PC	Backup & Recovery
	Privacy Plus	IBM PC	Encryption/Decryption
VM Software, Inc. Vienna, VA	VMSecure	IBM VM	Data Access Restriction
VM1 Los Angeles, CA	VM1Dataguard	IBM VM/SP	Data Access Restriction Encryption/Decryption

PROJECT MANAGEMENT SOFTWARE

PRODUCT	VENDOR	ENVIRONMENT	PRICE	COMMENT
PAC Micro	AGS Mgmt. Systems King of Prussia, PA	IBM PC/XT/AT	$990	Multiple project scheduling, CPM
PAC II		IBM BOS/MVS, DOS/VSE, VS/1, DEC VAX/VMS, Wang VS	$44K	Resource Allocation, cost analysis, reporting.
PAC III		IBM OS/MVS, VM, DOS/VSE; S/38; DEC VAX/VMS	$67K	Integrated networking, scheduling,
Estiplan		IBM PC/XT/AT		Software project mgmt. & control
Top down Project Planner	Ajida Technologies Santa Rosa, CA	IBM PC/XT/AT PS/2	$495	Top down approach, WBS

Guide to Software

PRODUCT	VENDOR	ENVIRONMENT	PRICE	COMMENT
Project Workbench Advanced	Applied Business Technologies, Inc., New York, NY	IBM PC/XT/AT, Wang PC	$1150	Complex projects; Gantt /resource screens
ABT Project Workbench Standard		IBM PC/XT/AT	$750	Small to medium-size projects
Pro Tracs	Applied Microsystems Roswell, CA	IBM PC/XT/AT	$59.95	Action/item tracking
Skyline	Applitech Software Cambridge, MA	IBM PC/XT/AT, PS/2	$295	Project out-liner, Uses CPM
APECS/800	Automatic Data Processing Ann Arbor, MI	DEC VAX, Micro VAX	Contact vendor	Project estimating & control
Synergy	Bechtel Software Acton, MA	IBM PC/XT, DEC VAX/VMS	Contact vendor	Budgeting, control, performance mgmt.
TRAK	The Bridge, Inc. Millbrae, CA	IBM OS/MVS, VS/1, DOS/VSE CICS, TSO	$13K-$23K	Calculates, reports time totals, cost
Pride PMS	M. Bryce & Associates Palm Harbor, FL	DEC VAX/VMS, IBM OS/MVS	$48K	Project mgmt. System for CASE
Who/What/When	Chronos Software, San Francisco, CA	IBM PC/XT/AT	$189.95	Personal Project, time manager
ViewPoint	Computer Aided Management, Inc., Petaluma, CA	IBM PC/XT/AT, PS/2	$1,995	Top-down Planning, scheduling
CA-Tellaplan	Computer Associates Garden City, NY	IBM MVS, VM, DEC VAX/VMS, Apollo, Sun	Contact vendor	CPM, Gantts, planning analysis
CA-Planmacs		IBM PC/XT/AT	$16,500	Planning tool, resource mgmt.
CA-Estimacs		IBM PC/MS-DOS	$15K	Estimates for mainframe

PRODUCT	VENDOR	ENVIRONMENT	PRICE	COMMENT
				application dev.
CA-SuperProject Expert		IBM PC/XT/AT, PS/2	$695	Pert, Gantt charts, CPM, probability analysis
Plantrac	ComputerLine, Inc. Pembroke, MA	IBM PC/XT/AT	$695+	Planning, tracking tool
ProjectAlert	CRI, Inc., Santa Clara, CA	DEC VAX, HP 3000, Apollo	$10,000+	Pert and Gantt, scheduling monitoring
Easytrak	Cullinet Software Westwood, MA	IBM mainframe	Contact vendor	Cost and resource mgmt. system
Capital Project Mgmt. System	Data Design Associates, Sunnyvale, CA	IBM OS/MVS, DOS/VSE	Contact vendor	Tracks large expenditure projects against budget
VAX Software Project Manager	Digital Equipment Corp., Maynard, MA	DEC VAX/VMS	$2,250-$71,250	Software development project mgmt.
AMS Time Machine	Diversified Information Services, Inc., Studio City, CA	IBM PC/XT/AT, HP 150	$2,500 (Base), $4,500 (w/graphics)	Scheduling, resource management, CPM
PEVA	Engineering Mgmt. Consultants, Troy, MI	IBM PC/XT/AT	$189	Project Earned Value
Action-Tracker	Information Research Corp., Charlottesville, VA	IBM PC/XT/AT	$198	Project tracking budget mgmt.
Action Network w/Project Query Language		IBM PC/XT/AT	$1,498	Project tracking budget mgmt. Multiproject control
InstaPlan	InstaPlan Corp., Mill Valley, CA	IBM PC/XT/AT, PS/2	$99	Top-down, out line-oriented
PREMIS	K & H Professional Management services, Wayne, PA	IBM OS, VM	Contact vendor	Time analysis resource mgmt.

Guide to Software

PRODUCT	VENDOR	ENVIRONMENT	PRICE	COMMENT
PICOM		IBM OS, VM	Contact vendor	Project cost information management
PROJECT-MANAGER	Manager Software Products, Lexington, MA	IBM MVS, VS1,DOS/VSE	$15k-$26K	Resource Management, budget control
MI-Project	Matterhorn, Inc., Minneapolis, MN	IBM DOS/VSE, OS/MVS, VS1	$7.5K-$15.5K	Project planning control
Artemis Project	Metier Management Systems, Houston, TX	IBM PC/XT/AT, PS/2	$3,500	What-if analysis, resource leveling
Artemis		IBM MVS, VMHP	Contact vendor	CPM project mgmt. database
Micro Planner	Micro Planning Software, San Francisco, CA	IBM PC/XT/AT	$495	Planning, resource management
Micro Planner Plus		Apple Macintosh	$495	Planning, resource management
Microsoft Project	Microsoft Corp., Redmond, WA	IBM PC/XT/AT	$495	Resource planning cost analysis, Gantt charts
Quick-Plan II	Mitchell Management Systems, Westborough, MA	IBMPC/XT/AT	$250	Planning resource scheduling
MAPPS		IBM PC, VM, HP150, Wang PC, DEC VAX, DG	$16K-$250K	Time, cost, resource planning & control
Task Monitor	Monitor Software, Los Altos, CA	IBM PC	$695	
Multitrak	Multisystems, Cambridge, MA	IBM MVS, DOS, CICS, IBM PC	Contact vendor	Resource allocation
Vue	National Info. Systems, Cupertino, CA	IBM PC/XT/AT, DEC VAX/VMS, Unix, HP 3000, Honeywell	$1,995	Scheduling uses CPM

PRODUCT	VENDOR	ENVIRONMENT	PRICE	COMMENT
Prothos	New Technology Association, Evansville, IN	IBM PC/XT/AT, DEC VAX, Unix Sys V	$600 +	
N5500	Nichols & Comp., Culver City, CA	IBM OS/MVS, DOS, Unisys, DEC, Wang, DG, HP, Honeywell Prime	$30K (Basicsystem)	Critical path system; network up to 3,000 activities
N1100		IBM PC, HP150, Wang PC	$1,800	Critical path system; project mgmt.; control
PMS-11	North America Mica, San Diego, CA	IBM PC/XT/AT	$1,295	
Pertmaster Advanced	Pertmaster International, Santa Clara, CA	IBM PC/XT/AT, PS/2	$1,500	Plan, schedule, manage projects with interrelated tasks
PMS-80 Advanced	Pinnell Engineering, Portland, OR	IBM PC/XT/AT	$2,500 (Base), $1,500 (graphics option)	
MicroMan II	Poc-It Management Systems Santa Monica, CA	IBM PC/XT/AT, PS/2	$2,895	Tracks, manages IS activity
Quick Schedule	Power Up, San Mateo, CA	IBM PC	$69.96	Scheduling
Primavera Project Planner	Primavera Systems, Bala Cynwyd, PA	IBM PC/XT/AT, PS/2	$2,500	Cost analysis & control, activity coding
Parade		IBM PC/XT/AT, PS/2	$2,000	Performance measurement, earned value analysis
Planner	Productivity Solutions, Waltham, MA	DEC VAX/VMS	$4,500 $18K	
Qwiknet Professional	Project Software & Development, Inc, Cambridge, MA	IBM PC/XT/AT, PS/2, DEC VAX/VMS	$1,495-$18,900	CPM multiproject scheduling
Project/2		IBM MVS, VM, DEC VAX/VMS	$75K-$750K	For complex project; schedule & cost mgmt.

Guide to Software

PRODUCT	VENDOR	ENVIRONMENT	PRICE	COMMENT
SAS/OR	SAS Institute, Cary, NC	IBM PC/XT/AT, PS/2, OS, DOS/VSE, DEC VAX/VMS, Prime	Contact vendor	Scheduling, control and analysis
Project Scheduler 4	Scitor Corp., Foster City, CA	IBM PC/XT/AT, PS/2, Wang PC, HP150	$685	Handles multiple projects
Advanced Pro-PATH 6	SoftCorp, Inc., Clearwater, FL	IBM PC/XT/AT, PS/2	$199	Uses CPM for planning; cost/resource mgmt.
Scheduling & Control	Softext Publishing Corp., New York, NY	IBM PC/AT	$95	Uses CPM
Micro Trak	SofTrak Systems, Salt Lake City, UT	IBM PC/XT/AT, PS/2, Unix, xenix, VMS	$595-$895	Project scheduling, control resource management using CPM
PlotTrak		IBM PC/XT/AT, PS/2, Unix	$295-$495	For MicroTrakgraphics, Ganttcharts & NetworkDiagrams
Harvard Project Manager	Software Publishing Corp., Mountain View, CA	IBM PC/XT/AT, PS/2	$595	WBS, project control/mgmt. ; Pert/Gantt charts
SSP's PROMIS	Strategic Software Planning Corp., Cambridge, MA	IBM PC/XT/AT, PS/2	$2,995	Subnetworking for large Projects
Project OUTLOOK		IBM PC/XT/AT, PS/2	$495	Interactive MS-Windows-based, builds networks on screen with mouse
Time Line	Symantec Corp., Break-through Software Division, Novato, CA	IBM PC/XT/AT, PS/2	$495	Project planning, resource allocation, cost tracking
VIS10N	Systonetics, Fullerton, CA	DEC VAX/VMS Prime	contact vendor	Scheduling, resource

PRODUCT	VENDOR	ENVIRONMENT	PRICE	COMMENT
				allocation, performance measurement
VIS10Nmicro		IBM PC/XT/AT	$995	Mouse-driven interface; project mgmt. & graphics
AcuVision		IBM MVS, VM	contact vendor	Evaluating, Scheduling, tracking
OpenPlan	Welcom Software Technology, Houston, TX	IBM PC/XT/AT, PS/2	$4,200	Critical path analysis, resource scheduling
Opera		IBM PC/XT/AT, PS/2	$2,200	Risk analysis extension

SPREADSHEET SOFTWARE

PRODUCT	COMPANY	SPECIFICATIONS	FEATURES
Quattro 1.0	Borland International, Inc.	256 columns by 8,192 rows matrix size; 1 maximum sheet on-screen	Consolidates different layouts; minimal recalculation; undo/redo
SuperCalc5	Computer Associates International Inc.	254 columns by 9,999 rows matrix size; 3 maximum sheets on-screen	Linking; consolidates different layouts; minimal recalculation, undo/redo
Lucid 3-D version 2.0	Dac Software, Inc.	254 columns by 9,999 rows matrix size; 9 maximum sheets on-screen	Linking; consolidates different layouts; minimal recalculation; undo/redo
Silk 1.1	Daybreak Technologies Inc.	256 columns by 2,048 rows matrix size; 1 maximum sheet on-screen	Consolidates different layouts; undo/redo
Smart Spreadsheet with Graphics 3.1	Informix Software Inc.	999 columns by 9,999 rows matrix size; maximum sheet on-screen	Linking, consolidates different layouts; undo/redo
Javelin Plus 2.02	Javelin Software Corp.	65,000 columns by 16,000 rows matrix size; 2 maximum sheets on-screen	Linking; 3-D; consolidates different layouts; minimal recalculation
Lotus 1-2-3 release 2.01	Lotus Development Corp.	265 columns by 8,192 rows matrix size; 2 maximum sheets on-screen	Minimal recalculation

Guide to Software

PRODUCT	COMPANY	SPECIFICATIONS	FEATURES
Lotus Symphony 2.0		256 columns by 8,192 rows matrix size; 1 maximum sheet on-screen	Linking consolidates different layouts; minimal recalculation; undo/redo
Microsoft Excel for Windows version 2.1	Microsoft Corp.	256 columns by 16,384 rows matrix size; maximum sheets on-screen limited by memory	Linking; consolidates different layouts; minimal recalculation; undo/redo
Legend Twin Level III	Mosaic Marketing Inc.	265 columns by 8,192 rows matrix size; 3 maximum sheets on-screen	Linking; consolidates different layouts; minimal recalculation
VP-Planner	Paperback Software International	265 columns by 9,999 rows matrix size; 1 maximum sheet on-screen	Consolidates different layouts
VP-Planner Plus		256 columns by 9,999 rows matrix size; 1 maximum sheet on-screen	Consolidates different layouts; minimal recalculation; undo/redo
Logistik	Precision Inc.	1,024 columns by 2,040 rows matrix size; 1 maximum sheet on-screen	Linking, consolidates different layouts
SCO Professional	The Santa Cruz Operation	256 columns by 8,192 rows matrix size; 1 maximum sheet on-screen	Consolidates different layouts
TM/1 release 3.0	Sinper Corp.	9,999 columns by 9,999 rows matrix size; 128 maximum sheets on-screen	Linking; 8-D spreadsheets; consolidates different layouts
Open Access II plus spreadsheet version 2.1	Software Products International Inc.	216 columns by 3,000 rows matrix size; 128 maximum sheets on-screen	Linking
Surpass version 1.01	Surpass Software Systems Inc.	256 columns by 8,192 rows matrix size; 31 maximum sheets on-screen	Linking, consolidates different layouts; minimal recalculation
Plan Perfect 3.0	WordPerfect Corp.	256 columns by 8,192 rows matrix size; 2 maximum sheets on-screen	Linking, consolidates different layouts;

APPENDIX B

Project Management Software Vendors

AccuraTech, Inc.
5422 Chevy Chase Drive
Houston, TX 77056
(713) 960-0889

AlderGraf Systems, Inc.
1080 W. Belt North, Suite 113
Houston, TX 77043
(713) 467-8500

AGS Management Systems, Inc.
880 First Avenue
King of Prussia, PA 19406
(215) 265-1550

Applied Business Technology Corp.
361 Broadway
New York, NY 10013
(212) 219-8945

Applied MicroSystems, Inc.
P. O. Box 832
Roswell, GA 30077
(404) 475-0832
Product(s): Protracs

Bechtel Software, Inc.
289 Great Road
Acton, MA 01720
(617) 635-0580

Breakthrough Software
505 San Marin Drive
Novato, CA 94947
(415) 898-1919
Product(s): Time Line

CDI Communication Dynamics, Inc.
7300 S.W. Hunziker, Suite 200
Tigard, OR 97223
(503) 684-5151
Product(s): Timepiece

Computer Aided Management, Inc.
24 Professional Center Parkway
San Rafael, CA 94903-2703
(415) 472-5120
Product(s): ViewPoint

Project Management Software Vendors

Computer Associates International
Micro Products Division
2195 Fortune Drive
San Jose, CA 95131
(408) 432-1727

Computerline, Inc.
P. O. Box 308
52 School Street
Pembroke, MA 02359
(617) 294-1111
Product(s): Plantrac

Dekker Ltd.
P. O. Box 2180
Redlands, CA 92373
(714) 793-7939
Product(s): Trakker Plus

Digital Marketing Corp.
P. O. Box 2010
Walnut Creek, CA 94595-0010
(415) 947-1000
(800) 826-2222
Product(s): Milestone

Diversified Information Services, Inc.
4370 Tujunga Avenue, Suite 130
Studio City, CA 91604
(818) 506-7265
Product(s): AMS Time Machine

Earth Data Corp.
P. O. Box 13168
Richmond, VA 23225
(804) 231-0300
Product(s): MicroGantt, MPert

Elite Software Development, Inc.
P. O. Box 1194
Bryan, TX 77806
(409) 846-2340
Product(s): CPM/PERT

Inmax Publishing Ltd.
560-1380 Burrard Street
Vancouver, B.C.
Canada V62 2H3
(604) 682-8700

InstaPlan Corp.
655 Redwood Highway, Suite 311
Mill Valley, CA 94941
(800) 852-7526

K & H Professional Management
  Services
48 Woodport Road
Sparta, NJ 07871
(201) 729-6142
Product(s): Prestige-PC

Kepner-Tregoe L.P.
P. O. Box 704
Princeton, NJ 08542
(800) 223-0482
Product(s): Planning Pro

McDonnell Douglas Information
  Systems Co.
Dept. L821, Building 302/4W
P. O. Box 516
St. Louis, MO 63166-0516
(314) 232-3037

Metier Management Systems, Inc.
2900 North Loop West, Suite 1300
Houston, TX 77092
(713) 956-7511

Micro Planning International
235 Montgomery Street, Suite 840
San Francisco, CA 94104
(415) 788-3324

Micro-Frame Technologies, Inc.
337 N. Vineyard Avenue, Suite 106
Ontario, CA 91764
(714) 983-2711
Product(s): software for government
  contracts

Micro Research Systems Corp.
P. O. Box 386, Snowdon
Montreal, Quebec
Canada H3X 3T6
(514) 487-2275

Microsoft Corp.
16011 N.E. 36th Way
P. O. Box 97017
Redmond, WA 98073-9717

Mitchell Management Systems, Inc.
Westborough Office Park
2000 W. Park Drive
Westboro, MA 01581
(617) 366-0800

Monitor Software
960 N. San Antonio Road, Suite
Los Altos, CA 94022
(415) 949-1688
(800) 367-7879
Product(s): Task Monitor

Multisystems, Inc.
1050 Massachusetts Avenue
Cambridge, MA 02138
(617) 864-5810
Product(s): Multitrak-PC

Multitrak Software Development
  Corp.
108 Lincoln Street
Boston, MA 02111-2502
(617) 482-6677

National Information Systems, Inc.
1190 Saratoga Avenue
San Jose, CA 95129
(408) 985-7100
Product(s): Accent R, Vue

North America Mica, Inc.
11772 Sorrento Valley Road
Suite 257
San Diego, CA 92121
(619) 792-1012
Product(s): PMS II

Pertmaster International
3235 Kifer Street
Santa Clara, CA 95051
(408) 736-6800
Product(s): Pertmaster

Pinnell Engineering, Inc.
5441 S.W. Macadam Avenue
Suite 208
Portland, OR 97201
(503) 243-2246
Product(s): custom products

Poc-It Management Services
606 Wilshire Blvd., Suite 512
Santa Monica, CA 90401
(213) 393-4552
Product(s): MicroMan II

Power Project Management, Inc.
4275 Executive Square, Suite 800
La Jolla, CA 92037
(619) 546-2939

Primavera Systems, Inc.
2 Bala Plaza
Bala Cynwyd, PA 19004
(215) 667-8600
Product(s): Primavera, Primavision,
  Parade

Project Software & Development
20 University Road
Cambridge, MA 02138
(617) 661-1444
Product(s): Qwiknet

Project Management Software Vendors

Projectronix, Inc.
4546 El Camino Real, Suite 324
Los Altos, CA 94022

Scitor Corp.
250 Lincoln Centre Drive
Foster City, CA 94404
(415) 570-7700
Product(s): Scheduler 5000
  Project Scheduler Network

Sheppard Software Co.
4750 Clough Creek Road
Redding, CA 96002
(916) 222-1553
Product(s): MicroPERT

Shirley Software Systems, Inc.
1930 La France Avenue
South Pasadena, CA 91030
(818) 441-5121

Simple Software, Inc.
2 Pinewood
Irvine, CA 92714-3274
(714) 857-9179
Product(s): ProjectMaster

SoftCorp, Inc.
2340 State Road 580, Suite 244
Clearwater, FL 33575
(813) 799-3984
(800) 255-7526
Product(s): Pro*Path*Plus

SofTrack Systems
P. O. Box 16750
Salt Lake City, Utah 84116
(801) 973-9610
Product(s): SofTrak, MultiGantt,
  CustomGantt

Software Publishing Corp.
1901 Landings Drive
P. O. Box 7210
Mountain View, CA 94039
(415) 962-8910
Product(s): Harvard Project Manager

Softext Publishing Corp.
17 E. 45th St., Suite 601
New York, NY 10017
(212) 986-5985
(800) 248-TEXT
Product(s): Scheduling and Control

Robert W. Starinsky Consulting
  Services
520 Pinebrook Drive
Lombard, IL 60148
(312) 495-7376
Product(s): Project Status Reporting
System I

Strategic Software Planning Corp.
245 First Street
Cambridge, MA 02142
(617) 577-8800
Product(s): Promis

Symantec Corp.
10201 Torre Avenue
Cupertino, CA 95014
(415) 898-1919

Systonetics, Inc.
1561 E. Orangethorpe Avenue
Suite 200
Fullerton, CA 92531
(714) 680-0910

Timberline Software
9405 S.W. Gemini
Beaverton, OR 97005
(503) 626-6775

VisiCorp (formerly Paladin Software
    Corp.)
2700 Augustine Drive, Suite 178
Santa Clara, CA 95054
(408) 970-0566
Product(s): VisiSchedule

Welcom Software Technology
1325 S. Dairy Ashford, Suite 125
Houston, TX 77077
(713) 558-0514
Product(s): Open Plan

Glossary

access arm—The disk drive mechanism used to position the read/write heads over the appropriate track.

access time—The time interval between the instant a computer makes a request for a transfer of data from a secondary storage device and the instant this operation is completed.

accumulator—The computer register where the result of an arithmetic or logic operation is formed.

acoustical coupler—A device in which a telephone handset is mounted for the purpose of transmitting data over telephone lines. It is used with a modem.

activity—A time-consuming element in a project plan. The nature of the start, content, and completion are embodied in the activity description.

activity-on-arrrows—A networking scheme in which the nodes represent events and the arrows represent activities.

activity-on-nodes—A networking scheme in which the nodes represent activities and the arrows represent precedence requirement only.

activity free slack—The number of time periods by which an activity's completion can be delayed beyond its earliest completion without affecting the earliest start of any succeeding activity.

activity total slack—The number of time periods by which an activity's completion may be delayed beyond its earliest completion without affecting the latest completion of the project.

activity variance—A measure of the variability associated with the activity duration.

Ada—A multipurpose, procedure-oriented language.

address—1. A name, numeral, or label that designates a particular location in primary or secondary storage. 2. A location identifier for terminals in a computer network.

alpha—Of or referring to the letters of the alphabet.

alphanumeric—Pertaining to a character set that contains letters, digits, punctuation, and special symbols (related to alpha and numeric).

analog—Of or referring to the transmission of information by converting it to a variable electrical signal. It usually refers to voice signals, like those over telephone lines.

APL (A Programming Language)—An interactive symbolic programming language used primarily for mathematical applications.

application—A problem or task to which the computer can be applied.

application generators—Fifth generation of programming languages in which programmers specify, through an interactive dialog with the system, which processing tasks are to be performed.

applications software—Software designed and written for a specific personal, business, or processing task.

arithmetic and logic unit—The portion of the computer that performs arithmetic and logic operations (related to accumulator).

ARPANET—A nationwide, packet-switched communications network developed for the Department of Defense by the Advanced Research Projects Agency and now an industry standard.

array—A programming concept that permits access to a list or table of values by the use of a single variable name.

arrow—A line carrying an indiction of direction. It also can represent an activity or a precedence relationship.

artificial intelligence (AI)—The ability of the computer to reason, learn, strive for self-improvement, and simulate human sensory capabilities.

ASCII (American Standard Code for Information Interchange)—A coding system for characters of seven bits plus one parity bit, for transmission over a data network.

assembly language—A low-level symbolic language with an instruction set that is essentially one-to-one with machine language.

asynchronous—A transmission sequence in which the intervals between characters are not equal, and start and stop bits are added for coordination.

asynchronous transmission—Data transmission at irregular intervals that is synchronized with start/stop bits (contrast with synchronous transmission).

automatic teller machine (ATM)—An automated deposit/withdrawal device used in banking.

auxiliary storage—*See* SECONDARY STORAGE.

back-end processor—A host-subordinate processor that handles administrative tasks associated with retrieval and manipulation of data (same as database machine).

backup—Pertaining to equipment, procedures, or databases that can be used to restart the system in the event of system failure.

backup file—Duplicate of an existing production file.

backward pass—The sequence of calculations that starts with the latest allowable time for the completion of the project and leads through the latest allowable start and complete times for all activities in the network.

badge reader—An input device that reads data on badges and cards (related to magnetic stripe).

bar code—A graphic encoding technique in which vertical bars of varying widths are used to represent data.

baseband—Transmission of signals directly onto the cable as voltage pulses, without modulation, one signal at a time.

BASIC—A multipurpose programming language that is popular on small computer systems.

batch processing—A technique in which transactions and/or jobs are collected into groups (batched) and processed together.

baud—Transmission speed according to the time duration of the shortest signal element.

binary notation—Use of the binary (base two) numbering system (10, 1) for internal representation of alphanumeric data.

bit—Short for a *bi*nary dig*it* (0 or 1).

block—A group of data that is either read from or written to an I/O device in one operation.

blocking—Combining two or more records into one block.

boot—To load the operating system to primary storage and ready a computer system for use.

BPI (bytes per inch)—A measure of data-recording density on secondary storage.

bridge—Circuitry used to connect networks with a common set of high-level protocols.

broadband—Or or referring to the transmission of signals through a modem onto a coaxial cable, with a wide range of frequencies available.

buffer—A small storage space for data, usually temporary, to hold transmitted data for processing.

bug—1. A logic or syntax error in a program. 2. A logic error in the design of a computer system. 3. A hardware fault.

burst event—An event that immediately precedes more than one activity.

bus—A network topology in which stations attach to a single transmission medium so that all stations hear all transmissions.

byte—A group of adjacent bits configured to represent a character.

Glossary

C—A transportable programming language that can be used to develop both systems and applications software.

CAD (Computer-Aided Design)—Use of computer graphics capabilities to aid in design, drafting, and documentation in product and manufacturing engineering.

CAI (Computer-Assisted Instruction)—Use of the computer as an aid in the educational process.

calendar—The specification of a standard calendar for a project. The calendar will indicate such things as work days, holidays, and working hours. A project management software package that allows for calendar modifications will automatically adjust project schedules to fit the specified calendar.

CAM (Computer-Aided Manufacturing)—A term coined to highlight the use of computers in the manufacturing process.

carrier, common—In data communications, a company that furnishes data communications services to the general public.

CASE—Abbreviation for Computer-Aided Software Engineering.

cathode ray tube—*See CRT.*

cell—The intersection of a particular row and column in an electronic spreadsheet.

cell address—The location, column and row, of a cell in an electronic spreadsheet.

central processing unit (CPU)—*See* PROCESSOR.

channel—The facility by which data are transmitted between locations in a computer network (e.g., workstation to host, host to printer).

character—A unit of alphanumeric datum.

CIM (Computer-integrated manufacturing)—Using the computer at every stage of the manufacturing process, from the time a part is conceived until it is shipped.

circuit switching—A method of directly connecting terminals by connecting the circuits they are attached to, where devices have full access to each other.

coaxial cable—A cable made up of a single conductor surrounded by insulation and covered with a metallic shield.

COBOL (Common Business Oriented Language)—A programming language used primarily for administrative information systems.

code—1. The rules used to translate a bit configuration to alphanumeric characters. 2. The process of compiling computer instructions in the form of a computer program. 3. The actual computer program.

collate—To combine two or more files for processing.

COM (Computer Output Microfilm/Microfiche)—A device that produces a microform image of a computer output on microfilm or microfiche.

common carrier—*See* CARRIER, COMMON.

communications—*See* DATA COMMUNICATIONS.

compatibility—1. Of or pertaining to the ability of one computer to execute programs of, access the database of, and communicate with, another computer. 2. Of or pertaining to the ability of a particular hardware device to interface with a particular computer.

compile—To translate a high-level programming language, such as COBOL, to machine language in preparation for execution (compare with interpreter).

compiler—Systems software that performs the compilation process.

computer—*See* PROCESSOR.

computer console—The unit of a computer system that allows operator and computer to communicate.

computer network—An integration of computer systems, workstations, and communications links.

computer system—A collective reference to all interconnected computing hardware, including processors, storage devices, input/output devices, and communications equipment.

computerese—Of or referring to the terms and phrases associated with computers and information processing.

concentrator—*See* DOWN-LINE PROCESSOR.

concurrent activities—Activities which are in progress simultaneously for one or more time periods.

configuration—The computer and its peripheral devices.

contention—1. A line control procedure in which each workstation "contends" with other workstations for service by sending requests for service to the host processor. 2. Access to a network that allocates capacity on a first-come-first-served basis.

contingency plan—A plan that details what to do in case an event drastically disrupts the operation of a computer center.

control clerk—A person who accounts for all input to and output from a computer center.

control field—*See* KEY DATA ELEMENT.

control total—An accumulated number that is checked against a known value for the purpose of output control.

control unit—The portion of the processor that interprets program instructions.

conversion—The transition process from one system (manual or computer-based) to a computer-based information system.

cottage industry—People using computer technology to do work-for-profit from their homes.

counter—One or several programming instructions used to tally processing events.

CPM (Critical Path Method)—The method that uses time-cost tradeoffs to determine the project length which gives the minimum sum of direct and indirect costs.

Glossary

crash cost—The minimum direct cost required to complete an activity in its crash time.

crash time—The minimum time in which an activity can be completed if the maximum resource augmentation is made.

critical path—The connected sequence of activities from the start of the project to the completion of the project which has the largest sum of activity durations. A delay along the critical path will cause the project to be delayed by the same number of time periods.

CRT (Cathode Ray Tube)—The video monitor component of a workstation.

cryptography—A communications crime-prevention technology that uses methods of data encryption and decryption to scramble codes sent over communications channels.

cursor—A blinking character that indicates the location of the next input on the display screen.

cyberphobia—The irrational fear of, and aversion to, computers.

cylinder—A disk storage concept. A cylinder is the portion of the disk that can be read in any given position of the access arm (*see* SECTOR.)

Daisy-wheel printer—A letter-quality serial printer, whose interchangeable character set is located on a spoked print wheel.

DASD (Direct-Access Storage Device)—A random-access secondary storage device.

data—A representation of fact and raw material for information.

database—1. An alternative terminology for microcomputer-based data management software. 2. An organization's data resource for all computer-based information processing in which the data are integrated and related such that data redundancy is minimized.

database administrator (DBA)—The individual responsible for the physical and logical maintenance of the database.

database machine—*See* BACK-END PROCESSOR.

database management system (DBMS)—A systems software package for the creation, manipulation, and maintenance of the database.

database record—Related data read from, or written to, the database as a unit.

data communications—The collection and/or distribution of data from and/or to a remote facility.

data communications specialist—A person who designs and implements computer networks.

data dictionary—A listing and description of all data elements in the database.

data element—The smallest logical unit of data. Examples are employee number, first name, and price (*see* FIELD, DATA ITEM).

data entry—The transcription of source data into machine-readable format.

data entry operator—A person who uses key entry devices to transcribe data into a machine-readable format.

data flow diagram (DFD)—A design technique that permits documentation of a system or program at several levels of generality.

data item—The value of a data element (compare with data element).

data PBX—A computer that electronically connects computers and workstations for the purpose of data communication.

data processing (DP)—Using the computer to perform operations on data.

debug—To eliminate ''bugs'' in a program or system (related to bug).

decimal—The base-10 numbering system.

decision support system (DSS)—A sophisticated information system that uses available data, computer technology, models, and query languages to support the decision-making process.

decision table—A graphic technique used to illustrate possible occurrences and appropriate actions within a system.

decode—The reverse of the encoding process (*See* ENCODE.)

density—The number of bytes per linear length of track of a recording media. Usually measured in bytes per inch (bpi) and applied to magnetic tapes and disks.

dependency—The relationship existing between one activity and another which must immediately precede it.

desktop computer—Any computer that can be placed conveniently on the top of a desk (e.g., microcomputer, personal computer).

deterministic activity time—If the duration of an activity would be essentially the same in each of several independent occurrences, that activity time (duration) would be regarded as deterministic.

diagnostic—The isolation and/or explanation of a program error.

digital—Binary, on-off signaling, consisting of 0s and 1s, as opposed to analog signaling.

digitize—To translate an image into a form that computers can interpret.

direct access—*See* RANDOM ACCESS.

direct-access file—*See* RANDOM FILE.

direct-access processing—*See* RANDOM PROCESS.

direct-access storage device—*See* DASD.

director of information services—The person who has responsibility for computer and information systems activity in an organization.

disk, magnetic—A secondary storage medium for random-access data storage. Available as micro-disk, diskette, disk cartridge, or disk pack.

disk drive—A magnetic storage device that records data on flat rotating disks (*see* TAPE DRIVE).

diskette—A thin flexible disk for secondary random-access data storage (*see* FLOPPY DISK, FLEXIBLE DISK).

distributed processing—Both a technological and an organizational concept based on the premise that information systems can be made more responsive to users by moving computer hardware and personnel physically closer to the people who use them.

distributed processor—The nucleus of a small computer system that is linked to the host computer and physically located in the functional area departments.

documentation—Permanent and continuously updated written and graphic descriptions of information systems and programs.

down-line processor—A computer that collects data from a number of low-speed devices, then transmits "concentrated" data over a single communications channel. Also called a multiplexor or concentrator.

download—The transmission of data from a mainframe computer to a workstation.

downtime—The time during which a computer system is not operational.

driver module—The program module that calls other subordinate program modules to be executed as they are needed.

dummy activity—An activity that has no real content and requires no time or resources. It is used in networking to extend dependencies, either to simplify the drawing of the network or to make possible the indication of all precedence requirements without indicating precedence requirements that do not exist.

dump—The duplication of the contents of a storage device to another storage device or to a printer.

duplex—The ability to transmit and receive over a network at the same time.

duration—The expected number of time periods which will be required to perform an activity.

earliest activity complete time—The earliest activity start time plus the expected activity duration.

earliest activity start time—The first time period in which all of an activity's predecessors are expected to be complete if all activities are performed as soon as all their predecessors are complete. It is equal to the earliest start time for the project plus the maximum sum of activity durations along the activity paths from the project start to the start of the activity.

earliest expected event occurrence time—The earliest project start plus the sum of the expected activity time along the longest path from the start of the project to the event. This is the maximum of the earliest activity complete times among all activities immediately preceding that event.

EBCDIC (Extended Binary Coded Decimal Interchange Code)—An encoding system.

education coordinator—The person who coordinates all computer-related educational activities within an organization.

EFT (Electronic Funds Transfer)—A computer-based system allowing electronic transfer of money from one account to another.

802—A family of standards for networks developed by the Institute of Electrical and Electronics Engineers (IEEE), from the 802.3 bus network to the 802.6 metropolitan area network.

electronic bulletin board—A computer-based "bulletin board" that permits external users access to the system via data communications for the purpose of reading and sending messages.

electronic funds transfer—*See* EFT.

electronic mail—A computer application whereby messages are transmitted via data communications to "electronic mailboxes." Also called E-mail.

electronic spreadsheet—*See* SPREADSHEET.

encode—To apply the rules of a code (contrast with decode).

encoding system—A system that permits alphanumeric characters to be coded in terms of bits.

end user—The individual providing input to the computer or using computer output. *See* USER.

end-of-file (EOF) marker—A marker placed at the end of a sequential file.

EPROM—Erasable PROM (programmable read-only memory).

ethernet—A baseband local area network developed jointly by Xerox, DEC, and Intel.

event—A point in time representing the start or completion of one or more activities.

expected activity time (duration)—The average number of time periods required to complete an activity if several independent occurrences of the activity in question could be observed.

expert system—An interactive computer-based system that responds to questions, asks for clarification, makes recommendations, and generally aids in the decision-making process (*see* KNOWLEDGE BASE).

export capability—The ability of a project management software package to export data to other computer programs.

facsimile—Transmission, either analog or digital, of page images.

feasibility study—A study performed to determine the economic and procedural feasibility of a proposed information system.

feedback loop—In a process control environment, the output of the process being controlled is input to the system.

fiber optics—Thin, glass strands bundled into cable that allow high-speed data transmission by on/off light signals.

field—*See* DATA ELEMENT.

file—A collection of related records.

firmware—"Hard-wired" logic for performing certain computer functions; built into a particular computer, often in the form of ROM or PROM.

file server—Hardware and/or software that provide users access to disks or other mass storage devices.

filtered task report—A feature that allows selective reporting on the status of particular tasks as opposed to a general reporting of all the tasks at one time.

flat files—A traditional file structure in which records are related to no other files.

flexible disk—*See* diskette.

float—*See* ACTIVITY FREE SLACK, ACTIVITY TOTAL SLACK.

floppy disk—*See* diskette.

flowchart—A diagram that illustrates data, information, and work flow via specialized symbols which, when connected by flow lines, portray the logic of a system or program.

FORTRAN (FORmula TRANslator)—A high-level programming language designed primarily for scientific applications.

forward pass—The sequence of calculations which starts with the earliest start time for the project and leads through the determination of the earliest start and complete times for all activities in the network.

front-end processor—A processor used to offload certain data communications tasks from the host processor.

full-screen editing—This word processing feature permits the user to move the cursor to any position in the document to insert or replace text.

Gantt Chart—A chart that shows a project schedule. It can also display the status of various tasks, personnel assignments, and costs.

gateway—System and software that permit two networks using different protocols to communicate with each other.

general-purpose computer—Computer systems designed with the flexibility to do a variety of tasks, such as CAI, payroll processing, climate control, and so on (*see* SPECIAL-PURPOSE COMPUTER).

gigabyte (G)—One billion bytes of storage.

grandfather-father-son method—A secondary storage backup procedure that results in the master file having two generations of backup.

hacker—A computer enthusiast who uses the computer as a source of enjoyment.

handshaking—The process of establishing a communications link between the source and destination.

hard copy—A readable printed copy of computer output.

hardware—The physical devices that comprise a computer systems (*see* SOFTWARE).

hashing—A method of random access in which the address is arithmetically calculated from the key data element.

hexadecimal—A base-16 numbering system that is used in information processing as a programmer convenience to condense binary output and make it more readable.

high-level programming language—A language with instructions that combine several machine-level instructions into one (*see* MACHINE LANGUAGE, LOW-LEVEL PROGRAMMING LANGUAGE).

HIPO (Hierarchical Plus Input-Processing-Output)—A design technique that encourages the top-down approach, dividing the system into easily manageable modules.

host computer—A system in a network that performs the actual processing operations and with which the network nodes communicate.

hot processor—The processor responsible for the overall control of a computer system. The host processor is the focal point of a communications-based system.

icons—Pictographs that are used in place of words or phrases on screen displays.

idea processor—A software productivity tool, also called an outliner, that allows the user to organize and document thoughts and ideas.

identifier—A name used in computer programs to recall a value, an array, a program, or a function from storage.

import capability—The ability of a project management software package to import data from other computer programs.

index sequential-access method (ISAM)—A direct-access data storage scheme that uses an index to locate and access data stored on magnetic disk.

information—Data that have been collected and processed into a meaningful form.

information center—A facility where computing resources are made available to various user groups.

information center specialist—Someone who works with users in an information center.

information resource management (IRM)—A concept advocating that information should be treated as a corporate resource.

information services department—The organizational entity or entities that develop and maintain computer-based information systems.

information system—A computer-based system that provides both data processing capability and information for managerial decision making (*see* MANAGEMENT INFORMATION SYSTEMS, MIS).

input—Data to be processed by a computer system.

I/O (Input/Output)—Input or output, or both.

inquiry—An on-line request for information.

instruction—A programming language statement that specifies a particular computer operation to be performed.

integrated software—The integration of data management, electronic spreadsheet, graphics, word processing, and communications software.

intelligent—Computer aided.

intelligent terminal—A terminal with a built-in microprocessor.

interactive—Pertaining to on-line and immediate communication between the end user and computer.

interblock gap (IBG)—A physical space between record blocks on magnetic tapes.

interpreter—Systems software that translates and executes each program instruction before translating and executing the next (*see* COMPILER).

ISAM—*See* INDEXED SEQUENTIAL ACCESS METHOD.

ISDN (Integrated Services Digital Network)—A communication standard that provides an integrated network of voice and data (analog and digital) to users on the same communications network.

job—A unit of work for the computer system.

K—1. An abbreviation for "kilo," meaning 1,000. 2. A computerese abbreviation for 2 to the 10th power or 1,024.

key data element—The data element in a record that is used as an identifier for accessing, sorting, and collating records (*see* CONTROL FIELD).

keyboard—A device used for key data entry.

knowledge base—The foundation of a computer-based expert system (*see* EXPERT).

latest activity complete time—The latest possible time period in which the completion of the activity can occur without delaying the project. It is the latest completion time for the project less the maximum path length from the activity in question to the end of the project.

latest activity start time—The latest activity complete time less the activity duration.

latest expected event occurrence time—The latest project completion time less the sum of the activity durations along the longest path from the completion of the project to the event. This is the minimum of the latest activity start time for all activities immediately following the event.

layout—A detailed output and/or input specification that graphically illustrates exactly where information should be placed/entered on a VDT display screen or placed on a printed output.

leased line—A permanent or semipermanent communications channel leased through a common carrier.

level of indenture—Level of detail appropriate for the level of management for which a project network is prepared.

lexicon—The dictionary of words that can be interpreted by a particular natural language.

librarian—A person who functions to catalogue, monitor, and control the distribution of disks, tapes, system documentation, and computer-related literature.

linkage editor—An operating system program that assigns a primary storage address to each byte of an object program.

load—To transfer programs or data from secondary to primary storage.

local area network (LAN or local net)—A system of hardware, software, and communications channels that connects devices on the local premises.

loop—A sequence of program instructions that are executed repeatedly until a particular condition is met.

low-level programming language—A language comprised of the fundamental instruction set of a particular computer (*see* HIGH-LEVEL PROGRAMMING LANGUAGE).

machine cycle—The time it takes to retrieve, interpret, and execute a program instruction.

machine language—The programming language in which a computer executes all programs, without regard to the language of the original code.

macro—A sequence of frequently used operations or keystrokes that can be recalled and invoked to help speed user interaction with microcomputer productivity software.

magnetic disk—*See* DISK, MAGNETIC.

magnetic ink character recognition (MICR)—A data entry technique used primarily in banking. Magnetic characters are imprinted on checks and deposits, then "scanned" to retrieve the data.

magnetic strips—A magnetic storage medium for low-volume storage of data on badges and cards (*see* BADGE READER).

magnetic tape—*See* TAPE, MAGNETIC.

main memory—*See* PRIMARY STORAGE.

mainframe—*See* HOST PROCESSOR.

maintenance—The ongoing process by which information systems (and software) are updated and enhanced to keep up with changing requirements.

management information system (MIS)—*See* INFORMATION SYSTEM.

master file—The permanent source of data for a particular computer application area.

megabyte (M)—One million bytes of primary or secondary storage capacity.

memory—*See* PRIMARY STORAGE.

menu—A workstation display with a list of processing choices from which an end user can select.

merge event—An event which occurs only when two or more immediately preceding activities are completed.

message—A series of bits sent from a workstation to a computer or vice versa.

methodology—A set of standardized procedures, including technical methods, management techniques, and documentation, that provides the framework to accomplish a particular function (e.g., system development methodology).

micro/mainframe link—Linking microcomputers and mainframes for the purpose of data communication.

microcomputer (or micro)—A small computer.

microcomputer speciality—A specialist in the use and application of micro-computer hardware and software.

microdisk—A rigid $3^1/_2$-inch disk used for data storage.

microprocessor—1. A computer on a single chip. 2. The processing component of a microcomputer.

milestone—A significant point in the development of a system or program.

minicomputer (mini)—Computers with slightly more power and capacity than a microcomputer.

MIPS—Millions of instructions per second.

MIS (Management Information System)—*See* INFORMATION SYSTEM.

mnemonics—Symbols that represent instructions in assembler languages.

modem (modulator-demodulator)—A device used to convert computer-compatible signals to signals suitable for transmission facilities and vice versa.

monitor—A televisionlike display for soft copy output in a computer system.

most likely activity time—The activity duration which has a higher probability of occurrence than any other duration.

motherboard—1. A microcomputer circuit board that contains the microprocessor. 2. Electronic circuitry for handling such tasks as input/output signals from peripheral devices, and "memory chips."

multidrop—The connection of more than one terminal to a single communications channel.

multiple projects—The simultaneous management of several projects. The projects can be independent, dependent, or mutually exclusive.

multiplexer—A device used for combining several lower-speed channels into one higher speed channel.

multiplexor—*See* DOWN-LINE PROCESSOR.

multiprocessing—Using two or more processors in the same computer system in the simultaneous execution of two or more programs.

multiprogramming—Pertaining to the concurrent execution of two or more programs by a single computer.

natural language—Sixth-generation language in which the programmer writes specifications without regard to instruction format or syntax.

nested loop—A programming situation where at least one loop is entirely within another loop.

network—A graphic representation of a project. It consists of nodes interconnected with arrows to represent all activities involved in the project and all dependency relationships existing among them.

network, computer—*See* COMPUTER NETWORK.

network logic—The feasibility of the dependency relationships indicated on a network.

node—1. An enclosed geometric figure such as a circle or a square. 2. A major point at which terminals are given access to the network.

normal cost—The minimum activity cost associated with the performance of an activity at the minimum feasible resource level.

normal time—The minimum time in which an activity can be performed at the normal cost.

numeric—A reference to any of the digits 0-9 (*see* ALPHA, ALPHANUMERIC).

object program—A machine-level program that results from the compilation of a source program.

octal—A base-8 numbering system used in information processing as a programmer convenience to condense binary output and make it easier to read.

off-line—Pertaining to data that are not accessible by, or hardware devices that are not connected to, a computer system (*see* ON-LINE).

office automation (OA)—Computer-based applications associated with general office work.

office automation specialist—A person who specializes in the use and application of office automation hardware and software (*see* OFFICE AUTOMATION).

on-line—Pertaining to data and/or hardware devices that are accessible to and under the control of a computer system (*see* OFF-LINE).

open system interconnection (OSI)—A model developed by the International Standards Organization (ISO) to describe a network open to equipment from different manufacturers.

operating system—The software that controls the execution of all applications and systems software programs.

operator—The person who performs those hardware-based activities necessary to keep information systems operational.

operator console—The machine-room operator's workstation.

optical character recognition (OCR)—A data entry technique that permits original-source data entry. Coded symbols or characters are "scanned" to retrieve the data.

optical laser disk—A read-only secondary storage medium that uses laser technology.

optimistic activity time—For a variable activity duration, the duration that will occur if every aspect of the performance of the activity goes as well as it possibly could.

output—Data transferred from primary storage to an output device.

packaged software—Software that is generalized and "packaged" to be used, with little or no modification, in a variety of environments (*see* PROPRIETARY SOFTWARE).

packer switching—Transmission method in which data is assembled into short bundles of information, then transmitted from node to node across the network.

page—A program segment that is loaded to primary storage only if it is needed for execution (*see* VIRTUAL MEMORY).

parallel host processor—A redundant host processor used for back-up and supplemental processing.

parallel transmission—Simultaneous transmission of bits over parallel wires.

parity—A method of error detection in a network by which one or two bits are appended to a character set to identify it as even or odd.

parity bit—A bit appended to a bit configuration (byte) that is used to check the accuracy of data transmission from one hardware device to another (*see* PARITY CHECKING, PARITY ERROR).

parity checking—A built-in checking procedure in a computer system to help ensure that the transmission of data is complete and accurate (*see* PARITY BIT, PARITY ERROR).

parity error—Occurs when a bit is "dropped" in the transmission of data from one hardware device to another (*see* PARITY BIT, PARITY CHECKING).

Pascal—A multipurpose procedure-oriented programming language.

password—A word or phrase known only to the end user. When entered, it permits the end user to gain access to the system.

patch—A modification to a program or information system.

path—Any series of predecessor and successor activities.

peripheral equipment—Any hardware device other than the processor.

personal computer (PC)—*See* MICROCOMPUTER.

personal computing—A category of computer usage that includes individual uses of the computer for both domestic and business applications.

PERT (Program Evaluation and Review Technique)—Technique that uses the three-time estimate system to calculate probabilities of meeting scheduled dates.

PERT Chart—A chart that shows the relationships between tasks. It is also referred to as a network chart.

pessimistic activity time—For a variable activity duration, the duration that will occur if every aspect of the performance of the activity goes as poorly as it possibly could.

PL/I—A multipurpose procedure-oriented programming language.

plotter—A device that produces hard copy graphic output.

point-of-sale (POS) terminal—A cash-register-like terminal designed for key and/or scanner data entry.

point-to-point—Dedicated communication between two terminals.

polling—A line control procedure in which each workstation is "polled" in rotation to determine whether a message is ready to be sent.

port—An access point in a computer system that permits communication between the computer and a peripheral device.

post-implementation evaluation—A critical examination of a computer-based system after it has been put into production.

precedence requirements—Restrictions on the sequencing of activities, based on an activity's need for the prior completion of other activities.

predecessor event—The event that must occur immediately before an activity can proceed.

primary storage—The memory area in which all programs and data must reside before programs can be executed or data manipulated (*see* MAIN MEMORY, MEMORY, RAM, and SECONDARY STORAGE).

printer—A device used to prepare hard copy output.

private branch exchange (PBX)—A private circuit-switching system designed to direct both voice and data traffic from within an organization to outside networks.

private line—A dedicated communications channel between any two points in a computer network.

problem-oriented language—A high-level language whose instruction set is designed to address a specific problem (e.g., process control of machine tools, simulation).

procedure-oriented language—A high-level language whose general-purpose instruction set can be used to model scientific and business procedures.

process control—Using the computer to control an ongoing process in a continuous feedback loop.

processor—The logical component of a computer system that interprets and executes program instructions [same as computer, central processing unit (CPU)].

program—1. Computer instructions structured and ordered in a manner that, when executed, cause a computer to perform a particular function. 2. The act of producing computer software (related to software).

programmer—One who writes computer programs.

programmer/analyst—A position title of one who performs both the programming and systems analysis function.

programming—To write a computer program.

programming language—A language in which programmers communicate instructions to a computer.

project—A generally noncyclical work effort which consists of distinct, interrelated phases.

project leader—The person in charge of organizing the efforts of a project team.

project management—The planning, scheduling, and control for the activities comprising a project.

PROM (Programmable Read Only Memory)—ROM in which the user can load read-only programs and data.

prompt—A program-generated message describing what should be entered by the end user operator at a workstation.

proprietary software—Vendor-developed software that is marketed to the public (*see* PACKAGED SOFTWARE).

protocol—A certain standard used to ensure compatibility of data transmissions between terminals.

prototype system—A model of a full-scale system.

pseudocode—Nonexecutable program code used as an aid to develop and document structured programs.

pull-down menu—A menu that is superimposed in a window over whatever is currently being displayed on a monitor.

Query language—A fourth-generation programming language with Englishlike commands used primarily for inquiry and reporting.

RAM (Random Access Memory)—*See* PRIMARY STORAGE.

random access—Direct access to records, regardless of their physical location on the storage medium (*see* SEQUENTIAL ACCESS).

random file—A collection of records that can be processed randomly.

random processing—Processing of data and records randomly (*see* DIRECT-ACCESS PROCESSING, SEQUENTIAL PROCESSING).

read—To access a record or a portion of a record from the magnetic storage medium (tape or disk) of a secondary storage device and transfer to primary storage for processing.

read/write head—The component of a disk drive or tape drive that reads from and writes to its respective magnetic storage medium.

record—A collection of related data elements (e.g., an employee record).

redundancy—A duplication of the indication of precedence requirements on a network.

register—A small, high-speed storage area in which data pertaining to the execution of a particular instruction are stored. Data stored in a specific register have a special meaning to the logic of the computer.

reserved word—A word that has a special meaning to a compiler or interpreter.

resolution—Referring to the number of addressable points on a monitor's screen. The greater the number of points, the higher the resolution.

resource allocation—The scheduling of activities on the basis of a criterion involving the level of resource utilization.

resource loading report—A report that presents information about the allocation of people, equipment, costs, and other resources that are available to a project.

resources per project—The number of variables (e.g., people, equipment, and costs) that will be considered in the planning of a project.

response time—The interval involved with transmission to the host computer, processing by the computer, and transmission back to the terminal (*see* TURNAROUND TIME).

reusable code—Modules of programming code that can be called and used as needed.

reverse video—Characters on a video display terminal presented as black on a light background, used for highlighting.

ring—A network topology in which the stations are arranged in an electrical circle.

robot—A computer-controlled manipulator capable of moving items through a variety of special motions.

robotics—The integration of computers and industrial robots.

ROM (Read-Only Memory)—Memory that can only be read, not written to.

RPG—A programming language in which the programmer communicates instructions interactively by entering appropriate specifications in prompting formats.

RS-232C—An electrical standard used for serial ports, established by the Electrical Industries Association.

run—The continuous execution of one or more logically related programs (e.g, print payroll checks).

scheduled activity start time—The time period selected for getting the activity under way, based on the limitations imposed by slack calculations and resource constraints.

scheduled activity complete time—The time period selected for bringing the activity to its conclusion. Usually the scheduled start time plus the activity duration. It can mean ''on this period,'' but more often means ''on or before this period.''

schema—A graphical representation of the logical structure of a CODASYL database.

secondary storage—Permanent data storage on magnetic disk and tape (*see* AUXILIARY STORAGE, PRIMARY STORAGE).

sector—A disk storage concept. A pie-shaped portion of a disk or diskette in which records are stored and subsequently retrieved (*see* CYLINDER).

sequential access—Accessing records in the order in which they are stored (*see* RANDOM ACCESS)

sequential files—Files that contain records that are ordered according to a key data element.

sequential processing—Processing of files that are ordered numerically or alphabetically by a key data element (*see* DIRECT-ACCESS PROCESSING, RANDOM PROCESSING).

serial port—An I/O port that transmits data out one bit at a time.

set—A CODASYL database concept that serves to define the relationship between two records.

slack path—A series of predecessor and successor activities sharing a common amount of slack.

slippage—Movement of an activity or event to a later time.

smart card—A card or badge with an embedded microprocessor.

soft copy—Temporary output that can be interpreted visually as on a workstation monitor (*see* HARD COPY).

software—The programs used to direct the functions of a computer system (*see* HARDWARE).

software package—*See* PROPRIETARY SOFTWARE.

sort—The rearrangement of data elements or records in an ordered sequence by a key data element.

source document—The original hard copy from which data are entered.

source program—The code of the original program (*see* OBJECT PROGRAM).

special-purpose computer—Computers that are designed for a specific application, such as CAD, video games, and robots (*see* GENERAL-PURPOSE COMPUTER).

spooling—The process by which output (or input) is loaded temporarily to secondary storage. It is then output (or input) as the appropriate device becomes available.

spreadsheet (electronic)—Refers to software that permits users to work with rows and columns of data.

star—A network topology in which terminals are connected to a central processor in a spoked configuration like points on a star.

statement—*See* INSTRUCTION.

structured programming—A design technique by which the logic of a program is addressed hierarchically in logical modules.

structured walkthrough—A peer evaluation procedure for programs and systems under development. It is used to minimize the possibility of something being overlooked or done incorrectly.

subroutine—A sequence of program instructions that is called and executed as needed.

successor event—The event involving the completion of the activity in question.

supervisor—The operating system program that loads programs to primary storage as the programs are needed.

switched line—A telephone line used as a regular data communications channel. Also called dial-up line.

synchronous—A transmission sequence in which characters are bundled into blocks, defined at the beginning and at the end of transmission by character codes.

synchronous transmission—Terminals and/or computers transmit data at timed intervals (*see* ASYNCHRONOUS TRANSMISSION).

syntax error—An invalid format for a program instruction.

system development methodology—Written standardized procedures that depict the activities in the systems development process and define individual and group responsibilities.

system life cycle—A reference to the four stages of a computer-based information system: birth, development, production, and death.

systems analysis—The analysis, design, development, and implementation of computer-based information systems.

systems analyst—A person who does systems analysis.

systems network architecture (SNA)—A communications model developed by IBM that integrates computer systems with data communications devices.

systems software—Software that is independent of any specific applications area.

tape drive—The secondary storage device that contains the read/write mechanism for magnetic tape.

tape, magnetic—A secondary storage medium for sequential data storage. Available as a reel or a cassette.

task—The basic unit of work for a processor.

technological precedence requirements—The precedence requirements that are based strictly on the necessity that the goals of the predecessor be met before the work involved in the successor would be possible and useful. For example, build the walls before installing the roof.

technology transfer—The application of existing technology to a current problem or situation.

telecommunications—Communication between remote devices.

teleprocessing—A term coined to represent the merging of telecommunications and data processing.

template—A model of a particular application of an electronic spreadsheet.

terminal—Any device capable of sending and/or receiving data over a communications channel.

throughput—1. A measure of computer system efficiency. 2. The rate at which work can be performed by a computer system.

timesharing—Multiple end users sharing time on a single computer system in an on-line environment.

token—A software message that circulates among nodes on the network, sometimes used in ring networks as an "all-clear" message.

top-down design—An approach to system and program design that begins at the highest level of generalization, design strategies are then developed at successive levels of decreasing generalization until the detailed specifications are achieved.

topological sort—A ranking of activities according to a selected criterion, such as total slack or activity cost.

trace—A procedure used to debug programs whereby all processing events are recorded and related to the steps in the program. The objective of a trace is to isolate program logic errors.

track, disk—That portion of a magnetic disk face surface that can be accessed in any given setting of a single read/write head. Tracks are configured in concentric circles.

track, tape—That portion of a magnetic tape that can be accessed by any one of the nine read/write heads. A track runs the length of the tape.

transaction—A procedural event in a system that prompts manual or computer-based activity.

transaction file—A file containing records of data activity (transactions) used to update the master file.

transaction-oriented—Transactions are recorded and entered as they occur.

transcribe—To convert source data to machine-readable format.

transmission rate—The number of characters per second that can be transmitted to/from primary storage from/to a peripheral device.

transparent—A reference to a procedure or activity that occurs automatically and does not have to be considered in the use or design of a program or an information system.

tree—A network arrangement in which stations of equal status are aligned along a common bus cable.

trunk—A specialized circuit used to connect circuit switches to one another.

turnaround document—A computer-produced output that is ultimately returned to a computer system as machine-readable input.

turnaround time—Elapsed time between the submission of a job and the distribution of the results.

twisted pair—Electrical cable used for communications, most commonly found as telephone wire.

uninterruptible power source (UPS)—A buffer between an external power source and a computer system that supplies clean and continuous power.

universal product code (UPC)—A 10-digit machine-readable bar code placed on consumer products.

updating—The incorporation of progress information into the network and related project management records.

upload—To transmit data from a workstation to the mainframe computer.

user—*See* END USER.

user friendly—Pertaining to an on-line system that permits a person with relatively little experience to interact successfully with the system.

user liaison—A person who serves as the technical interface between the information services department and the user group.

utility program—An often-used service routine (e.g., a program to sort records).

value added network (VAN)—A specialized common carrier that "adds value" over and above the standard services of common carriers.

variable—A primary storage location that can assume different numeric or alphanumeric values.

variable activity time—If several independent occurrences of an activity could be expected to result in durations of differing length, with some stable underlying pattern describing the long-run frequencies of the values possible, the activity is said to be variable.

variable name—An identifier in a program that represents the actual value of a storage location.

variable schedule units—The capability of a project management software package to schedule tasks based on desired time units (e.g., hours, days, etc.)

VDT (Video Display Terminal)—A terminal on which printed and graphic information is displayed on a televisionlike monitor and data are entered on a typewriterlike keyboard.

videodisk—A secondary storage medium that permits storage and random access to "video" or pictorial information.

videotext—The merging of text and graphics in an interactive communications-based information network.

virtual machine—The processing capabilities of one computer system created through software (and sometimes hardware) in a different computer system.

virtual memory—The use of secondary storage devices and primary storage to effectively expand a computer system's primary storage.

walkthrough, structured—*See* STRUCTURED WALKTHROUGH.

window—1. A rectangular section of a display screen that is dedicated to a specific activity or application. 2. In integrated software, a "view" of a designated area of a worksheet, such as a spreadsheet or word processing text.

window panes—Simultaneous display of subareas of a particular window (*see* WINDOW).

wireband—A transmission medium capable of passing more frequencies than the standard 3-KHz voice channel.

word—For a given computer, an established number of bits that are handled as a unit.

word processing—To the computer to enter, store, manipulate, and print text.

workstation—The hardware that permits interaction with a computer system, such as a mainframe or a multiuser micro. A VDT and a microcomputer can be workstations.

write—To record data on the output medium of a particular I/O device (e.g., tape, hard copy, workstation display; *see* READ).

X.25—A packet-switching standard adopted by the Consultative Committee of International Telephone and Telegraph (CCITT).

zoom—An integrated software command that expands a window to fill the entire screen.

Bibliography

Adrian, James. *Quantitative Methods In Construction Management*. New York: Elsevier Publishing Co., 1973.

Ahl, David H. "How to buy an Electronic Spreadsheet." *Creative Computing*, (June 1984).

Allmendinger, Glen. "Management Goals for Manufacturing Technology." *Manufacturing Engineering* (November 1985): 83-84.

Amrine, Harold T., John A. Ritchey, and Colin L. Moodie. *Manufacturing Organization and Management*, 5th ed., Englewood Cliffs, N. J.: Prentice-Hall, Inc., 1987.

Archibald, Russell D. *Managing High-Technology Programs and Projects*. New York: John Wiley & Sons, 1976.

Assad, Michael G., and G. P. J. Pelser. "Project Management: A Goal-Directed Approach." *Project Management Quarterly* (June 1983): 49-58.

Badiru, Adedeji Bodunde. "Communication, Cooperation, Coordination: The Triple C of Project Management." *Proceedings of IIE Spring Conference*, Washington, DC (May 1987): 401-404.

_____."Cost-Integrated Network Planning Using Expert Systems." *Project Management Journal*, vol. 19, no. 2 (April 1988b): 59-62.

_____."Expert Systems and Industrial Engineers: A Practical Guide to a Successful Partnership." *Computers & Industrial Engineering*, Vol. 13, nos. 1-4 (1988): 1-13.

_____."Graphic Evaluation of Amortization Schedules." *Industrial Engineering*, vol. 20, no. 9 (September 1988b): 18-22.

_____."Microcomputer Applications for Project Planning and Control." Presented at the Eighth Annual Computers & Industrial Engineering Conference, Orlando, Fla., March 1986.

Bibliography

_____."Minimum Annual Project Revenue Requirement Analysis." *Computers and Industrial Engineering,* vol. 13, nos. 1-4, 366-370, 1987.

_____."Process Capability Analysis on a Microcomputer." *Softcover Software,* Norcross, Georgia: Industrial Engineering & Management Press, (1985): 7-14.

_____. *Project Management in Manufacturing and High Technology Operations.* New York: John Wiley & Sons, 1988a.

_____."Towards The Standardization of Performance Measures For Project Scheduling Heuristics." *IEEE Transactions on Engineering Management,* Vol. 35, no. 2 (May 1988): 82-89.

Badiru, Adedeji Bodunde, and Gary E. Whitehouse. "The Impact of the Computer on Resource Allocation Algorithms." Presented at the Fall ORSA/TIMS Conference, Miami, Fla., October 1986.

_____."Introduction to STARC—A Project Scheduling Package." *Proceedings of IIE Spring Conference,* Los Angeles (May 1985): 539-545.

Badiru, Adedeji Bodunde, and James R. Smith. "Setting Tolerances by Computer Simulation." *Proceedings of IIE Fall Conference,* Cincinnati, Ohio (November 1982): 284-288

Bahouth, Saba B. *Project Management: Why, Who, and How,* Unpublished M.S. Thesis, Vanderbilt University, Nashville, Tennessee, 1981.

Ballou, Paul O. "Decision-Making Environment of a Program Office." *Program Manager: The Journal of the Defense Systems Management College* (Sept.-Oct. 1985): 36-39.

Bedworth, D. D., and James E. Bailey. *Integrated Production Control Systems: Management, Analysis, Design.* New York: John Wiley & Sons, 1982.

Bennis, Warren, and Burt Nanus. *Leaders: The Strategies For Taking Charge.* New York: Harper & Row Pubs. Inc., 1985.

Bersoff, E. H. "Elements of Software Configuration Management." *IEEE Transactions On Software Engineering,* vol. SE-10, no. 1 (January 1984): 79-87.

Borovits, Israel. *Management of Computer Operations.* Englewood Cliffs, N. J., Prentice-Hall, 1984.

Boulding, Kenneth E. "General Systems Theory: The Skeleton of Science." *Management Science,* vol. 2, no. 3 (April 1956): 197-208.

Brand, J. D., W. L. Meyer, and L. R. Shaffer. "The Resource Scheduling Method for Construction." *Civil Engineering Studies Report,* no. 5, University of Illinois, 1964.

Bright, Deborah S. *Gearing up for the Fast Lane: New Tools For Management in a High-Tech World.* New York: Random House Publishing Co., 1985.

Broadwell, Martin M., and Ruth S. House. *Supervising Technical & Professional People.* New York: John Wiley & Sons, 1986.

Bruno, G., A. Elia, and P. Laface. "A Rule-Based System to Schedule Production." *IEEE Computer,* vol. 17, no. 9 (1986): 32-40.

Bryan, Marvin. "Spreadsheets Stress Connectivity, Graphics." *PC Week* (February 6, 1989): 105.

Buchanan, Bruce G., and Edward H. Shortliffe. *Rule-Based Expert Systems: The MYCIN Experiments of the Stanford Heuristic Programming Project.* Reading, Mass.: Addison-Wesley, 1984.

Carlson, Edmond W., and William G. Carlson. "A Case Study in the Application of Microcomputer Technology in the Construction Industry." *Computers and Industrial Engineering,* vol. 13, nos. 1-4 (1987).

Carlson, Edmond W. "Use of Microcomputers in Construction Management." Project management seminar presented to the project management class, School of Industrial Engineering, University of Oklahoma, March 1987.

Carroll, John M. *Simulation Using Personal Computers.''* Englewood Cliffs, N. J.: Prentice-Hall, 1987.

Catalyst. "Managing Sexual Tension in the Workplace." Manhattan, New York, 1987.

Chase, Richard B., and Nicholas J. Aquilano. *Production Operations Management.* Revised Edition, Richard D. Irwin, 1977.

Clark, C. E. "The Optimum Allocation of Resources Among the Activities of a Network." *Journal of Industrial Engineering,* vol. 12 (January-February 1961).

Clarke, Darral G. *Marketing Analysis and Decision Making: Text and Cases with Lotus 123.* Redwood City, Calif.: The Scientific Press, 1987.

Cleland, D. I., and W. R. King. *Systems Analysis and Project Management.* 3rd ed., New York: McGraw-Hill, 1983.

Cleland, David I., and Dundar F. Kocaoglu. *Engineering Management.* New York: McGraw-Hill, 1981.

Clews, G., and R. Leonard. *Technology and Production.* Oxford, England: Philip Allan Publishers Limited, 1985.

Cohen, William A. *High-Tech Management.* New York: John Wiley & Sons, 1986.

Collier, Mel, ed. *Microcomputer Software for Information Management: Case Studies.* Brookfield, Vt.: Grover Publishing Co., 1986.

Cooper, D. F. "Heuristics for Scheduling Resource-Constrained Projects: An Experimental Investigation." *Management Science,* vol. 22 (July 1976): 1186-1194.

Cooper, Dale, and Chris Chapman. *Risk Analysis for Large Projects: Models, Methods, and Cases.* New York: John Wiley & Sons, 1987.

Cooper, John D., and Matthew J. Fisher. *Software Quality Management,* New York: Petrocelli Books, 1979.

Cunningham, Mary. *Powerplay: What Really Happened At Bendix.* New York: Linden Press/Simon & Schuster, Inc., 1984.

Daly, E. B. "Organizing for Successful Software Development." *Datamation,* vol. 25, no. 10 (December 1979): 106-120.

Bibliography

Davies, B. J., and I. L. Darbyshire. "The Use of Expert Systems In Process Planning." *Annals of CIRP*, vol. 33 (1984): 303-306.

Davies, C., A. Demb, and R. Espejo. *Organization for Project Management*. New York: John Wiley & Sons, 1979.

Davis, E. W., and J. W. Patterson. "A Comparison of Heuristic and Optimum Solutions in Resource-Constrained Project Scheduling." *Management Science*, vol. 21 (April 1975): 944-955.

Day-Copeland, Lisa. "Project Management Software Market Shows Indications of Growth." *PC Week* (August 22, 1988): 102.

Department of Energy. *Cost & Schedule Control Systems: Criteria for Contract Performance Measurement: Work Breakdown Structure Guide*. US Department of Energy, Office of Project & Facilities Management, Washington, DC 20585, 1981.

Dinsmore, Paul, C. *Human Factors In Project Management*. American Management Association, New York, 1984.

Drucker, Peter F. *Innovation and Entrepreneurship*. New York: Harper & Row, 1985.

Dumbleton, J. H. *Management of High-Technology Research and Development*. Elsevier, New York, 1986.

Duncan, Acheson J. *Quality Control and Industrial Statistics*. 3rd ed., Homewood, Ill.: Irwin, Inc., 1965.

Dutta, Amitava, and Amit Basu. "An Artificial Intelligence Approach to Model Management in Decision Support Systems." *IEEE Transactions*, (September, 1984): 89-97.

Dybvig, Phillip H. *Personal Computing for Managers with Lotus 123*. Palo Alto, Calif.: The Scientific Press, 1986.

Ein-Dor, Phillip, and Carl R. Jones. *Information Systems Management: Analytical Tools and Techniques*. New York: Elsevier Science Publishing Co., 1985.

Elmaghraby, S. E. *Activity Networks: Project Planning and Control by Network Models*. New York: John Wiley & Sons, 1977.

Elmaghraby, S. E., and Willy S. Herroelen. "On The Measurement of Complexity in Activity Networks." *European Journal of Operations Research*, vol. 5 (1980): 223-234.

Elsayed, E. A. "Algorithms for Project Scheduling With Resource Constraints." *International Journal of Production Research*, vol. 19 (1982).

Fathi, Eli T., and C. V. W. Armstrong. *Microprocessor Software Project Management*. New York: Marcel Dekkar, Inc., 1985.

Fawcette, James E. "How to Pick the Perfect Spreadsheet." *Personal Software* (September 1984): 117-121.

Filley, Richard D. "1986 Project Management Software Buyer's Guide." *Industrial Engineering*, vol. 18, no.1 (January 1986): 51-63.

Flynn, Roger R. *An Introduction to Information Science*. New York: Marcel Dekker, Inc., 1987.

Ford R. D., and B. J. Schroer. "An Expert Manufacturing Simulation System." *Simulation*, vol. 48, no. 5 (May 1987): 193-200.

Frame, J. Davidson. *Managing Projects in Organizations*. San Francisco: Jossey-Bass Publishers, 1987.

Galbraith J. R. "Matrix Organization Design." *Business Horizons* (February 1971): 29-40.

Gallimore, Jack M. "Planning To Automate Your Factory," *Production Engineering* (May 1983): 50-52.

Gessner, Robert A. *Manufacturing Information Systems: Implementation Planning*. New York: John-Wiley & Sons, 1984.

Gido, Jack. *Project Management Software Directory*. New York: Industrial Press, Inc., 1985.

Gilbreath, Robert D. *Winning At Project Management: What Works, What Fails, and Why*. New York: John-Wiley & Sons, 1986.

Glasser, Alan. *Research and Development Management*, Englewood Cliffs, N. J.: Prentice-Hall, 1982.

Goldstein, Larry J. *Microcomputer Applications*. Reading, Mass.: Addison-Wesley, 1987.

Gordon, Maynard M. *The Iacocca Management Technique*, New York: Dodd, Mead, & Company, 1985.

Gorenstein, S. "An Algorithm for Project (Job) Sequencing With Resource Constraints." *Operations Research*, vol. 20 (July-August 1972): 835-850.

Graham, Robert J. *Project Management: Combining Technical and Behavioral Approaches for Effective Implementation*. New York: Van Nostrand, 1985.

Grant, T. G. "Lessons for OR from AI: A Scheduling Case Study." *Journal of Operations Research*, vol. 37, no. 1 (1986): 41-57.

Greiner, L. E., and V. E. Schein. "The Paradox of Managing a Project-Oriented Matrix: Establishing Coherence Within Chaos." *Sloan Management Review* (Winter 1981).

Grubbs, F. E. "Attempts to Validate Certain PERT Statistics or 'Picking on PERT'." *Operations Research* 10 (1962): 912-915.

Guenthner, Franz, H. Lethamann, and W. Schonfeld. "A Theory for the Representation of Knowledge." *IBM Journal of Research and Development*, vol. 30, no. 11 (January 1986): 39-56.

Hajek, V. G. *Management of Engineering Projects*. New York: McGraw-Hill, 1977.

——————. *Project Engineering: Profitable Technical Program Management*. New York: McGraw-Hill, 1965.

Harmon, Paul, and David King. *Expert Systems: Artificial Intelligence in Business*. New York: John Wiley & Sons, 1985.

Harrison, F. L. *Advanced Project Management*. 2nd ed., New York: John Wiley & Sons, 1985.

Hartzband, D. J., and F. J. Maryanski. "Enhancing Knowledge Representation in Engineering Databases." *IEEE Transactions* (September, 1985): 39-46.

Bibliography

Haugeland, John. *Artificial Intelligence, The Very Idea*. Cambridge, Mass.: The MIT Press, 1985.

Hayes-Roth, Frederick. "The Knowledge-Based Expert System: A Tutorial." *IEEE Transactions* (September, 1984): 11-28.

Herzberg, Frederick. "One More Time: How Do You Motivate Employees?" *Harvard Business Review*, vol. 45, no. 1 (1968): 53-62.

_____. *Work and the Nature of Man*. Cleveland, Ohio: World Publishing Co., 1960.

Hicks, Philip E. *Introduction to Industrial Engineering and Management Science*. New York: McGraw-Hill, 1977.

Hink, R. F., and D. L. Woods. "How Humans Process Uncertain Knowledge: An Introduction for Knowledge Engineers." *AI Magazine*, vol. 8, no. 3 (Fall 1987): 41-51.

Hoffman, Thomas R. *Production Management and Manufacturing Systems*. Belmont, Calif: Wadsworth Publishing Co., Inc., 1967.

Holloway, C. A., R. T. Nelson, and V. Suraphongschai. "Comparison of a Multi-Pass Heuristic Decomposition Procedure With Other Resource-Constrained Project Scheduling Procedures." *Management Science*, vol. 25 (September 1979): 862-872.

Hribar, John P. "Development of An Engineering Manager." *Journal of Management In Engineering*, Vol. 1, 1985, 36-41.

Humphrey, Watts S. *Managing For Innovation: Leading Technical People*. Englewood Cliffs, New Jersey: Prentice-Hall, 1987.

Humphreys, Kenneth K., ed. *Project and Cost Engineer's Handbook*. 2nd ed., New York: Marcel Dekkar, Inc., 1984.

"Individual Training for Project Management." Foster City, Calif.: Individual Software, Inc., 1986.

Jenkins, Avery. "Industry Reluctantly Accepts SQL Emergence," *PC Week*, January 26, 1988, 53-63.

Jennett, Eric. "Guidelines for Successful Project Management." *Chemical Engineering* (July 1973): 70-82.

Johnson, J. R. "Advanced Project Control." *Journal of Systems Management* (May 1977).

Johnson, L. A., and D. C. Montgomery. *Operations Research in Production, Scheduling, and Inventory Control*. New York: John Wiley & Sons, 1974.

Johnson, R. A., F. E. Kast, and J. A. Rosenzweig. *The Theory and Management of Systems*. 2nd ed. New York: McGraw-Hill, 1967.

Kangari, Roozbeh, and LeRoy T. Boyer. "Risk Management By Expert Systems: Basic Concepts of the Theory of Fuzzy Sets." *Project Management Journal*, vol. 20, no. 1 (March 1989): 40-46.

Kannewurf, Adolf S. "How to Present Your Proposals to Management." *Achieving Success in Manufacturing Management*, Society of Manufacturing Engineers, Charles F. Hoitash (ed.), 1980.

Karger, Delmar W., and Franklin H. Bayha. *Engineered Work Measurement*. 3rd ed., New York: Industrial Press, Inc., 1977.

Karni, Reuben. "Heuristic Resource Analysis." *Management Information*, vol. 2 (April 1973): 57-70.

Kasevich, Lawrence S. *Harvard Project Manager/Total Project Manager: Controlling Your Resources*. Blue Ridge Summit, Pa.: TAB BOOKS Inc., 1986.

Keen, Peter G. W. "Information Systems and Organizational Change." *Communications of the ACM*, vol. 24, no. 1 (January 1981): 24-33.

Keller, Robert T. "Project Group Performance in Research and Development Organizations." *Academy of Management Proceedings*, San Diego, Calif. (Aug. 11-14, 1985): 315-318.

Kelley, Albert J., ed. *New Dimensions of Project Management*. Lexington, Mass.: Lexington Books, 1982.

Kerzner, Harold. *Project Management: A Systems Approach To Planning, Scheduling, and Controlling*. 2nd ed., New York: Van Nostrand Reinhold, 1984.

_____. *Project Management Operating Guidelines: Directives, Procedures, and Forms*. New York: Van Nostrand Reinhold, 1986.

KharBanda, O. P., and E. A. Stallworthy. *Management Disasters and How to Prevent Them*, England: Gower Publishing Company, 1986.

Kilpatrick, Michael. *Business Statistics Using Lotus 1-2-3*. New York: John Wiley & Sons, 1987.

King, Ronald S., and Bryant Julstrom. *Applied Statistics Using the Computer*. Sherman Oaks, Calif.: Alfred Publishing Co., Inc., 1982.

Kintner, Stephen S. "Using Harvard Total Project Manager for Public Facilities Construction and Administration." in Levine, Harvey A., *Project Management Using Microcomputer,* Berkeley, Calif.: Osborne McGraw-Hill, 1986: 334-346.

Kochhar, A. K. *Development of Computer-Based Production Systems*. New York: John Wiley & Sons, 1979.

Koenig, Michael H. "Management Guide to Resource Scheduling." *Journal of Systems Management*, vol. 29, (January 1978): 24-29.

Koontz, Harold, and Cyril O'Donnel. *Principles of Management*. 2nd ed., New York: McGraw-Hill, 1959.

Krakow, Ira H. *Project Management with the IBM PC*. Bowie, Md.: Brady Communications Co., 1985.

Kurtulus, I. S., and E. W. Davis. "Multi-Project Scheduling: Categorization of Heuristic Rules Performace." *Management Science*, vol. 28 (February 1982): 161-172.

Levine, Harvey A. *Project Management Using Microcomputer*. Berkeley, Calif.: Osborne McGraw-Hill, 1986.

Lewis, Barry. "Things to Consider for an Ideal Security Match." *Software Magazine* (February 1989): 43-52.

Liebowitz, Jay. "Introduction to Expert Systems." Santa Cruz, Calif.: Mitchell Publishing, Inc., 1988.

Bibliography

Lilien, Gary L. *Marketing Mix Analysis with Lotus 1-2-3*. Redwood City, Calif.: The Scientific Press, 1986.

Lindsey, D.V. "The Probability Approach to the Treatment of Uncertainty in Artificial Intelligence and Expert Systems." In *Proceedings of Uncertainty in Artificial Intelligence and Expert Systems Conference*, George Washington University, Washington, DC, 1984.

Long, Larry. *Computers In Business*. Englewood Cliffs, N. J.: Prentice-Hall, 1987.

Lucas, John. "Using QWIKNET and PROJECT/2 To Plan The 1988 Olympic Winter Games." in Levine, Harvey A. *Project Management Using Microcomputer*, Berkeley, Calif.: Osborne McGraw-Hill, 1986: 385-391.

MacCrimmon, Kenneth R., and Charles A. Ryavec. "An Analytical Study of the PERT Assumptions." *Operations Research* 12 (1964): 16-21.

Mackie, Dan. *Engineering Management of Capital Projects: A Practical Guide*. Toronto, Canada: McGraw-Hill Ryerson Ltd., 1984.

Magers, C. S. "Managing Software Development in Microprocessor Projects." *IEEE Computer*, vol. 11, no. 6 (June 1987): 34-42.

Malcolm, D. G., J. H. Roseboom, C. E. Clark, and W. Fazar. "Application of a Technique for Research and Development Program Evaluation." *Operations Research* 7 (1959): 646-669.

Malstrom, Eric M. *What Every Engineer Should Know About Manufacturing Cost Estimating*, New York: Marcel Dekkar, Inc., 1981.

Maslow, Abraham H. "A Theory of Human Motivation." *Psychological Review*, vol. 1 (1943): 370-396.

——————. *Motivation and Personality*. New York: Harper & Brothers, 1954.

McBride, William J. and Charles W. McClelland. "PERT and the Beta Distribution." *IEEE Transactions on Engineering Management*, EM-14, (1967): 166-169.

McDermott, Kevin J. "Microcomputer and Spreadsheet Software Make Time Studies Less Tedious, More Accurate." *Industrial Engineering* (July 1984): 78-81.

McFadden, Fred R., and Jeffrey A. Hoffer. *Data Base Management*. Menlo Park, Calif.: Benjamin/Cummings Publishing, 1985.

McGill, Franks. *Factory Automation Case Books*. Walker-Davis Publication, Inc., 1986.

McGregor, D. *The Human Side of Enterprise*. New York: McGraw-Hill, 1960.

McKeown, Patrick G. *Living With Computers*. Orlando, Fl.: Harcourt Brace Jovanovich, 1986.

Melcher, R. "Roles and Relationships: Clarifying the Manager's Job." *Personnel* (May-June 1967).

Meredith, Jack R., ed. *Justifying New Manufacturing Technology*. Norcross, Ga.: Industrial Engineering & Management Press, 1986.

Meredith, Jack R., and Samuel L. Mantel, Jr. *Project Management: A Managerial Approach*. New York: John Wiley & Sons, 1985.

Meredith, Jack R., and T. E. Gibbs. *The Management of Operations*. 2nd ed., New York: John Wiley & Sons, 1984.

Metz, Horst J., and James A. Gingrich. "Managing Complexity In Mature Industries." *Manufacturing Issues*, New York: Booz-Allen & Hamilton, Inc., (1986): 1-8.

Miller, Jule A. *From Idea To Profit: Managing Advanced Manufacturing Technology*. New York: Van Nostrand Reinhold, 1986.

Minsky, M. "A Framework for Representing Knowledge." *The Psychology of Computer Vision*, P. Winston, ed., New York: McGraw-Hill, 1975: 211-277.

Mintzberg, H. *The Nature of Managerial Work*. New York: Harper & Row, 1973.

Mishkoff, Henry. *Understanding Artificial Intelligence*. Dallas: Texas Instruments Learning Center, 1985.

Moder, Joseph J., C. R. Phillips, and E. W. Davis. *Project Management With CPM, PERT, and Precedence Diagramming*. 3rd ed., New York: Van Nostrand Reinhold, 1983.

Moore, Franklin G. *A Management Sourcebook*. New York: Harper & Row, 1964.

_____. *Production Management*. 6th ed., Homewood, Ill.: Richard D. Irwin, Inc., 1973.

Mueller, Frederick W. *Integrated Cost and Schedule Control For Construction Projects*. New York: Van Nostrand Reinhold, 1986.

Murdick, Robert G., and Joel E. Ross. *Information Systems For Modern Management*. 2nd ed., Englewood Cliffs, N. J.: Prentice-Hall, 1975.

Murphy, Kathleen J. *Macroproject Development In The Third World: An Analysis of Transnational Partnerships*. Boulder, Colo.: Westview Press, 1983.

Naisbitt, John, and Patricia Aburdene. *Re-Inventing The Corporation*. New York: Warner Books, 1985.

Newell, Allen, and Herbert A. Simon. *Human Problem-Solving*. Englewood Cliffs, N. J.: Prentice-Hall, 1972.

Newman, William H., E. K. Warren, and A. R. McGill. *The Process of Management: Strategy, Action, Results*. Englewood Cliffs, N. J.: Prentice-Hall, 1987.

Niebel, Benjamin W. *Motion and Time Study*. 6th ed., Homewood, Illinois: Richard D. Irwin, Inc., 1976.

O'Neal, Kim Rogers. "Project Management Microcomputer Software Buyer's Guide." *Industrial Engineering*, vol. 19, no. 1 (January 1987): 53-63.

Odiorne, G. S. *Management by Objectives: A System of Management Leadership*. New York: Pitman Co., 1965.

Ouchi, William G. *Theory Z: How American Business Can Meet the Japanese Challenge*. Reading, Mass.: Addison-Wesley, 1981.

Paperback Software International. "Multidimensional Database vs 3-D Worksheets," *Readme.PSI*, vol. 4, no. 1 (1989): 1, 6.

Bibliography

Parkinson, C. N. *Parkinson's Law*. Boston: Houghton Mifflin, 1957.

Pascale, Richard T., and Anthony G. Athos. *The Art of Japanese Management*. New York: Penguin, 1982.

Patterson, J. H. "Comparison of Exact Approaches for Solving Multicon-strained Resource Project Scheduling." *Management Science*, vol. 30, no. 7 (1984): 854-867.

——————. "Project Scheduling: The Effects of Problem Structure on Heuristic Performance." *Naval Research Logistics Quarterly*, vol. 23, no. 1 (1976): 95-123.

Peters, Thomas J., and Robert H. Waterman Jr. *In Search of Excellence: Lessons from America's Best-Run Companies*. New York: Harper & Row, 1982.

Peterson, Robert O. *Managing The Systems Development Function*. New York: Van Nostrand, 1987.

Phillips, Don T., and A. Garcia-Diaz. *Fundamentals of Network Analysis*. Englewood Cliffs, N. J.: Prentice-Hall, 1981.

Pinchot, Gifford III. *Intrapreneuring*. New York: Harper & Row, 1985.

Pritsker, A. Alan. *Introduction To Simulation and SLAM II*. 3rd ed., New York: Halsted Press, John Wiley & Sons, 1986.

Pritsker, A. Alan, C. Elliot Sigal, and R. D. Jack Hammersfahr. *SLAM II Network Models for Decision Support*. Englewood Cliffs, N. J.: Prentice-Hall, 1989.

Pritsker, A. Alan, L. J. Walters, and P. M. Wolfe. "Multi-Project Scheduling With Limited Resources: A Zero-One Programming Approach." *Management Science*, vol. 16 (September 1969).

Quinn, James Brian. "Managing Innovation: Controlled Chaos." *Harvard Business Review*, (May-June, 1985): 73-84.

Rajaram, N. S. "Expert System Building Tools: Present Trends and Future Needs." *ISA Transactions*, vol. 26, no. 1 (1987): 53-55.

Ravindran, A., Don T. Phillips, and James J. Solberg. *Operations Research: Principles and Practice*. New York: John Wiley & Sons, 1987.

Reifer, D. J. "The Nature of Software Management: A Primer." IEEE Computer Society Tutorial, *Software Management* (1981): 9-12.

Rhodes, David, M. Wright, and M. Jarrett. *Computers, Information & Manufacturing Systems*, New York: Praeger Publishers, 1984.

Riggs, Henry E. *Managing High-Technology Companies*. Belmont, Calif.: Lifetime Learning Publications, 1983.

Roche, W. J., and N. L. MacKinnon. "Motivating People With Meaningful Work." *Harvard Business Review* (May-June, 1970).

Rogers, William P., et al. *Report of the Presidential Commission on the Space Shuttle Challenger Accident: Executive Summary*. Washington, DC, June 6, 1986.

Rohm, Tapie C. E., and Walter T. Stewart. *Essentials of Information Systems*. Santa Cruz, Calif.: Mitchell Publishing, Inc., 1988.

Roman, Daniel D. *Managing Projects: A Systems Approach*. New York: Elsevier Science Publishing Co., Inc., 1986.

Rosenau, M. D., Jr. *Successful Project Management*. Belmont, Calif.: Lifetime Learning Publications, 1981.

_____. *Project Management for Engineers*. Belmont, Calif.: Lifetime Learning Publications, 1984.

Rubin, Charles. "Power Spreadsheeting." *Personal Computing* (July 1984): 218-223.

Ruskin, Arnold M., and W. Eugene Estes. *What Every Engineer Should Know About Project Management*. New York: Marcel Dekker, 1982.

Russell, Robert A. "A Comparison of Heuristics for Scheduling Projects with Cash Flows and Resource Restrictions." *Management Science*, vol. 32, no. 10 (Oct. 1986): 1291-1300.

Sadler, Philip. "Designing An Organizational Structure." *Management International Review*, vol. 11, no. 6 (1971): 19-33.

Samaras, Thomas T., and Kim Yensuang. *Computerized Project Management Techniques for Manufacturing and Construction Industries*. Englewood Cliffs, N. J.: Prentice-Hall, 1979.

Sasieni, M. W. "A Note On PERT Times." *Management Science*, vol. 32, no. 12 (1986): 1652-1653.

Saul, Ken. "Anatomy of a 1-2-3 Graph." *Lotus* (January 1989): 43-48.

Schindler, Max, "Expert Systems Poised To Reshape Industry." *Electronic Design* (March 19, 1987): 29-32.

Schonberger, R. J. "Why Projects are Always Late: A Rationale Based on Manual Simulation of a PERT/CPM Network." *Interfaces* (Oct. 1981).

Sell, Peter S. *Expert Systems—A Practical Introduction*. New York: John Wiley & Sons, 1985.

Semprevivo, Philip C. *Systems Analysis: Definition, Process, and Design*. 2nd ed., Chicago: Science Research Associates, Inc., 1982.

Shaiken, Harley. "The Automated Factory: The View from the Shop Floor." *Technology Review* (January 1985): 17-27.

Silverman, Melvin. *The Art of Managing Technical Projects*. Englewood Cliffs, N. J.: Prentice-Hall, 1987.

Skinner, Wickham. *Manufacturing: The Formidable Competitive Weapon*. New York: John Wiley & Sons, 1985.

Slowinski, R. "Two Approaches to Problems of Resource Allocation Among Project Activities: A Comparative Study." *Journal of the Operational Research Society*, vol. 31 (August 1980): 711-723.

Spinner, M. *Elements of Project Management: Plan, Schedule, and Control*, Englewood Cliffs, N. J.: Prentice-Hall, 1981.

Steiner, George A. and William G. Ryan. *Industrial Project Management*. New York: MacMillan, 1968.

Steiner, Henry M. *Basic Engineering Economy*. Glen Echo, Md.: Books Associates, 1988.

Bibliography

Stephanou, S. E. *Management: Technology, Innovation, & Engineering*, Malibu, Calif.: Daniel Spencer, 1981.

Stephanou, S. E., and M. M. Obradovitch. *Project Management: System Developments and Productivity*. Malibu, Calif.: Daniel Spencer Publishers, 1985.

Stepman, Kenn. *1986 Buyer's Guide to Project Management Software*. Milwaukee, Wis.: New Issues, Inc., 1986.

Stevens, Jr., G. T. *Economic and Financial Analysis of Capital Investments*. New York: John Wiley & Sons, 1979.

Stinson, J. P., E. W. Davis, and B. M. Khumawala. "Multiple Resource Constrained Scheduling Using Branch and Bound." *AIIE Transactions* vol. 10 (January 1962): 138-167.

Stuckenbruck, Linn C. "The Matrix Organization." *Project Management Quarterly* (September 1979).

Stuckenbruck, Linn C., ed. *The Implementation of Project Management: The Professional's Handbook*. Reading, Mass.: Addison-Wesley, 1981.

Summers, Edward L. *An Introduction To Accounting For Decision Making and Control*. Homewood, Ill.: Richard D. Irwin, Inc., 1974.

Szymanski, Robert A., Donald P. Szymanski, Norma A. Morris, and Donna M. Pulschen. *Introduction to Application Software Using Open Access*. Columbus, Ohio: Merrill Publishing Company, 1988.

Talbot, F. B., and J. H. Patterson. "An Efficient Integer Programming Algorithm With Network Cuts for Solving Resource-Constrained Scheduling Problems." *Management Science*, vol. 28, (July 1978): 1163-1174.

Taylor, Frederick, W. *Scientific Management*. New York: Harper & Row Publishers, Inc., 1911.

Thayer, R. H., A. Pyster, and R. C. Wood. "The Challenge of Software Engineering Project Management." *IEEE Computer*, vol. 14, no. 8 (August 1980): 51-59.

Thesen, Arne. "Heuristic Scheduling of Activities Under Resource and Precedence Restrictions." *Management Science*, vol. 23 (December 1976): 412-422.

Topkins, G. B. *Project Cost Control for Managers*. Houston: Gulf Publishing Co., 1985.

Turner, W. S., III. *Project Auditing Methodology*. Amsterdam: North-Holland, 1980.

Ullmann, John E., D. A. Christman, and Bert Holtje. *Handbook of Engineering Management*. New York: John Wiley & Sons, 1986.

Van Slyke, Richard M. "Monte Carlo Methods and the PERT Problem." *Operations Research* 11 (1963): 839-860.

Waterman, D.A. *A Guide to Expert Systems*. Reading, Mass.: Addison-Wesley Publishing Co., 1986.

Webster, Robin. "Expert Systems On Microcomputer." *Computer and Electronics*, vol. 23, no. 3 (1985): 69-73, 94-95, 104.

Weight, Alec C. "Computer Integrated Manufacturing." *Manufacturing Issues*, New York: Booz-Allen & Hamilton, Inc., 1986.

Weiss, S., and C. A. Kulikowski. *A Practical Guide to Designing Expert Systems*. Totowa, N. J.: Rowman & Allanheld, 1984.

Wheelwright, James C. "How to Choose the Project Management Microcomputer Software That's Right For You." *Industrial Engineering*, vol. 18, no. 1 (January 1986): 46-50.

White, A.P. "Inference Deficiencies in Rule-Based Expert Systems." *In Proceedings of the 4th Technical Conference of the British Computer Society Specialist Group on Expert Systems*, Cambridge University Press, 1985.

Whitehouse, Gary E. "Electronic Spreadsheets and their Applications." Presented at the Sixth Annual Computers & Industrial Engineering Conference, Orlando, Fla., March 1984.

_____. *Practical Partners: Microcomputers and the Industrial Engineer.* Norcross, Ga.: Industrial Engineering and Management Press, 1985.

_____. *Systems Analysis and Design Using Network Techniques.* Englewood Cliffs, N. J.: Prentice-Hall, 1973.

Whitehouse, Gary E., and Ben L. Wechler. *Applied Operations Research: A Survey*. New York: John Wiley & Sons, 1976.

Whitehouse, G. E., and J. R. Brown. "Genres: An Extension of Brooks Algorithm for Project Scheduling With Resource Constraints." *Computers and Industrial Engineering* (December 1979).

Wiest, Jerome D. "A Heuristic Model for Scheduling Large Projects With Limited Resources." *Management Science*, vol. 13 (February 1967): B-359-B377.

Wiest, Jerome D., and F. K. Levy. *A Management Guide to PERT/CPM With GERT/PDM/DCPM and Other Networks*. 2nd ed., Englewood Cliffs, N. J.: Prentice-Hall, 1977.

Wilemon, D. L., and J. P. Cicero. "The Project Manager: Anomalies and Ambiguities." *Academy of Management Journal* (September 1970).

Wittry, Eugene J. *Managing Information Systems: An Integrated Approach*. Dearborn, Mich.: Society of Manufacturing Engineers, 1987.

Wolfgram, Deborah D., Teresa J. Dear, and Craig S. Gailbraith. *Expert Systems for the Technical Professional*. New York: John Wiley & Sons, 1987.

Woods, W. A. "What's Important About Knowledge Representation?" *IEEE Computer,* vol. 16, no. 22 (1983).

Wortman, Leon A. *Effective Management for Engineers*, New York: John Wiley & Sons, 1981.

Zadeh, L. A. "Fuzzy Sets." *Information and Control*, vol. 8, (1965): 338-353.

Zarley, Craig. "Low-End Packages Take Advantage of LAN Technology." *PC Week* (January 9, 1989): 87-89.

Bibliography

Zeyher, Lewis R. *Production Manager's Desk Book*. Englewood Cliffs, N. J.: Prentice-Hall, 1969.

Zimmerman, Steven M., Leo M. Conrad, and Stanley M. Zimmerman. *Electronic Spreadsheets and Your IBM PC*. Rochelle Park, N. J.: Hayden Publishing Company, Inc., 1984.

Index

Index

Index

graphical evaluation of amortizing payments (GAMPS), 134, 136, 137

graphics (*see also* charts and graphics), 9, 10, 160

H

hard disks (*see also* optical disks), 6, 16

hardcopy (*see* output)

hardware, microcomputers, 4, 5

Harvard Graphics, 10, 164

Harvard Project Manager, 141, 211

help functions, 47

heuristic reasoning, 173

hierarchical databases, 90

Hitachi, 7

host processor, mainframe computers, 3

HP LaserJet/PaintJet, 14

hybrids, expert systems, 183

I

IBM, 7, 141, 151

if-then rules, knowledge base, expert systems, 172

IFPS/Personal, 55

impact printers, 13

indexed sequential access files, 100

inductive reasoning, 184

inference engine, expert systems, 170

information filtering, 45

Informix, 54, 94

ink jet printers, 13

Innovative Software Inc., 54

input, 2, 3, 11, 39

InstaPlan, 141

integrated applications software, 10, 46

integrated imaging, fax machines for, 147

integrated services digital network (ISDN), 216

integrating data, databases, 106-107

Intel, 7

InterAct, 215

Interactive Picture Systems Inc., 146

interfaces (*see* user interfaces)

internal commands, 22

internal rate of return (IROR), 79

interval scale, 42

J

Jenkins, 95

K

Kangari, 222

Kerzner, 27

keyboards, 6

kilobytes (K), 12

knowledge base, expert systems, 170-172

  if-then rules, 172, 180

  structure of, 193

knowledge representation, 176-184

  deep vs. surface, 176

  frames, 177-180

  hybrids, 183

  O-A-V triplets, 183

  predicate logic, 181-182

  production rules for (if-then rules), 180

  scripts, 183

  semantic networks, 177-178

L

laser disks (*see* optical disks)

laser printers, 13, 14

learning curve analysis, 72-77

lifecycle, 81

light pen, 6

line graphs, 64, 65

line printers, 13

linking columns, relational databases, 88

LISP, 170

local area networks (LAN), 140-141, 147-154

  access in, 148

  baseband vs. broadband, 147

  bus configuration, 149

  bus-shaped ring configuration, 151, 152

  contention, 148

  logical ring configuration, 152-153

  media for, 148

  mesh configuration, 150

  multiple access networks, 149

  planning and management for, 153-154

  protocols for, 148

  ring configuration, 151

  signaling in, 148

  star configuration, 149

  star-shaped ring configuration, 151, 152

  token passing, 148

  topologies, 148

logic, predicate, expert systems, 181-182, 188

logical operators, SQL, 93

logical ring LAN configuration, 152-153

Look & Link, 57

Lotus 1-2-3, 9, 55, 57, 64-69, 78, 94, 157, 160, 162, 165

Lotus Freelance Plus, 10, 157, 160, 164

Lotus Graphwriter II, 160

Lotus Manuscript, 9, 157

Lotus Symphony, 10, 157, 160

Lotus/DBMS, 57

M

magnetic media, 15-17

  diskettes, 15

  formatting, 16, 19

  hard disks, 16

  microdisks, 16

  optical disks and tape, 16-17

  sectors and tracks in, 22

  tape, 15

mainframe computers, 2-4

managerial decision analysis, 124-126

Mantel, 27

MasteriskPM software, 143

MCI Mail, 10

measurement processes, 30

media, LAN, 148

megabytes (MB), 12

memory (*see also* storage), 2, 11-12

  bits and bytes, 11

  capacity of, 12

  expert systems, 170

  primary storage unit for, 11

  random-access (RAM), 11

  read-only (ROM), 11

  secondary storage (*see* magnetic media)

  words, 12

menus, 47

Meredith, 27

mesh LAN configuration, 150

meta rules, expert systems, 181

Metier Management Systems, 107, 206

Micro Planner, 141

microcomputers, 2, 4-8

microdisks, 16

microprocessors, 7

Microsoft Corp., 55, 94

Microsoft Excel, 55, 56

Microsoft Project, 141, 204-205

Ming Telecomputing, 55

minicomputers, 2, 5

minimum annual revenue requirements (MARR), 80, 138

modularity, expert systems, 171

monitoring projects, 28, 49, 216

monitors, 6, 14

  clear screen, 20

  color vs. monochrome, 14

  extended graphics adapter (EGA) for, 15

  pixels in, 14

Index

Other Bestsellers of Related Interest